GOLD RUN

The Rescue of Norway's Gold Bullion
from the Nazis, April 1940

GOLD RUN

*The Rescue of Norway's Gold Bullion
from the Nazis, April 1940*

Robert Pearson

CASEMATE
uk
Oxford & Philadelphia

Published in Great Britain and the United States of America in 2017 by
CASEMATE PUBLISHERS
The Old Music Hall, 106–108 Cowley Road, Oxford OX4 1JE, UK
and
1950 Lawrence Road, Havertown, PA 19083, USA

© Casemate Publishers 2015

Paperback Edition: ISBN 978-1-61200-462-4
Digital Edition: ISBN 978-1-61200-287-3

A CIP record for this book is available from the British Library

Typeset and design by Casemate Publishers

Printed and bound in the United Kingdom by TJ International

Originally published as Redd Gullet! by Dinamo Forlag, Norway
© Dinamo Forlag 2010; © Robert Pearson 2010

For a complete list of Casemate titles, please contact:

CASEMATE PUBLISHERS (UK)
Telephone (01865) 241249
Fax (01865) 794449
Email: casemate-uk@casematepublishers.co.uk
www.casematepublishers.co.uk

CASEMATE PUBLISHERS (US)
Telephone (610) 853-9131
Fax (610) 853-9146
Email: casemate@casematepublishing.com
www.casematepublishing.com

To my wife Juliette and our three children,
Matthias, Jared & Enya.

Also, for my family and friends
and those who fought and continue to fight
for freedom, truth and justice.

Contents

"When bad men combine, the good must associate; else
they will fall one by one, an unpitied sacrifice in
a contemptible struggle."

Edmund Burke 1770

A cartoon from the now defunct Daily Sketch by Clive Upton

Preface

The purpose of this book is to document the transportation of Norwegian gold bullion from Norway to the United Kingdom during WWII when Norway was facing the darkest period in her history. Where required, I have given a brief over-view of events peripheral to the transport, but it is not within the domain of this account to go into fine detail the reasons why Norway was invaded during April 1940. For further and more detailed information on books available I refer the reader to the bibliography.

The objective from the outset has been to present the information as a balanced, factual account based on primary evidence from people directly and indirectly involved with the bullion. On occasions I have relied on documented evidence submitted to museums and archives and have used the material as supporting evidence to the story. Where evidence has been presented in Norwegian or German I have sought translation and submitted this evidence without attempting to compromise the original text. Invariably, some words are lost in translation and I apologise for this. All translations into English are my responsibility and mine alone.

The operation of the gold transport and its influence on the Norwegian Government, the armed forces in exile and the Norwegian people has, in my opinion, been overshadowed by the subsequent calamitous events that surrounded the allied attempt to free Norway followed quickly by the Dunkirk evacuation after the fall of France. Yet the movement of almost 50 tons of gold bullion from Oslo to three west coast ports and then in three separate shipments to the UK, one of which included the rescue of King Haakon, Crown Prince Olav, members of the Norwegian Storting and various foreign officials is as astonishing as it is remarkable.

The invasion of Norway was an imperative strategic repositioning by the Germans who were fearful of the Allies outflanking them. It enabled the Germans to break the British blockade of the North Sea, but it was also a strategic encumbrance tying up valuable capital ships, aircraft and troops. The Germans also misunderstood and miscalculated the reaction of the Norwegian mercantile fleet - the third largest and most modern merchant marine fleet, which was promptly given over to the Allies. For Britain, an opportunity to secure vital iron-ore supplies had been lost: the German invasion of Norway was more than just a thorn in the side of the Allies. But as Geirr Haarr observes in his book, *'The German Invasion of Norway',* the full strategic significance of Norway only emerged after the German invasion of Russia. Later, during the allied invasion of Europe, Norway once again proved to be of strategic importance, but this time to the advantage of the Allies as the Germans, fearful of an allied invasion of Norway, retained nearly 400,000 troops there.

In the UK, the Norwegian Government-in-exile wisely moved the bullion once more, fearing a possible invasion of the UK during 1940, but this time the bullion was transported to the very safe havens of Canada and America, save for a small amount retained in the UK. The significance of the bullion, along with the merchant marine fleet then became fully apparent with the Norwegian Government able to financially administer its part in the war effort on an equal footing with the Allies.

The loss of the bullion was a blow to the Germans. They had gained a country, but lost a King, a government, a merchant marine fleet and nearly 50 tons of bullion that would have financed their war machine. That loss is directly attributed to a visionary bank chief, a Colonel, a hastily assembled body of Norwegians and the ships and men of the Royal Navy. Ever resourceful, brave and loyal to their respective countries; this is their story.

Robert Pearson

Acknowledgments

There are many people who have generously, willingly and unselfishly given their time and assistance to help me with my research; I am indebted to their knowledge, support and encouragement throughout. I have not just benefited from their expertise and wisdom, but have also been fortunate in gaining their friendship, which for me is beyond measure. I hope it is not seen as crass and is certainly not intended to be, but without their guidance and comprehension of the subject area, historical corrections, and grammatical amendments as well as their plenteous assistance – and at times going way beyond the boundaries of hope and expectation to contribute, then this book would have been nigh on impossible to research and complete. In particular I would like to mention Geirr Haarr for his consummate comprehension of Norwegian WW2 history, particularly in all matters relating to the period of 1940 as well as for his guidance and direction when I needed it; Arild Bergstrom who has unstintingly, efficiently and without compromise provided information that has enabled me to further my research when I thought I had reached an impasse. To Juliette, my wife and my family of Matthias, Jared & Enya for their understanding and patience. Also, significant to the research of this book and without whom little would have been achieved are the following:

Hans Olav Henanger, Ivar Kraglund, Roger Tobbell, Professor Dag Tangen, Professor Tore Pryser, Christian Falch, Tor Christian Jevanord, Merry Swan, Gunnar Bolsø, Ian Bowater, the late Edward du Cann, Cato Guhnfeldt, Howard Davies, Unni Dorum, Tore Eggan, Ivar Enoksen, Berit Fougner, Mette Krefting, Ian Foulkes, Frode Sæland, Roald Gjelsten, Steve Griffin, Rob Guyatt, Gunnar Sønsterby, Ragnar Ulstein, William Hakvaag, Ron Hogg, Kai Isaken, Richard Karlsseon, Erling Krange, Magne Lien, Ole-Johan Larsen, Gunnar Arne Løvlund,

John Makie, Anita Erin Melkevik, Michael Smith, Sarah Millard, Charles Millnar, Arnfinn Moland, Oddvar Naas, Professor Ole Kristian Grimnes, Oddbjorn Skarbovik, Don Oliver, Per Martinsen, Dag Reppe, Sven Erik Rognes, Rolf Dahlø, Liv Ronneberg, Jostein Saakvitne, Ole Gunnar Sætre, Graham Salt, Øivind Solvik, Tore Tomter, Stian Trovik, Janet Voke, Ove Voldsrud, Inge Voldsrud, Ole Voldsrud, Aksel Melsæter, Anis Bonsor, Asbjørn Nakke, Boutwood family, Dorothy Baden-Powell, Grace Burns, Guttorm Reppe, Hans Olaf Brevig, Horace Grant RN, Jack Hall RN, James Irvine, Jan Reimers MBE, Per Haugerud, Per Åsmundstad, Olaf Hartmann-Johnsen, Joe Kynoch, Doris Kynoch, Lita Deinboll, Jan Tystad, Kjell Thoresen, Liv Karin Lange, Erik Birkeland, Leif Aagard, Reg Samways RN, John Frederick Baker, Martin Carroll, S W. Crabb RM, Donald M. Edwards RN, Harold Hall RN, Alfred Hunt RN, John Kelleher RN, Jack A. Lovelock RN, Alfred A. H. Luke RN, Cyril Kenwyn Milner RN, Thomas W. Morton RN, Leif Arneberg, Peter Bell, Arnfinn Haga, Arvid Witzoe, Christopher Sporborg, the late Joan Bright-Astley, Erling Iversen, Randi Bell, Julia Korner, Mark Florman, the Fougner family (Lillehammer), Barbara Melkavik, Robert Binks, Cath Piddington, Peter Cann, Tracey Bishop, Stian Beinset, the Palmer family, Lene Bøckman-Pedersen, Pat Gruber, Asbjørn Nakken, Heather Johnson, and the Torgersen family (Bergen), Sue Laughlin. Hjemmefrontmuseet – (Oslo Resistance Museum), Romsdalmuseet (Molde), Norges Bank, North Sea Traffic Museum – Shetland Bus (Bergen), RAF Tempsford Museum, Møres Fylkes Rutebåtar (MFR), Rica Hotel (Molde), Riksarkivet (Oslo), The Navy News (UK), Romsdal Budstikke, Per Kåre Tveeikrem, The National Archives, London, E. Birkeland AS (Molde), Gemini Recording Studios (Ipswich), Samlerhuset, Kolbotn, The London Gazette, Royal Naval Museum, Portsmouth, Imperial War Museum, www.godebilder. no, www.nuav.net, www.samlerhuset.no.

Introduction

The story of the Norwegian gold transport of 1940 is truly an amazing one. In terms of leadership, human endurance, and dogged persistence coupled with a grim determination to deny the invaders of Norway a valuable bonus, it must rank as one of the greatest gold snatches in history. But how was it that Norway, a peaceful nation with absolutely no desire or need to become embroiled in war should become a theatre of hostilities? The answer of course is far from straightforward and it is not the purpose of this book to delve deeply into such reasons. However, there is justification to set the outline context of events that led up to the invasion of Norway.

> There were no German plans whatsoever for an attack on Scandinavia in September 1939. The rationale for Hitler to unleash his dogs of war on Norway and Denmark seven months later developed during the winter through a series of intertwined incidents and processes involving the German fear of being outflanked, Norwegian neutrality policy, and Allied aspirations to sever German iron-ore supplies and to establish an alternative front in Scandinavia.[1]

Events in Europe during the 1930s had deteriorated dramatically. Hitler had become the autocratic leader of Germany in January 1933 having risen to power on a wave of economic discontent. The reasons for this can be levelled at the Versailles Treaty and the depression that followed from World War I. As AJP Taylor states. *'In his view, [Hitler] the German Depression was the legacy of defeat, and the instruments for overcoming the Depression would also carry Germany to political victory.'* [2] Taylor comments further that the initial gains by Germany were small and Hitler was gambling upon the World Powers' reluctance to go to war again. The gamble almost worked. Hitler's intention was to *'creep forward, as it were, unobserved or at least unchecked until they emerged as World Powers too strong to be challenged'*.[3]

For many historians the countdown to war began in 1936, although interestingly in 1929 a senior German naval officer, Vizeadmiral Wolfgang Wegener, stated in his book, *Die Seestrategie des Weltkriges (The Naval Strategy of the World War)* that in the event of a war Germany should invade and occupy Norway so that it had access to the Atlantic for its naval forces.[4]

By the mid 1930s Italy had invaded Abyssinia, Germany was rearming; Britain and France followed suit. November 1936 saw Germany signing an anti-communist pact with Japan and it was clear that *The League of Nations,* which had been set up after World War I was now virtually dead.[5]

The Prime Minister of Great Britain, Neville Chamberlain, viewed Germany's eastward extensions as a barrier against communism and in 1937 Chamberlain and Lord Halifax made it known to Hitler that Danzig, Austria and Czechoslovakia *'could be settled in Germany's favour, provided there were 'no far-reaching disturbances'.* Consequently, Austria was annexed followed quickly by Czechoslovakia; Britain's policy of appeasement, along with the agreement of France and Italy had very generously favoured Germany.[6] Hitler now turned his attentions to Poland whom he believed would agree to becoming a German satellite. The British Government became anxious and yet despite ignoring the appeals of the Chiefs of Staff, who stated that nothing could be done to help Poland, Chamberlain signed a guarantee on 30th March 1939 to come to her aid if she was attacked.[7]

On September 1st 1939 German forces crossed into Poland in an act of aggression. There had been no declaration of war and Hitler stated that his offer of a settlement with Poland prior to the invasion had been ignored.

On that infamous, yet memorable Sunday morning of September 3rd 1939, Prime Minister Chamberlain spoke to the nation via the radio at 9am.[8] His tone was understandably dour and despondent as he presented to the listening nation the consequences of Germany's action against Poland.

> I am speaking to you from the cabinet room of 10 Downing Street. This morning the British Ambassador in Berlin handed the German Government a final note stating that, unless we heard from them by 11 o'clock that they were prepared at once to withdraw their

troops from Poland, a state of war would exist between us. I have to tell you now that no such undertaking has been received, and that consequently this country is at war with Germany…

Chamberlain, perhaps realising the irony in its content, concluded the broadcast with this pronouncement.

…we have a clear conscience, we have done all that any country could do to establish peace, but a situation in which no word given by Germany's ruler could be trusted, and no people or country could feel itself safe, had become intolerable. And now that we have resolved to finish it, I know that you will all play your parts with calmness and courage.

A French ultimatum delivered to Germany the same day was ignored and so Britain's ally was also dragged into war. Ironically, no aid of consequence to Poland from her Allies was forthcoming and Germany's subsequent victory in Poland was decisive. Britain's response was to pour troops into France to support her ally who was strengthening the Maginot Line against invasion by the Germans. Thus British troops were initially stationed along the Belgian frontier and placed under French control.[9] Battle with the Germans had not yet materialised and although Hitler had instigated plans as early as October 1939 to attack the west circumstances had intervened to postpone this. The so-called *phoney war* had begun.

When Britain declared war on Germany, Neville Chamberlain quickly formed his War Cabinet. There were few surprises except for one; Winston Churchill, who was re-appointed as First Lord of the Admiralty.[10] On that fateful day the Prime Minister called for Winston Churchill to attend 10 Downing Street.[11] Accompanied by Mrs Churchill he took the short drive from the House of Commons to the residence of the PM. A short time later he emerged from his meeting with Chamberlain declaring to his wife, '*it's the Admiralty,* adding with a chuckle, *that's a lot better than I thought'.* Churchill was back in government and, more importantly, in Chamberlain's war cabinet. That evening an Admiralty signal was flashed across the free world … '*WINSTON IS BACK.'* Once again, Churchill was First Lord of the Admiralty, a position he had previously held during the First World War. Patrick Beesly, in his excellent book, '*Very Special Admiral – The Life of J H Godfrey C.B'* ponders if that famous signal was in fact a warning to senior RN officers *'to keep a weather eye open for unusual squalls?'* However, many at that time saw it as a prodigious move. Churchill had long been a thorn to many in the government and it was seen as advantageous to have Churchill *'pissing out from inside the tent rather than pissing in'*. Ironically, prior to Churchill coming back into Government, Lieutenant Colonel Count von Schwerin, head of the British Section of German Military Intelligence, who was a trusted representative of Admiral Canaris and seen as an honourable German, was on a mission to Britain to determine whether Britain would come to Poland's aid if she was attacked. At one particular meeting with Gladwyn Jebb of the Foreign Office, it was stated by Schwerin that Hitler thought Britain would easily surrender Central and Eastern Europe to Germany. Schwerin perhaps in an attempt to counter Hitler's thoughts and so avert war, proffered a suggestion that Britain should *'take Winston Churchill into the cabinet'*, but the suggestion was ignored until war had been declared.

Churchill long remembered the importance of Norway during WW1, as he was instrumental in attempting to persuade Norway to mine her Inner Leads so that the mine barrage laid by the British across the North Sea could be completed. This would then deny sea passage to the Germans, but Norway's undertaking was not needed as the war came to an end. Churchill, somewhat prophetically, realised that the Inner Leads and ports of Western Norway would once again be very important to Britain, although the War Cabinet was reluctant to sanction any action that would violate Norwegian neutrality.

Unbeknown to the British, the Germans had also looked ahead and took a more pro-active approach to their needs. During the autumn months of 1939, so called *'tourists'* visited Norway to take photos of all that they could see including important features such as towns, fjords, harbours and military establishments. But it was only after the German invasion of Poland in September 1939 that Britain slowly awoke from its slumber to events in Scandinavia.

Neutral Norway, with its long, rugged, western coastline incised with deep fjords and ports, offered natural protection to the German iron-ore ships that plied their trade. During peacetime the Germans were importing around 10 million tons annually from Sweden, with another 10 million tons being imported from France; with the advent of war the Swedish iron-ore became vital to Germany's war industry. A small amount of ore came out from central Sweden, but the main bulk was exported from the Swedish port of Lulea. However, the Baltic port was prone to becoming ice-bound during the winter months and so the ore was transported by train overland to the Norwegian port of Narvik then shipped out by freighter via the territorial waters of the Leads, south to Stavanger, across the Skagerrak and then on to German ports. Churchill, ever alert to the material needs of the Germans, badgered the Cabinet for action, but his plans were thwarted by political heavyweights such as Lord Halifax, the Foreign Secretary who bitterly opposed any infringement of Norwegian neutrality. Churchill noted, somewhat inaccurately, in his memorandum to the First Sea Lord on 19th September 1939:[12]

> I brought to the notice of the cabinet this morning the importance of stopping the Norwegian transportation of Swedish iron ore from Narvik, which will begin as soon as the ice forms in the Gulf of Bothnia. I pointed out that we had laid a minefield across the 3-mile limit in Norwegian territorial waters in 1918, with the approval and co-operation of the United States. I suggested that we repeat this process very shortly.

Halifax had in fact been dampening many of Churchill's desires and ideas to take the war forward and consequently Churchill was reined in.[13] Halifax was seen as the senior figure in Chamberlain's government and, despite Churchill's remarkable oratory skills, he was not in any way over-awed by him. Churchill, for his part, had every respect for a man that stood up to him. Despite Churchill writing an informative paper on the iron-ore traffic, and twice bringing the matter to the attention of the cabinet, Churchill was continually thwarted in his efforts to bring direct action against the traffic.[14] He later wrote:

> When all was agreed and settled at the Admiralty I brought the matter a second time before the cabinet. Again there was general agreement upon the need; but I was unable to obtain assent to action. The Foreign Office arguments about neutrality were weighty, and I could not prevail. I continued, as will be seen, to press my point by every means and on all occasions. It was not however until April 1940 that the decision that I asked for in September 1939 was taken. By that time it was too late.

Churchill's vision of defeating Germany took on a new lease of life when the Soviet Union attacked Finland causing worldwide protests. The Allies, supposedly keen to assist Finland, now had their eyes firmly fixed on the iron-ore coming out of Sweden and once again Narvik became the centre of attention. Churchill, astute as ever to an opportunity, foresaw it becoming an ideal Allied base for supplying the brave Finns. The British Foreign Secretary, Lord Halifax, had now become vociferous in his disgust at the Soviet attack on Finland and Churchill sensed that the mood had shifted to his way of thinking. Yet it was Halifax who again frustrated Churchill's ideas about supporting the Finns with British troops. Halifax realised that infringing the sovereignty of Norway and Sweden could force the Russians, and perhaps the Germans, to invade those countries as a direct result of British violation. Understandably, Norway and Sweden were also very fearful of Churchill's plans and point blank refused access through their territories, although aircraft, guns and supplies were eventually sent as aid. Thankfully though, the Finnish-Russo war came to an end on March 12th 1940 and this surely must have been a relief to all, particularly the Norwegians and Swedes as well as the British who had not particularly wanted to start a fight with the Soviet Union.

For Churchill's plans for naval operations at Narvik to be accepted he would need the full backing of General Sir Edmund Ironside, Chief of the Imperial Staff from September 1939 to May 1940, but this was far from straightforward as arguments persisted between the two men. Churchill's idea of naval action to bring an abrupt halt to the German transport was not to Ironside's liking. He wanted to put into operation an overland expedition, which would culminate in the occupation of the iron-ore mines. The arguments raged wearily on serving only to alienate Prime Minister Chamberlain and Foreign Secretary Halifax from the idea of taking any form of action. Still Churchill would not give in to inaction and the many, frequently tedious debates wore on, often late into the long winter nights of 1939.

Meanwhile, on December 10th 1939 in Germany, Vidkun Quisling, a name later to be synonymous world-wide with the word traitor, was visiting Berlin as leader of the Norwegian Nationalist Socialist Party in an attempt to become more politically informed of events in Germany and to garner support for his movement. Through his intermediary, Albert Hagelin, Quisling participated in a meeting with Grossadmiral Erich Raeder, the C-in-C of the German Navy, who had previously expressed his favour of the Third Reich expanding their affairs in Scandinavia. Quisling, for his part, spoke readily about his fears of a British invasion of Norway and naturally Raeder was keen to hear what he had to say. The next day, December 12th, Raeder recounted Quisling's views positively to Hitler, the result of which led directly to the Führer inviting Quisling for talks the following day at the Reichskanzlei (Reich Chancel). Quisling did not hold back. He informed Hitler [wrongly] that the Norwegian Government had surreptitiously agreed to Allied forces occupying southern Norway and that the British would not respect Norwegian neutrality. Hitler could see that if the Allies were invited to Norway then his northern flank would be exposed. Quisling went further by offering to get his party followers, many of whom he claimed were in significant positions of civil responsibility, to seize Norway via a coup. He would then, as the leader, invite German forces to occupy Norway. Quisling's standpoint, which was without foundation, had influenced Hitler's thinking. The talk concluded and after Quisling had departed Generalmajor Alfred Jodl, chief of the operations office at OKW, was instructed to initiate a low-key investigation into how Norway could be occupied should the need arise. Jodl busied himself and by January the outline framework for 'Studie Nord' was in place. Even at that stage it was still a contingency plan against any British threat against Norway. Hitler knew that it was in his country's best interests for Norway to remain neutral, but if the Allies made moves towards Norway then they would be ready.

Whilst Churchill kept the debates on Norway simmering even he, as a visionary, could not forsee that events in Norway would erupt so quickly in the aftermath of an event considered by some to have finally persuaded Hitler on Britain's intentions as regards to Norwegian neutrality...the *Altmark* affair.

The *Altmark* – described in the official 1939 list as *'Deutschen Kriegsmarine trossschiff'* (German Navy supply ship) for the so called 'pocket battleship' *Graf Spee*, had been used to hold captured British merchant sailors from the ships that the *Graf Spee* had sunk.[15]

The Royal Navy, having thankfully seen the demise of the *Graf Spee* after she had been scuttled off the coast of Montevideo, now widened their search for the *Altmark*. The British authorities were convinced that the *Altmark* had merchant navy prisoners aboard taken from the *Graf Spee* after she had earlier sunk her mercantile quarry… and the British wanted them back. The hunt was on and the First Lord of the Admiralty, Winston Churchill, demanded results.

The *Altmark* fortuitously evaded detection by sailing northwards crossing over the equator line and into the North Atlantic. Her skipper, Captain Dau made good use of lookouts and at the slightest hint of smoke or superstructure on the horizon he would alter course and steer away from the sighting. After many days at sea the *Altmark,* skirting south east of Iceland, but north of the Faeroes, eventually reached Norwegian waters on Wednesday February 14th 1940; Dau was seeking the relative safety of the neutral fjords with their high snow covered mountains that have stood sentinel for an eternity over the dark, enigmatic waters that lay below. The *Altmark* had arrived just north of Trondheimsfjord and Dau's plan was to travel down the rugged western coastline keeping his ship well hidden from prying British eyes and then steal into the Skagerrak Sea during darkness. This tactic would afford him and his crew a furtive cloak of anonymity as the prison ship headed for a German port. Hamburg was the favoured choice, but the port of Kiel was also an option.

The *Altmark's* voyage around the Norwegian coastline was not without problems. The ship was stopped several times and boarded by Norwegian naval officers, although a full search was never conducted and the hopes of the prisoners stowed below were cruelly dashed.

At last the RAF finally spotted the *Altmark* and a message was immediately sent to all Royal Navy ships in the area using plain signal rather than code, such was the urgency of the situation. The *Altmark* sighting caused much excitement within the Admiralty and the senior naval men knew that the net was closing in as lookouts of the Royal Navy ships intensified their sweeping of the sea. Eventually the *Altmark* was spotted by HMS *Arethusa* and chased into Jossingfjord.[16] As collaboration with the Norwegian authorities was not possible, Captain Vian of HMS *Cossack* was ordered to take his destroyer alongside *Altmark* and board her. To the cries and shouts of *'the Navy's here!'* 299 British prisoners were released. The date was February 16th 1940.

Cossack came home to a hero's welcome, but to Germany it seemed that the Norwegians were either unable or unwilling to defend their neutrality. Equally, the Germans felt humiliated and Hitler, apoplectic with rage, ordered that plans for *'Operation Weserübung'* be intensified. In Hitler's view the loss of Norway to the Allies could not be tolerated. The countdown to invasion had begun in earnest.

On February 21st General der Infanterie Nicolaus von Falkenhorst, C-in-C of the German XXI Army Corps was summoned to Berlin and appointed in charge of the invasion of Norway. The appointment had come of something as a shock to Falkenhorst who was then ordered by Hitler to go away for a few hours and consider how to occupy Norway. Falkenhorst duly returned armed with the only piece of information he could find on Norway – a Bädeker tourist guide and map. Following that inauspicious start, Falkenhorst's preparations became rather more focused. Norway was to be taken by land, sea and air with Oslo, Bergen, Stavanger, Narvik, Kristiansand, Arendal, Egersund and Trondheim falling to German forces with little if any bloodshed…if the Norwegian forces proved not to be hostile.

Subsequently, on March 1st 1940, Hitler issued the directive for implementing *Operation Weserübung*. The Allies, not realising or predicting Germany's intentions were about to play 'catch up'.

The consequences of Britain's actions in Norwegian waters in the *'Altmark Affair'* had now brought about a chain of events that were to result in far more serious repercussions for all, particularly Norway. For the Admiralty, the *Altmark* affair was fully justified by the release of a large number of British and foreign national prisoners but for Norway there was understandable anger and dismay that their neutrality had been breached so blatantly. Foreign Minister Koht dispatched a strongly worded diplomatic note of protest to Britain, whilst according to Kersaudy, King Haakon voiced his concern by confiding to the French minister, Count de Dampierre, that Norway was being used as a football field by the two antagonists. Meanwhile in Germany, Admiral Raeder was told by an enraged Hitler that Norway could no longer maintain her neutrality and that as a result there was only one option to take: invade. The German press and radio also added their collective voice of scorn. Planning for *Operation Weserübung* now took on a renewed urgency and by early April 1940,

German naval units and their merchant support were slipping quietly out of port: the simultaneous invasion of Denmark and Norway had begun.

It was to be Britain who first seriously violated the neutral waters surrounding Norway by implementing *Operation Wilfred,* the laying of mines at the entrance of Vestfjord on April 8th. British and French ministers sent diplomatic notes to the Norwegian Foreign Secretary stating that their reasons for sowing the mines were to interrupt the passage through Norwegian territorial waters of all ships *'carrying war contraband'.*[17] Later that day the Norwegian Government gloomily debated the issue and as a result a solemn note of protest was sent to the British and French governments. All that had been achieved was for attentions to be drawn away from the German fleet that had already sailed in number towards Denmark and Norway and although there had been plenty of warnings to the Allied and Norwegian governments, their reactions to the news of a possible German invasion was one of total disbelief. With the exception of a few alert and farsighted types the reactions of Britain, France and Norway in view of the information received could be considered nothing short of shameful and shambolic.

During the night of the 8th and early hours of the 9th April 1940, Germany invaded Norway and Denmark with a proclamation from Joseph Goebbels that both countries had been *'taken under the protection of the Reich to forestall Allied occupation'.*[18]

Despite some resistance from the Norwegians the invasion was largely successful, although the loss of the Hipper class cruiser, *Blücher,* was to be a significant blow to the German plan of taking Oslo quickly.

For their part Britain and the Allies had been caught napping and the response to the invasion is considered by many to have bordered on the farcical at times, although the resourcefulness and professionalism of sailors, soldiers and airmen cannot be brought into question. Important clues as to the intentions of the Germans were on offer; reports to the Foreign Office and Britain's Secret Service indicated that an attack on Norway was forthcoming, but these reports were largely ignored. Harry Hinsley, a Cambridge undergraduate who was on the staff of the Naval Section of Bletchley Park, had been monitoring German naval W/T traffic and had noted a dramatic increase on the Baltic frequency. He also noted that a completely new frequency had been born and was in use. He duly reported his findings to his seniors, but it appears that no deductions were made or further action taken. Clearly, the different departments being handed these clues were not coordinating their resources and any indication about the intentions of the Germans were ignored.[19]

Meanwhile, Captain Henry Denham, the British naval attaché in Denmark had noted significant German warship movements heading for Norway from his vantage point at Rödby. One of the ships he identified was the *Blücher*, but his report to the Admiralty warning them that Norway was the probable destination, and ironically received by his friend, Captain Ralph Edwards (Duty Captain at the Admiralty) on the evening of April 7th, was ignored by Winston Churchill, who had retorted, *'I don't think so'* after Edwards had advised him of Denham's telegram.[20] It wasn't just the UK that was ignoring the many warning signals. Similar shortcomings were occurring in Norway, France and Denmark. Interestingly, Sweden was aware of what was going on, but decided to keep her counsel, although there was an instance on April 5th when the Head of Swedish Intelligence, Oberst Carlos Adlercreutz called his counterpart in Oslo, Oberstløytnant Wrede-Holm to warn him that Sweden had reliable information that the Germans were going to attack Denmark and then Norway. Similar information was also received from the Danes; again no action was taken.[21] It would appear then that the collective eyes and minds of the Allies and their neutral neighbours were rendering themselves blind and oblivious to the approaching danger.

By late evening of April 7th, it was obvious that a major German naval undertaking was in progress and, attempting to prevent what the Allies considered would be a German break-out into the Atlantic, Admiral Sir Charles Forbes dispatched the Home Fleet north-east out of the British naval base of Scapa Flow late that day. Meanwhile, the 2nd Cruiser Squadron under the command of Vice-Admiral Collins departed Rosyth and headed towards Stavanger. The plan was to arrive at a point off the Norwegian coast the next day and then sweep northwards, but a combination of poor weather, misreading of signals and miscalculating the German intentions meant that the Royal Navy failed to locate their quarry, with the exception of the destroyer HMS *Glowworm* (pennant H92), which happened by chance to locate and engage German destroyers, although *Glowworm* later lost contact with the ships due to the atrocious weather. Events then turned fully against *Glowworm* when the German cruiser *Admiral Hipper* appeared out of the gloom. It was a one-sided affair, but *Glowworm's* skipper, Lieutenant Commander Roope and his crew fought bravely as they took on the mighty cruiser. German shells smashed into the destroyer killing and wounding a great many sailors. The bridge was taken out and steering was completely lost. It was at this point that the *Glowworm*, still making smoke, turned towards the *Admiral Hipper* and rammed her. The collision caused the bow of the *Glowworm* to shear off and as she drifted clear of the *Admiral Hipper* the destroyer was subjected to further shelling until Kapitän zur See Heye ordered a ceasefire. *Glowworm* was lost and sinking fast. Lt Commander Roope gave the command to abandon ship and the survivors took to the water.

Kapitän Heye, considering that there was the possibility of British ships close by, bravely chose to heave to positioning his ship so that the currents would bring the stricken survivors towards the *Admiral Hipper* and so began the humanitarian rescue of British sailors. Forty-four men were eventually saved and brought aboard via the ship's nets, although some unfortunately succumbed later to their wounds and the effects of a very cold sea. Lt Commander Roope made it to the scramble nets, but mortally wounded, and with any lingering strength being sapped away by the intense numbing cold, slipped the safety of the nets. He was lost to the sea.[22]

The Royal Navy hurriedly abandoned its *Plan R4*, the somewhat vague military objective of taking Narvik and securing the iron ore routes in the event of a German invasion of Norway.[23] The troops that had already embarked at Rosyth were taken quickly off, along with their kit, and on April 8th the 1st Cruiser Squadron put to sea to join up with the Home Fleet. Meanwhile, alarming news was filtering through to the Admiralty that a procession of German warships was sailing northwards and was passing through the Kattegat. Few at the Admiralty actually believed that Norway and Demark were the targets thinking instead that the German naval force was preparing to breakout into the Atlantic; the stable door was open. The confused state of affairs continued, and it was only the beginning. A few days later the Royal Navy later scored a tremendous victory at Narvik with the sinking of a number of enemy destroyers, but at some cost to their own.

In the UK the reaction to the German invasion was one of complete surprise. The War Cabinet met immediately to discuss the response, but it wasn't until April 13/14th that the Allies took part in the first operation to land troops on Norwegian soil at Namsos with *'Operation Henry',* the landing of 350 Royal Marines and soldiers. Subsequent landing operations followed with allied troops pouring in, yet the whole process was hamstrung with virtually no air support or artillery, poor communications, changes of leadership and inadequate war kit complete with confused, countermanded and perplexing orders that merely added to the disorder and turmoil.

From the German perspective, the invasion of Norway had been largely very successful, save for the sinking of the *Blücher* in Oslofjord. All objectives had been met and generally *Operation Weserübung* (Weser Exercise), the code name for the simultaneous invasion plan of Denmark and Norway, had been effective.[24] The plan to ensure a *fait accompli* was that all the designated targets of Oslo, Bergen, Stavanger, Trondheim, Narvik and Tromsø were to be occupied concurrently. This would ensure

German troops landing at Fornebu – Oslo. Picture credit: Tore G Eggen

resistance was kept to an absolute minimum. If the Norwegian Royal Family, government and media were captured then complete capitulation would inevitably follow. With the capture of Norway would also come the resources for extended warfare against the Allies, in particular Britain. Airfields and naval bases would permit the Germans to control the north Atlantic with their U-boats able to freely attack allied shipping as well as secure virtually unhindered supplies of iron-ore for their war machine. Norway was also seen as a very useful embarkation point for a proposed invasion of Britain.

However, the loss of the *Blücher* was a significant blow to the invasion plans of the Germans; the Norwegian capital of Oslo was vitally important for the invaders and an unopposed occupation sweeping up all in their path including capturing the country's gold bullion would have enabled the Germans to control a whole nation; to determine, force and administer laws; to engage a work force for the good of the Fatherland, and to strip a sovereign nation of its moral, mineral and monetary resources so that the Germans could construct an even bigger empire. Far more important to Hitler though, was the securing of the ports and airfields that would allow Germany to be within striking distance of Britain. Conversely, the invaders had also stopped Britain from possibly taking Norway for her own purposes. But in their eagerness to conquer they made mistakes, the biggest of which was to underestimate the gritty determination of a few Norwegians to protect their country as best they could, albeit with very limited means.

The Germans for their part had captured yet another country enslaving its people and securing material resources to feed their war machine, but the cost was not insignificant. They lost three cruisers and ten destroyers as well as various other ships during the campaign and nearly all of the surface fleet had been damaged in some way. If there had been thoughts of using Norway as a stepping-stone to the invasion of Britain then this was put on hold. The *Kriegsmarine* were far from ready.

The Allied response to the German invasion was muddled at best and by late May it was clear that the campaign to oust the Germans had failed dismally, though in many minds it had finished long before then. Evacuation quickly followed and by June 8th 1940 the Allies had completely withdrawn from Norway. Two days later on June 10th Norway

CLOSING PRICES · *EVENING STANDARD* April 9 1940 · FINAL NIGHT EXTRA

Evening Standard

Amusements 12
Radio 14

BLACK-OUT 8.15 pm, 5.48 am
NOON
Rises 7.4 am ; Sets 9.38 pm

No. 36,066   LONDON, TUESDAY, APRIL 9, 1940   ONE PENNY

NORWAY AND DENMARK INVADED: THE ALLIES WILL GIVE FULL AID

Nazi Battle-Cruiser Reported Sunk

"BRITISH FORCE ON WAY," SAYS NEW YORK

IT WAS REPORTED IN STOCKHOLM TO-NIGHT THAT NORWEGIAN COASTAL BATTERIES SANK A GERMAN BATTLE CRUISER, BELIEVED TO BE THE GNEISENAU, IN OSLO FIORD, SAYS BRITISH UNITED PRESS.

THE British and French Governments are to extend full aid to Norway, following the invasion of Norway and Denmark by German troops to-day.

The British Foreign Office announced this afternoon that the necessary naval and military steps are being taken in conjunction with the French. They have informed Norway that they will fight the war in full association with them.

It is learned that the British statement refers only to Norway because it is impossible at the moment to say what the position is in Denmark, as all communications are cut off.

REPORTS THAT A BRITISH EXPEDITIONARY FORCE IS ON THE WAY TO NORWAY HAVE BEEN RECEIVED IN NEW YORK, STATES REUTER.

GERMAN FORCES LANDED ON THE SOUTH COAST OF NORWAY AT 3 A.M., AND ARE REPORTED TO HAVE OCCUPIED A NUMBER OF TOWNS. DENMARK WAS INVADED AT 4.30 A.M. BY OVERWHELMING FORCES. THE GERMANS CLAIM THAT COPENHAGEN WAS IN THEIR HANDS BY 8 A.M.

OSLO WAS BOMBED SEVERAL TIMES FROM THE AIR. IMMEDIATE EVACUATION WAS ORDERED. TO-NIGHT IT WAS STATED IN BERLIN THAT THE CITY HAD BEEN "OCCUPIED WITHOUT INCIDENT."

A Reuter message from Malmo, Sweden, states that Denmark is entirely in German hands. Armed forces have occupied virtually all the important towns and military points.

German airplanes bombed Christiansand, at the southern tip of Norway. The town was evacuated and coastal batteries at Oakarsberg shelled German warships which were attempting to land troops.

Oslo radio stated at 11 a.m. that four German warships were trying to get through the Oslo Fiord. One got through and then ran aground in shallow water.

During the night warships which had tried to force an entry

(Continued on PAGE THREE, Column One)

Our Larders Will Keep Full

A MINISTRY of Food official stated to-day that loss of Danish provisions would not mean that Britain would have to draw on the national food reserves. Arrangements made elsewhere would enable us to keep the larders full.

The invasion of Denmark did not constitute a serious assault on the home front, which remained strong.

"PROPHECY FULFILLED" —PREMIER

Nazi 'Mining' Excuse Is Exploded

MR. CHAMBERLAIN told the House of Commons this evening that the Nazi expedition to invade Norway must have sailed before the British mining of Norwegian waters was announced.

If they had left their nearest port, Cuxhaven — 700 miles away—immediately after the announcement, they could not yet have arrived.

Ever since the beginning of the war Germany had attempted to dominate Scandinavia and to control both the political and economic policy of the Scandinavian States.

Germany's pressure on these States had been steadily increasing, and they claimed and exercised the right to dictate their policy towards Finland during the Finnish-Soviet war.

The Premier reminded the House, that speaking on March 19 after the Finnish-Soviet peace, he said :

"What is the result to Scandinavia? Has the security of Norway and Sweden been preserved?" On the contrary, the danger has been brought nearer than ever to these two countries till it stands upon their doorsteps.

He had said then that these States would not be safe unless they showed their determination to save themselves and to join with others who were ready to come to their defence.

"Double Advantage"

Mr. Chamberlain continued: " Some of my listeners may have thought those words exaggerated, but now we see the fulfilment to the letter of the prophecy they contained.

"Since that date the situation has further

(Continued on Back Page, Column One)

THE NEW WAR

Evening Standard Naval Correspondent, the Military Correspondent, and George Malcolm Thomson explain the German Invasion, with MAP—PAGE SEVEN.
How Denmark was invaded—PAGE THREE.
Cabinets meet—PAGE FIFTEEN.

Headline from the *Evening Standard* of April 9th 1940

capitulated. The Norwegian Campaign was over and it would be five long years before Norway was once again free of tyranny.

Perhaps the words of General Archibald Wavell, written as an introduction to Dudley Clarke's superb account of his time in the British Army 'Seven Assignments', best sum up the debacle that was the Norwegian Campaign:

> The beginnings of any war by the British are always marked by improvidence, improvisations, and too often, alas, impossibilities being asked of the troops.

Yet it would be wrong to completely harangue everything that surrounded this calamitous debacle. There are many accounts of immense bravery; outstanding leadership, seamanship, airmanship and remarkable soldiering that lay incongruous with the campaign, but arguably none more deserving of being retold than the story of the Norwegian gold transport. Taking place at the very beginning of the invasion it resulted in muted success for the Norwegian Government and its people when the prospect of occupation was devastating and overwhelming. Yet, this story could not have been told without the intervention of one man, Colonel Eriksen, a Norwegian officer, who if he had not taken upon himself to give the order to fire upon invaders and defend his country's neutrality at Oscarsborg Fort then a Royal family, a government and 50 tons of gold would have been lost to the invaders. This man, along with notables such as Nicolai Rygg, Fredrik Haslund, Nordahl Grieg, and ably supported by many other loyal Norwegians as well as the men of the Royal Navy, performed a duty whose legacy can still be seen today.

1

The Sinking of the *Blücher*
April 8–9th

During the night of April 8th 1940, a procession of blacked-out warships from gruppe (group) V (also known as *Gruppe Oldenburg*) entered Norwegian waters intent on taking Oslo. Other gruppes were attacking Norwegian ports simultaneously: Narvik (gruppe I), Trondheim (gruppe II), Bergen (gruppe III), Kristiansand and Arendal (gruppe IV) and Egersund (gruppe VI). Norway was being invaded.

Oslo – the prized capital city of Norway was within a few hours of being taken by the Germans, but events were not to prove straightforward for the invaders. It could be argued that it was sheer arrogance that was to prove their downfall at such a crucial moment of the invasion or at the very least pure misfortune. Leading the invasion force was the brand new 18,000-ton Hipper-class cruiser *Blücher*, Flagship of Konteradmiral Oskar Kummetz and commanded by 47-year-old Kapitän zur See Heinrich Woldag. *Blücher* was named after the Großer Kreuzer *Blücher* (1908–1915), which was sunk during the *'Battle of the Doggerbank'*. Laid down at the Kiel Works in August 1935, she was commissioned in September 1939 at a cost of around 87 million Reichmarks. *Blücher* had had only just enough time to 'work up' sufficiently before she was sent to Norway with a novice crew. Sea trials are crucial to the 'working up' of any ship prior to becoming fully operational and *Blücher* had spent a mere 20 days in total at sea accompanied by *Emden*, an ageing light cruiser, in preparation for *Operation Weserübung*. Weather conditions in the Baltic at that time were nothing short of atrocious and coupled with the restrictions of limited sea-trials meant that there had simply not been enough time to test fire her 20.3cm guns, or her torpedo batteries;

damage control training and action station drills were also inadequate…a deficiency that would later contribute to a tragic outcome for many of the German crew.

The crew assigned to the *Blücher* assembled whilst the ship was being completed in the yard allowing the crew to become familiar with each other. This was one encouraging point in what was otherwise a very hurried affair. Only a few of the sailors had previously been drafted to other ships and to hinder matters further many of the officers were also inexperienced, with only a handful having previous battle experience of some description. On April 6th *Blücher* docked at Swinemünde and once darkness had fallen crews immediately started the process of embarkation of troops, propaganda, war material, civilian and administrative staff. Secrecy was of the essence and only Kummetz, Woldag and their senior staff officers had been briefed of their task. Soldiers were quartered below decks and ordered to remain there whilst their equipment was stowed atop. Rumours of their destination were rife amongst those not senior enough to be informed, but the rumours remained just that; the destination would remain a secret until orders permitted otherwise.

The loading of war material began in earnest, but due to the urgency of the operation, and also for security reasons, training ammunition was not removed from *Blücher's* magazines to dockside to prevent any hint of what *Blücher* was preparing for; live ammunition was merely stowed on top of the practice rounds. To compound matters further, and due to the severe lack of space below decks, the soldiers stowed their ammunition in the Torpedo Room and in the aircraft hangar. Lifejackets for the soldiers were not issued, but strapped to the guardrails along the superstructure: crucial decisions that would later have far reaching consequences.

On April 7th, *Blücher* departed Swinemünde for Kiel with *Emden* and two torpedo boats – *Albatros* and *Kondor* as escorts. At Kiel, *Blücher* anchored beside *Lützow*, a so-called 'Pocket Battle-ship'. She was originally destined for Trondheim, but re-ordered to sail with *Blücher*. This however, was initially against the wishes of Admiral Raeder who wanted her to begin distant ocean raiding.

With the group assembled, Rear Admiral Kummetz convened a conference aboard *Blücher* with captains, army commanders and navigational officers invited to attend. Finalised details of the invasion

German troops of 183th Mountain Regiment and 83rd Pioneer Unit embarking *Admiral Hipper* on the afternoon of April 6th at Cuxhaven, Germany. Meanwhile, a similar scenario was being played out on the *Blücher*.

Men of the Kriegsmarine look on whilst troops board the *Admiral Hipper*.

plans were discussed and for many this was the first indication of their intended operation.

It was during the early hours of April 8th 1940 that *Blücher, Lützow, Emden, Albatros*, and *Kondor* raised anchor and sailed north; with torpedo boat *Möwe* joining the convoy. Their destination: neutral Norway.

Timing was fundamental to the success of the operation and there was no doubt as to what was required of the invasion force with the following Decree for the Execution of *Operation Weserübung*:[25]

> The operation in itself is contrary to all the principles in the theory of naval warfare. According to this theory, it could be carried out by us only if we had naval supremacy. We do not have this; on the contrary, we are carrying out the operations in the face of a vastly superior British fleet. In spite of this the C-in-C Navy believes that, provided surprise is complete, our troops can and will successfully be transported to Norway. On many occasions in the history of war those very operations have been successful which went against all the principles of warfare, provided they were carried out by surprise.
>
> The critical moment is the penetration of the harbours while passing the coastal fortifications. It is expected that this will succeed if carried out by surprise, and that the Norwegians will not make the decision to fire quickly enough, if they decide to do so at all.
>
> Report of the Commander-in-Chief of the Navy
> to the *Führer*, 9 March 1940

The following is an unconfirmed decree from Grand Admiral Raeder supposedly issued to the combined German force prior to the invasion.

> The Führer and Supreme Commander, in order to ensure vital German interests, has imposed upon the Wehrmacht a task, the success of which is of decisive importance to the war.
>
> The execution and protection of the landing operations by the Kriegsmarine will take place mainly in an area in which not Germany, but England with her superior naval forces, is able to exercise control of the sea. In spite of this we must succeed, and we will, if every leader is conscious of the greatness of the task and makes a supreme effort to reach the objective assigned to him. It is impossible to anticipate the course of events and the situations that may arise locally. Experience shows that luck and success are

on the side of him who is eager to discharge his responsibilities with boldness, tenacity and skill.

The pre-requisite for the success of the operation are surprise and rapid action. I expect the senior officer of every group and every commanding officer to be governed by an inflexible determination to reach the port assigned to him in the face of any difficulty that may arise. I expect them to enter the ports of disembarkation with the utmost resolution, not allowing themselves to be deterred by the holding and defence measures of the local commanders, nor by guard ships and coastal fortifications.

Any attempt to check or hinder the advance of our forces must be repulsed. Resistance is to be broken ruthlessly in accordance with the directives in the operational orders.

Gruppe V sailed through a flat-calm Kattegat sea during the early hours of April 8th unmolested by the Royal Navy, and by 06:00 (German Time) had passed the Danish minefield in the Great Belt – the tensions high and palpable to the invaders. At 12:00 restrictions were lifted and soldiers and sailors paraded on deck to be informed of their target. Excitement and apprehension engulfed the ranks of the servicemen as the reality of their mission enveloped them. British submarines were known to be nearby, but how near nobody knew, but they would attack if they were in a position to do so. Were the Norwegians on alert? Would they bring their coastal guns to bear on the armada?

At around 19:00 an alarm from *Albatros* warned the invading convoy of a confirmed submarine contact and almost immediately torpedo tracks were sighted heading for *Lützow*. The ships breathed a sigh of relief as they all passed harmlessly by the cruiser, which was already operating a standard zigzag manoeuvre. *Albatros* broke off from the convoy and followed the tracks in an attempt to engage the submarine with depth charges, but the submarine, HMS *Triton*, somehow evaded the onslaught and escaped.

The convoy continued unabated with *Albatros* rejoining as darkness descended. The night began cold and clear with sea conditions ideal for the group, but as the evening wore on a mist developed. *Blücher*, as Flagship, ordered 'Action Stations!', a total blackout, battle ensigns lowered and distance between the larger ships reduced to 600 metres with all ships in standard line astern. Shrouded aft lamps were the only means of ensuring that ships remained on station with each other.

The approach to Oslo necessitated a long, slow passage up the Oslofjord. Rain showers and occasional fog hindered visibility. At 23:25 on April 8th (Norwegian time) the Norwegians became alert to unnamed ships entering the fjord. One by one the warning beacons of the lighthouses were extinguished and it was now clear to Kummetz that the Norwegians knew of their presence. The convoy edged forward ever closer to their intended target. A request from Captain Thiele of the *Lützow* to increase speed was summarily rejected by an irritated Kummetz. Thiele's judgement was that an increase in speed would greatly reduce the readiness of the Drøbak Battery to engage the invaders, but Kummetz's thinking opposed Thiele's – that the Norwegians would not attack. If Kummetz harboured any vestiges of hope for an unopposed invasion then he was sadly mistaken when at around midnight the port side of *Blücher* was illuminated by a single searchlight.

The converted Norwegian whaler, *Pol III*, a 214-ton patrol vessel armed only with a single 76 mm gun and a searchlight, had received orders to be at readiness. Manned by 15 sailors called up for the duration of the Neutrality Watch and commanded by Captain Leif Welding-Olsen, a reserve naval officer from Horten, it became clear to all that something was up, but they knew no more than that. Consequently, Welding-Olsen ordered his men to keep a sharp lookout for anything out of the ordinary. The captain's suspicions were confirmed when at 22:00 the lights from the lighthouses were extinguished.[26] A few minutes later at 23:06 (Norwegian time), and to the utter amazement of *Pol III's* crew, a procession of large warships emerged from the misty haze that had cloaked Oslofjord. *Pol III* immediately focused her searchlight upon the lead ship.

The torpedo boat *Albatros* abandoned her station and turned menacingly towards *Pol III* countering the whaler with her searchlight. *Albatros* signalled and ordered *Pol III* to stop engines and not transmit from her radio, but the small Norwegian auxiliary fired off a warning signal to Horten naval base – *'Alien ships incoming at high speed'*. The German radio operator onboard *Albatros* vainly attempted to jam the signal, but more was to come from *Pol III* as she then bravely attempted to ram *Albatros*, holing the torpedo boat, although not enough to disable and sink her. The action took the Germans totally by surprise, though they soon recovered their senses as during the ramming two Norwegian

Gruppe II force enroute to attack neutral Norway. Men on the *Blücher* would have experienced a similar scene.

Close up of main armament on the *Admiral Hipper*. *Blücher* was unable to bring her main armament to bear on Oscarsborg Fort when she came under attack from the Norwegians.

sailors either jumped or were thrown onto *Albatros* due to the impact of ramming and were immediately captured and arrested. At the same time coloured flares were fired from *Pol III* in an attempt to warn Norwegian naval auxiliaries upstream and the coastal forts that '*Enemy ships are forcing the line*'. In response the Germans fired twice upon the small boat with their 105mm gun and raked the whaler with small calibre machine gun fire mortally injuring Captain Welding-Olsen. *Pol III* did not return fire as by now she was stricken. Welding-Olsen was carried and placed in the lifeboat, which was then lowered into the water, but as the Norwegians sailors clambered into the boat it capsized throwing all into the icy cold water. The majority of the sailors managed to climb back on to *Pol III,* but Welding-Olsen was by this time too weak through blood loss; succumbing to his injuries he let go of the upturned hull of the lifeboat and drifted away to his death.

The 13 remaining crewmen of *Pol III* were summarily hauled aboard the *Albatros,* and taken prisoner earning the dubious distinction of becoming the first Norwegian prisoners of war. Sadly, Captain Welding-Olsen's body was never recovered and was deemed lost forever to Oslofjord.

Albatros commander Kapitänleutnant Siegfried Strelow then ordered the destruction of *Pol III* and the gunners soon turned the whaler into a burning wreck.

> (NB some unconfirmed sources state that a German officer from *Albatros* boarded *Pol III* on the pretence of negotiating, but just after he left, and at a given signal, *Albatros* shelled *Pol III*. Other unconfirmed sources have said that *Pol III* accidentally bumped *Albatros*, which then opened fire on the Norwegians). It is reasonable to conclude that the captain and crew of *Poll III* were extremely brave to take on and engage the might of the Kriegsmarine and execute their duty as best they could that fateful night, especially under the neutrality circumstances that were currently in force.

The element of surprise was now utterly lost, and Kummetz fully realised this, but knew there was no other option than to carry on in obedience to Hitler's orders...to be in Oslo Harbour at 05:00 without deviation:

> I expect them to enter the ports of disembarkation with the utmost resolution, not allowing themselves to be deterred by the holding

and defence measures of the local commanders, nor by guard ships and coastal fortifications…

Kummetz left *Albatros* to deal with the aftermath of *Pol III* and the invading force headed northwards, having now been joined by 8 R-boats of the 1st R-Boat Flotilla.[27] Mist and fog now both shrouded and protected the invaders from the searching eyes of the Norwegian defenders, but sharp-eyed lookouts on Rauøy and Bolærne Forts managed to spot the large, shadowy grey shapes as they made their way up the fjord and despite the gloom, the forts trained their searchlights on the warships. *Blücher* replied focusing her own searchlights on the forts. The guns of the invaders were trained on the forts, but no shots were fired either from the ships or the forts. A signal lamp from a Norwegian minesweeper also challenged *Blücher*, but the signal was ignored and *Blücher* continued up the fjord and into the relative safety of thick fog. A little further on the force stopped momentarily to disembark troops, who then went on to quickly capture the Norwegian forts to the rear, including the Norwegian naval base of Horten.

Having disgorged troops and assigned various R-boats to support them gruppe V continued their journey at a slow pace. The fog was now lifting. The force approached the Drøbak Narrows determined that nothing would stop the invasion. Kummetz's group was ahead of schedule. His orders were to pass the Narrows at 04:15 – a simultaneous point in time as the other groups were nearing or reaching their intended targets. But Kummetz pushed on towards the Narrows early – 03:30 – his thinking possibly being that the Norwegians were aware of the force and that the element of surprise had evaporated. Only the old fort at Oscarsborg Fort stood in Kummetz's way. This was regarded as obsolete by the Germans, along with many other elements of the Norwegian forces, and therefore not considered a threat. Kummetz was confident that the firepower of the invasion force would deal adequately and ruthlessly with any defence measures that the Norwegians cared to put up. Whether arrogance played a part is unclear, but the decision to place *Blücher* as the lead ship, without a protective screen, can only be seen as naval folly of the highest order.

(NB Vidkun Quisling, on his visit to Berlin, had advised that there were no minefields in Oslofjord and that the coastal forts would not open fire unless specific orders were issued from the Government.)

At 02:30 *Kondor* was dispatched, along with two R-boats, to Horten. Meanwhile, as they closed in on their intended target the battle order for the three cruisers was *Blücher* followed by *Lützow* and *Emden* at 600m intervals. *Möwe* and R-boats 18 and 19 made up the rear. The speed of the convoy was now 7 knots. A short while later two Norwegian auxiliaries, *Alpha* and *Furu* spotted the slow moving warships and opened up with their searchlights. No shots were fired from either side, but the tension on the ships must have risen dramatically. The invading convoy continued on their way up Oslofjord closing in on the Drøbak Narrows and Oscarsborg Fort. The order for increased speed did not come. *Blücher* was now just moments away from disaster as Admiral Kummetz, having dismissed the fort as obsolete manoeuvred *Blücher* into the narrows, and unknown to him, towards a watery grave.

Oscarsborg Fort commanded the Drøbak Narrows – effectively the sea gateway to Oslo. The fort, built during the Crimean War and reputed then to be the strongest defence of its time in Northern Europe, was ideally situated on South Kaholmen, a small island in the middle of the fjord where the channel narrows to around 1000 metres. The fort has stood

Guarding the approaches; a view looking over the top of one of the guns at Oscarsborg Fort. Photo credit: Tore G Eggen.

sentinel over all who have entered the capital by the sea routes, carefully observing the traders, tourists and armed warships of visiting nations. It was armed, ironically, with three German built Krupp 28cm (11inch) cannons named Josva, Aron and Moses. The cannons required their own manually operated crane to lift the 600lb shells to the breach. The rate of fire was approximately one round every five minutes, but only a few drafted men manned the guns, so any chance of firing off a succession of rounds was somewhat improbable.

Flanked on the mainland eastern side of the fjord, and just north of Drøbak were three smaller guns – 15cm (6inch) – based at Husvik along with two 57mm (6pdr) guns sited on the foreshore. But it was Oscarsborg Fort that was to deliver the first telling blows.

Oberst (Colonel) Birger Eriksen, a private, laconic man, but totally professional in manner had been warned that a significant naval invasion force was on its way. At this point he was probably unaware of the intentions of the force or the nationality, but he began preparations in readiness for any actions the fort would have to take to protect the neutrality of Norway. With only two sergeants and 23 drafted men Eriksen was able to muster crews for two of the guns only. Another crucial factor for Eriksen to consider was the darkness and fog…how would they see their targets? The answer was to station two small patrol boats south of the fort so that Eriksen could be given advanced warning of the invader's approach. At around 04:00 Eriksen ordered the torpedo battery to be readied and to open fire if necessary.

To enable him to identify the number of ships, type of target, and distance from his guns, Eriksen climbed onto the grassy hill that formed part of the earthwork defence of the fort and placed himself between two of the cannons. Suddenly a searchlight illuminated the profile of *Blücher* and Eriksen could now clearly see his target. He estimated and ordered range for sights to be set at 1400 metres. The small Norwegian force replied that they were ready. With his guns standing by and batteries at Kopås and Husvik reporting prepared and ready Oberst Birger Eriksen gave the order to fire! It was 04:21.

Norwegian army recruit, Private Fevang, then stationed at Oscarsborg Fort recalled the moments when the fort opened fire on the *Blücher*:[28]

No one around where we were thought that it [the war] would spread to Norway. We believed that Norway would remain neutral and avoid it, but on the 8th of April we heard about ships that had violated and so on. But we trusted the British; they ruled the sea. Norwegians have always had a good relationship with the British; we thought we would get aid from the British.

I arrived as a 22 year old recruit, and received the supplies that I needed. We were quartered by the torpedo battery, in a room by the officer school, with bunks for 36 men. It was quite crowded. That's where we stayed on the night of 9th of April. On the evening of 8/9th we were sitting in the mess, when we heard about ships in Sørlandet, and it started to sound a bit strange. But we were young and didn't think too much about it, so we went to our bunks. Everyone went to bed and went to sleep.

The cannons started firing during the night and woke us up. We told ourselves that it was the soldiers (former soldiers drafted to Oscarsborg Fort) drilling with the cannons. But then we heard more and more shooting. Someone climbed up onto the window ledge to see out – it was a window high above the ground and shouted 'it's a ship going down the fjord, in full flames!' Then a Fenrik (Lieutenant) opened the door and shouted: "Are you up men? It's war, get out, get your clothes on and get out!" We got our clothes on, and while we got dressed we heard the torpedo battery fire two torpedoes and then hit the *Blücher*. When we went outside we saw *Blücher*, going through Drøbakksundet in flames. It went a little further and went on its side, still burning, then oil started to appear on the water. We saw them [the Germans] go from the deck and up on the side, we saw the propellers. The Germans sang 'Deutschland Deutschland'. Then the *Blücher* went down, and there was a lot of oil on the water and it started burning. We heard a lot of shouting for help. They were screaming. They were swimming in oil. Some were swimming towards land towards Drøbak. We were rallied up and the captain came over to speak to us and asked how we were. We talked for a while, but then our captain received a message about planes coming in from the south and that he was afraid that they would bomb us. We were told to follow him down some stairs, and we ended up at the ammunition depot, which was empty, except with lots of empty shelves. More than a hundred men went down there. The big iron doors were then closed behind us. We were now safe from enemy bombing. The planes came and started to bomb the fort.

Wave upon wave of planes attacked and dropped their bombs on us. A lieutenant told us to keep our mouths open, because then we would stand the pressure from the bombs much better. We were pretty safe down there, because of 7–8 metres of concrete. There was a tunnel that went all the way from the top and down to the dock, where ammunition was delivered at Borgen. During the day, it became calmer and quieter and some of us opened the iron door and went outside. But then more planes attacked us. Then we ran and they came straight down on us, shooting. I was one of the last ones to come in and close the door. They shot straight at the door, with me just on the other side of it, and as I remember it made a lot of noise!

Blücher's First Lieutenant Fregattenkapitän Erich Heymann took it upon himself, with complete professionalism and incredible foresight, to complete a report after the loss of the *Blücher*. This was because all official books, including the War Diary and Ship's log were lost with the *Blücher* when she went down. Heymann completed his report in Oslo as soon as he was able to. Magnanimously he freely admits that the recollections are his own and of individual serving officers who survived the sinking, but that his '*considerations, impressions, and conclusions*' may not have been shared by his commander, Kapitän zur See Woldag, who was intending to comment upon the report, but a short time later lost his life in an air crash in Oslo Fjord.

In his report Heymann gives many clues to how the loss of the *Blücher* came about and as with all accidents it is a catalogue of errors leading to the final conclusion. Some have placed the loss of the *Blücher* directly at the lack of planning by the German Naval Staff and poor execution of the operation by its commander, Admiral Oscar Kummetz, but there appears to be no single overwhelming factor, just accumulative errors.

The *Blücher* was laid down in August 1935 and launched in June 1937 with characteristic Third Reich celebration. However, some design changes were implemented almost immediately, the most dramatic being the change of the bow from a straight stem to a curved clipper bow (also known as an 'Atlantic' bow) giving her a most elegant, graceful appearance. On September 20th 1939 the *Blücher* was finally handed over to the Kriegsmarine. Her main armament was eight 203mm (8 inch) guns arranged in four twin turrets mounted fore and aft. Her anti-aircraft battery was impressive with twelve 105mm (4.1 inch) guns and supplemented with smaller weapons of various calibre.

The next few months were supposed to be spent on extensive, demanding sea trials in the Baltic, but *Blücher's* crew were denied this due to the severe weather of 1939/40 – one of the worst on record. The clock was ticking down on *Blücher* and her crew. Despite the setback of limited trials, the Kriegsmarine had hoped the *Blücher* would be fully operational by May 7th, but with winter raging in the Baltic this hope was dashed, in fact the *Blücher* only spent 20 days at sea up until April 1st – not nearly enough time for the crew to be fully proficient in the working up of their ship. Ominously, on April 7th the ship was listed as available for *"simple tasks"*; but it was Hitler's lust for Norway that sealed the fate of *Blücher* and much of her crew.

Heymann writes:[29]

> At the conclusion of dockyard building work, on March 30th 1940, the cruiser *Blücher* was released from the trials programme, which had already been extended as a consequence of the preceding winter's especially unfavourable ice conditions. Battle training (including engine room and damage control) had been restricted to individual exercises and theoretical instruction at the battle station. The battle regulations manual for all weapons and sections had been prepared (with the exception of the engine room, which was still in the drafting stage) and numerous emergency scenarios had been played out, with a run-through of solutions. These would be practised over and over if time permitted. On the other hand there had been no battle "exercises" for damage control and the engine room; furthermore, neither the heavy guns nor the torpedo installation had been fired – this had been planned for April, and the ship to be battle ready by May 3rd. In response to an enquiry of OKM on April 7th 1940, it had been reported: "Cruiser *Blücher* operational for simple tasks; heavy guns not fired, no battle exercises or engine room procedures, no damage control exercises." The commander and I put the report in this form because (1) the ship had already been in commission for 6 months and the ship's company was keen for action, and (2) it was still necessary to point out the existing deficiencies. At this point, however, in order that no incorrect conclusions be drawn, I would like to make it clear that when the critical hour came on 9 April 1940 there was no deficiency in the defence of the ship which might have contributed to its' loss.

Heymann's report goes on to list more clues:

> After leaving the dockyard *Blücher* was fitted out for five weeks; as a subterfuge, the gunnery officers had been told that the ship was to undergo an extended period of battle training in the eastern Baltic. Despite a great deal of persistence we had still not received delivery of the Marx floats – to my recollection ten to twelve of them each holding from 15 to 40 men – and eventually they arrived the day before sailing after much pressure had been exerted, together with life-jackets for the crew. About 700 of these lifejackets were the rubber type: these were distributed to those men whose action stations were below decks, while the remaining kapok vests were strapped to the guardrails on the superstructure deck. It had been intended to begin gunnery training following our release from the shipyard, and we now had aboard live ammunition plus a year's supply of practice ammunition for all calibres. The former had to be stowed on top of the latter before sailing, the commander having forbidden the unloading of the practice ammunition for security reasons. This meant ultimately that there was no room in the magazines for the ammunition brought aboard by the army personnel. All ship's boats, which we might have used for the purpose, were already secured aboard in readiness for the troop landings when we reached Norway.
>
> *Blücher* was supplied finally with two of the three aircraft promised, both fully crewed. One lodged on the catapult with a small quantity of fuel in the tank and the other in the hanger with an empty tank, but otherwise operational. The four 50kg bombs – two for each aircraft – were also stored in the hangar.
>
> 6th April: 'During the hours of darkness, about 800 men embarked aboard *Blücher*, bringing with them all their weapons and equipment, including four anti-tank guns plus crates of anti-tank shells, machine-gun and rifle ammunition and hand grenades. It weighed 21 tonnes as I remember. Because of the stowage problem in the magazine rooms, it had to be stowed in the torpedo workroom. Army personnel had not been supplied with life jackets ashore and it was not possible to have the items brought aboard subsequently for security reasons.

From Erich Heymann's well written and concise report it is clear that many of the men aboard *Blücher* would be lost due to poor decision making, reckless and dangerous stowage of kit and ammunition and a lack of personal safety equipment. His account of April 8/9th makes for very interesting reading:

By now the group was nearing the Norwegian coast and "Clear ship for battle" status was ordered for midnight. The army contingent remained in their assigned locations below decks in their respective groupings. The ship's landing party would only be piped on deck once the Drøbak Narrows had been passed, in order to avoid confusion with the army groups. It was a clear, but dark night. Shortly before the battle group entered Oslo Fjord a blacked-out vessel appeared ahead, turned on a searchlight and morsed a message. It was apparently a Norwegian patrol boat (*Pol 111*). *Albatros* was ordered by Konteradmiral Kummetz to capture it.

9th April – After I had received the reports of the senior gunnery officers I informed the commander at midnight that the ship was "clear for battle." Kapitän zur See Woldag ordered me to remain on the bridge. *Blücher* was illuminated by the searchlight batteries situated on either side of the fjord, presumably Bolearne and Rauöy. We responded with our own searchlights. On the bridge we heard the coastal guns fire a round, but as no splash or hit was observed it was assumed to be a warning shot. A little later the coastal beacons at the southern entrance to the fjord were extinguished.

At 00:15 the first motor minesweeping flotilla came up on the cruiser from astern, and towards 01:00 two boats (R18 and R19?) drew alongside the main after turrets port and starboard. 150 men of 5 company, 307th Infantry Regiment, with full equipment, were shipped out to the R-boats within 25 minutes. Once all ships had discharged according to plan, the voyage up-fjord continued.

At 03:00 *Albatros* reported having rammed and sunk a Norwegian patrol vessel and rescued her crew. At 03:30 the assault group for Horten naval base was detached.

It is worth pointing out that Heymann neglects to state in his otherwise comprehensive report how this patrol vessel was dealt with. Heymann continues:

As most coastal lights had now been doused Konteradmiral Kummetz announced his intention to pass through the Drøbak Narrows at first light. The ships therefore reduced speed to 7 knots and increased to 12 knots shortly before Drøbak. At about 04:40 (*German time*), at the approach to the Narrows, *Blücher* was illuminated by the searchlight from a patrol vessel. Soon afterwards, a small Norwegian patrol vessel (possibly a floating crane) took station to starboard ahead of *Blücher* for a short while. The entrance to the Narrows was flooded with light from searchlights situated on either side of the fjord. It was about 05:18. A searchlight raked the ship from stem to stern and back. We were dazzled by it. Our orders were to respond to light with light; we were only to open fire if the Norwegians began to shoot in earnest. The events recorded here happened so quickly within a very short time frame that no station was able to give an exact account of the sequence.

Passing through this narrowest part of the Oslo fjord, the activity of the searchlights created a very tense atmosphere aboard the cruiser, made worse by a mistiness through which no batteries or other details could be distinguished. The tension was dispelled suddenly at 05:19 when the Oscarsborg battery, about 500–600 metres away on the port bow, fired a 28cm shell, which passed above the fully staffed bridge and struck the main flak fire control position. The No 2 Gunnery Officer, Kapitänleutant Pochharnmer, was killed, together with several ratings. Flak Medium Weapons Officer Oberleutnant zur See Schiirdt was seriously wounded, but no injuries were reported from the foretop. On the bridge we felt a powerful air pressure and splinters were flying about. The commander gave permission at once to open fire and ordered the engines to maximum speed.

The heavy guns did not fire because no military target could be identified. Neither the foretop, the forward fire control, the night control centre, nor the after fire control had located the position from where the shell had been fired; nevertheless, both heavy and light flak opened up a lively fire following the first shell hit. Some houses, the shoreline and a Norwegian patrol vessel which was spraying our upper deck with machine gun fire were raked by our flak. Then one or two 28cm shells hit the aircraft hangar, which burst into flames. The aircraft on the catapult with 40 litres of fuel in the tank and the second aircraft housed in the hangar caught fire at once. Port 111 10.5cm gun was put out of action as a result of this hit. At the same time the Drøbak 15cm battery on the starboard beam fired about 25 rounds from a range of 400–600m, and at least twenty of these shells hit, mainly amidships on the port side between compartments IV and IX. Although the battery was to starboard, it was in a high position and could look down into the ship. Flak control B and Port 1 10.5cm guns were rendered unserviceable.

One of the first three hits put the rudder and engine telegraph out. The rudder lay slightly to port and the ship had a starboard tendency. Steering was attempted by rudder telegraph in Compartment 1, but because all message relay systems were unserviceable, engine commands were passed to the command centre by voice tube. The ship was very close to Kaholmen, and in order to move her away from the island the commander stopped the starboard shaft and ordered maximum speed astern. At that moment two heavy reverberations were felt through the ship, which led me to believe that we had run into a minefield marked on our charts. We discovered much later that we had been hit by two torpedoes fired from a land-based battery built into a rock on Kaholmen Island. After about three or four minutes the enemy guns fell silent as *Blücher* passed out of their field of fire. The speed of the ship had only increased to 15 knots. The commander ordered "cease fire" but the flak batteries did not conform because the order was not received owing to the destruction of the main flak fire control and most command relay systems.

Despite all the hits, we did not have the impression that the ship would not survive. The list was only 8–12 degrees. She was making a little way through the main channel after the commander corrected the effects of the rudder failure by the use of the other propellers. Shortly, the Chief Engineer reported that the centre turbine was no longer in use. The ship was now barely under way. Next the engine room reported that the other two plants had been closed down and that the ship was unmanoeuvrable. The Chief Engineer added later that he thought he could have the other turbines in service again in about an hour. In order to stop the ship drifting ashore under the effect of wind and current, the commander decided to anchor while awaiting repairs. A short while later communications with the engine room was lost. The forepeak anchor could not be freed owing to the list, the starboard anchor finding the bottom at 60m with 175m of chain run out. Without engine power there was no prospect of arriving at the arranged disembarkation point for the army contingent, and any idea of getting the ship's landing party ashore to capture Fornebu airfield had been abandoned since saving the ship took priority.

The serious damage in the aircraft hangar combined with the smaller calibre shell hits in the area of compartments IV to IX allowed the fire to take hold and develop into a roaring conflagration since damage control had not been able to take early measures to combat the spread.

When I informed the commander that the No 1 Damage

Control Officer in the command centre had reported that he did not have an overall picture of the flooding and fires in the ship, the commander ordered me to make a survey of the situation on deck. Below the Port 1 10.5cm gun the ship's side was torn open over a large area and folded back. Thick smoke and fierce flames were coming out of the opening. Where the torpedo workroom had been there was now a large hole in the deck. In the vicinity of the aircraft hangar and inside it a conflagration was raging through several decks. In the area of the starboard forward torpedo tube set rifle cartridges were detonating continuously. Great clouds of smoke and steam were rising from the funnel and amidships. Everywhere I went I found pump-master groups below decks and gun crews above decks engaged on fire-fighting duties. Ammunition threatened by the fire was thrown overboard; in some locations endangered ready ammunition was passed down into the magazines.

According to the battle regulations manual, and corresponding to the rules laid down on other ships, lines for fire-fighting purposes were not to be laid via the armour deck. This proved disastrous. When water pressure was requested later, it was found that sections of the lines had been ripped to shreds as a result of the hits and that at many stations where the under deck pumps or auxiliary machinery had been damaged no water could be supplied. For similar reasons the foam extinguishers could not be used. When men managed to connect up new lengths of hose, at first a little water could come through, then gradually the flow would become weaker and finally cease. In some places Minimax fire extinguishers were employed, but these proved of little or no use pitted against fires of the magnitude we were facing. In further inspections by the fire teams it was found that in some rooms, in preparation for the land fighting, Army personnel had been priming hand grenades when the fire arrived and caused the weapons to explode. In the battery deck many soldiers met their deaths engaged on this work.

In my inspection of the ship what I found most depressing was the fire teams were making inroads into the fire even though no possibility existed that it could be brought under control from the ship itself. Wherever I went and gave instructions, I found the crew working calmly and purposefully, but with insufficient equipment for the job.

After hearing Heymann's report Kummetz ordered all gunnery teams to focus on fire-fighting duties, he also attempted to order – via shortwave radio and searchlight – the torpedo boat *Möwe* alongside to help with fire-fighting, but this was to no avail as the crew on the *Möwe* failed to respond to the desperate messages. A fresh wind was assisting the fires and blowing the smoke forward choking all those in its thick, poisonous path. To compound matters further the currents were now controlling the *Blücher* – with her one operational anchor insufficient in holding her on station, she was now out of control. Kummetz ordered the starboard torpedoes be fired off as a precaution against premature explosions and these detonated themselves harmlessly against rocks in the fjord. The pistol charges from the port torpedoes were removed.

> Up to this point, and though the list had increased to 18 degrees, neither the commander nor I, nor probably any of the senior officers, had the impression that the ship could not be saved. My opinion changed when at about 06:30 as I was making my way from the starboard forward torpedo tube set, where I had had the Army ammunition jettisoned, to the bridge behind me the 0.5cm VII.8.2 magazine exploded with a great column of smoke which reached as high as the masthead. The magazines had not been fully flooded because of the lack of pressure in the seawater fire-fighting lines. There was a perceptible jolt felt throughout the ship and the list increased appreciably.
>
> Measures were set in hand to disembark the crew and remaining soldiers. Korvettenkapitän Zöpfel succeeded in getting the starboard cutter afloat. Kapitänleutnant Mihatsch received orders from me to take command of the cutter, which was to be reserved for the seriously wounded and two sick berth officers. The portside cutter had been badly damaged and was not worth lowering away. Korvettenkapitän Cyzan, whom I had stationed on the quarterdeck after the ship anchored, got two dinghies afloat and released the motor pinnance and motor yawl from their cradles, but the latter could not be lowered because the cranes were unserviceable. The commander gave the orders "all hands on deck" and "don lifejackets". However, most of the Kapok lifejackets strapped to the guardrail were burnt.
>
> The distance from the stern to the island of Askerholmen was less (about 300m) than that from the foredeck to the mainland (about 400–500m). The attempt to slip the anchor chain, so as to

allow the ship to drift ashore or go aground and thus avoid deaths caused by swimming in the icy water, failed.

The conflagration had divided the ship into two parts at amidships and it was no longer possible for one part to communicate with the other. On the foredeck and afterdeck all objects which could possibly be adapted for use as lifebuoys were laid out ready, Officers, NCOs and men all participated energetically in this work. In the stern Korvettenkapitän Cyzan and later the Chief Engineer had command. When the angle of heel reached 45 degrees, Korvettenkapitän Cyzan gave the order to abandon ship aft. I had the crew in the forward part of the ship and the remaining Army personnel assemble on the foredeck for a short address by the commander. Then the commander called for three cheers for the cruiser *Blücher*. Following this I called for three cheers for the commander and Konteradmiral Kummetz. The list increased drastically and the port guardrail was touching the water. Fuel oil was seeping into the sea amidships, but was fortunately not on fire. Kapitän zur See Woldag gave the orders to abandon ship at about 07:00. The behaviour of all was exemplary. Despite the great angle of heel all men remained calm

Blücher ablaze and sinking. Photo credit: Collection of The Norwegian Naval Museum

and disciplined then and while abandoning. Many Blücher crew members made the great sacrifice of giving their lifejackets to Army personnel who could not swim. With the exception of the wounded, crew and soldiers had to swim ashore. Some succumbed to the intense cold of the water. Some suffered injury because of the hot oil. The cutter, which had orders to land its' wounded and then return to help those in the water, struck a rock and was holed. Konteradmiral Kummetz, Kapitän zur See Woldag, the Navigation Officer, the Senior Gunnery Officer and I, all without life-jackets, went into the sea over the forepeak as the ship settled. I was in the sea about 200m away when I watched *Blücher* capsize at 07:32, her battle ensigns flying at the head of the mainmast and at the foretop near the admiral's pennant. She had a list of 50 degrees for a while, which then increased to 100 degrees and then to 110 degrees, so that it was possible to see the entire length of the burning upper deck. Then she raised her stern and sank by the bow.

Heymann's account of *Blücher* is fascinating and thought provoking, although he neglected to mention two of the most important passengers that were to feature so prominently in the invasion: the commanding designate admiral for Norway, Herman Boehm (4/1940–1/1943) and Generalmajor Erwin Engelbrecht (163rd Infantry Division). The two officers, unharmed, eventually scrambled ashore safely and began to reorganise their otherwise stalled invasion plans in earnest. The wounded men and survivors landed at two sites on the main land – Digerud and Hallangen, just north of Drøbak and also on the island of Askholmen. Close to 750 men grouped at Hallagen where they were placed under the command of Engelbrecht, who was keen to move out as soon as possible. A reconnaissance of the surrounding area was taken and then the order to move out along the shore was given. However, many of the survivors were wet and without suitable clothing or shoes. It was very cold and snow was still on the ground: movement was very difficult, which was further compounded by the wounded that needed shelter and immediate care.

The Germans located some huts and ensconced their wounded in them, but the huts were then later surrounded by a group of Norwegian soldiers led by Kaptein Aksel Thulow Petersson, with 7 officers and 62 men of the 4th Guards Company. The Germans were quickly rounded up and disarmed, although they only possessed a few pistols. There was no resistance from the Germans. They were then marched to the Garder family's farm at Søndre Hallangen, arriving around 11:00 where as many as possible were settled in the farmhouse, although not everyone could be catered for. Improvised shelters were constructed outside for the unlucky ones and turns were taken to warm up in the farmhouse. Only the wounded were spared this inconvenience.

That night the survivors had their first and only meal of potato and milk, provided by the farmer. It was noted by the Germans that their captors acted correct, polite, and were even friendly. At approximately 18:30 that evening, Kaptein Petersson received further orders to withdraw and to leave the Germans to fend for themselves; the fortunes of war had changed. The Norwegian soldiers duly obeyed their orders and moved off without fuss. Later that evening, Engelbrecht, Kummetz and their chosen staff left for Oslo in a requisitioned bus arriving in Oslo around midnight...it had not been a good day for 'gruppe V' and one can only imagine their disappointment upon finding out that the consummate prize of a Norwegian Government, the Royal family and nearly 50 tons of gold had already fled.

Whilst Kummetz, Engelbrecht and their men were battling for their very survival the following invading armada were confused as to what had happened to the *Blücher*, the general opinion being she had hit a mine. At once the invaders halted their approach to reassess their plans. Kapitän Thiele, as the senior officer still actively engaged in the invasion, took command, but his ship had also received hits from shore based defences and he quickly decided not to pass the *Blücher*, but turned the squadron south towards Horten, Son and Tronvik; the orders of Admiral Raeder now seeming very hollow.

With daylight giving the position of Oscarsborg away to the Luftwaffe efforts were made by the Germans to silence the fort and Stukas from gruppe 1/ StG1 bombed the fort relentlessly. Fortuitously, little damage was sustained and there were no losses of Norwegian personnel. The Lützow returned to the narrows at 14:17 and commenced shelling Oscarsborg Fort. Kapitän Thiele, still unwilling to risk his ship through the narrows, lowered a small boat and under the cover of a white flag made its way towards the fort. Realising that their cause was now over, Eriksen responded by sending a Norwegian boat to meet the Germans and surrender terms were negotiated, written and signed. Interestingly, the Norwegians at Oscarsborg were permitted to keep their flag flying next to the German flag, perhaps in recognition of such gallant defending against such a superior force.

The sinking of the *Blücher* had bought valuable time and now, thanks to the actions of Colonel Eriksen and his men, the flight from Oslo of the Royal Family, Government, officials and gold bullion began in earnest.

2

The Flight & Fight Begins
April 9th

On that fateful night of April 8/9th in Oslo, the air-raid sirens wailed and the streetlights went out. It had just turned midnight and the Norwegian Foreign Secretary, Halvdan Koht, had earlier taken supper with a friend, but was on his way home when the sirens first sounded. The wails of the siren only compounded what had been a difficult day for him. The British had sown mines off the Norwegian coast and Koht had spent the best part of the day preparing a protest to the British Government. Koht had been aware that the press was full of strange reports of Germans in uniform coming ashore after a transport ship had been sunk by a British submarine and that there had been a significant loss of life.[30] Also, there were reports to the Norwegian Foreign Office of German warships heading towards Narvik coupled with a telegram from the British Admiralty stating that the Royal Navy had sighted German warships and a transport ship off the Norwegian coast. The reports were duly passed on. Understandably, it was very late by the time Koht had retired exhausted from his duties.

Initially, Koht thought the sirens soundings were just a test, but as the sirens continued their ominous wailing he considered that something was seriously amiss. Managing to find a public telephone he contacted the Foreign Office who immediately informed him that warships had entered the Oslofjord. The office also informed Koht that the Prime Minister, Johan Nygaardsvold had called a Cabinet meeting for 01:30. Koht at once set about trying to find a taxi, but was thwarted, probably due to the air-raid alarm. Undeterred he set out on foot stumbling his way through the darkened city arriving at the Foreign Office just after 01:00. Koht said:[31]

...it was like seeing a drama unfolding itself before us and at the same time participating in it. At short intervals, the telephone went on ringing and bringing news from all parts of Norway.

Meanwhile, King Haakon was working late into the night in his study when during the early hours of the 9th his adjutant presented him with a message from Koht that the forts were engaging enemy warships.[32] The King received the message and then carried on working by candlelight as the lights went out all over Oslo. Various officials, military and civilian, began to hurry about their business. The situation was now dire and although confusion reigned supreme at Victoria Terrasse in Oslo, it was also in the ascendancy at the War Office in Britain. Reports flooded in of German warships penetrating deep in to Norwegian fjords and by the early hours of the 9th it was clear that Norway was being invaded.

Foreign Secretary Koht telephoned the British Minister, Sir Cecil Dormer just after 02:00 to inform him of events. Koht advised Dormer that he was confident that the defences at Oslo would hold off the invaders, but clearly stated to Dormer 'now we are at war.' Telegrams were sent to London informing the various British authorities that Norway was under attack.[33]

Later, Koht telephoned Dormer again to further advise him that German warships were now approaching Trondheim. Koht was aware that the British Legation was in possession of a Wireless Telegraphy set (W/T) and that an up to date report would get through to Britain describing Norway's predicament.

Hampering matters further was the call to mobilisation of Norwegian forces. The procedures laid down were clear, but the politicians either were not aware of those procedures or had failed to understand them; once again confusion reigned. (The uncertainty, disorder and misunderstanding of the mobilisation on April 9th continue to this day and therefore do not fall within the auspices of this book to debate further).

As the German cruiser Blücher advanced her way slowly up Oslofjord, the German Minister for Norway, Dr Bräuer, had sought an audience with Koht.[34] Unbeknown to Koht, Herr Bräuer had been unaware of the intention to invade Norway, but nonetheless, and despite being taken by complete surprise, Bräuer had been ordered by his superiors to deliver the German ultimatum at exactly 04:15 hours having been assured by

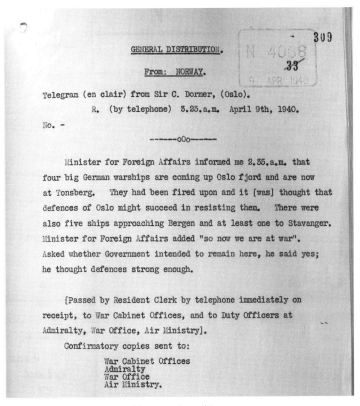

Photo credit: author

the same superiors that German forces would have landed shortly after in Oslo. For unexplained reasons, Dr Bräuer was five minutes late arriving at Koht's Office at Victoria Terrasse: Koht later stated:[35]

> After three hours of strained tension, the German Minister in Oslo was announced, asking to see me…I received the minister in one of the library rooms just outside [*his office*].

In a darkened room, lit only by two small candles, Bräuer presented Koht with a 19-page ultimatum, which he proceeded to read out. Bräuer's tone, according to Koht, was cold but with polite firmness. Koht struggled to keep quiet whilst Bräuer proceeded with his diplomatic rant and his mind worked overtime as it placed in order the many possible outcomes of Bräuer's ultimatum as well as the likely response of the British. Koht expected Britain would come to Norway's aid as Sir Cecil Dormer had stated to Koht that an attack on Norway would be regarded as an attack on Britain. He was also in no doubt that his government would reject the ultimatum, but he informed Bräuer that he would consult and respond to him directly. What Bräuer did not know at that time was that *Blücher* had been hit and was in the process of sinking. The fortunes of war, at least momentarily, had swung the way of the Norwegian Government.

After consultation, Koht replied to Bräuer: it was a complete rejection of the ultimatum. Koht later stated:[36]

> I think it was not yet half-past five when I brought their answer to the German Minister. The day was just beginning to dawn, and in the grey morning light we could talk without candlelight. "We cannot see that Germany is in any way justified in taking such measures of force as she now intends, or rather has begun, to carry out against the Norwegian nation..."

Dr Bräuer was taken by surprise, as it was a reaction he had not expected; Norway to take on the might of the German war machine? Brauer snapped at Koht. *"Then there will be fighting and nothing can save you."* Koht retorted quickly. *"The fight is already in progress."* A chastened and dismayed Bräuer hastily returned to his Embassy. Essentially the plan was to employ a pre-determined code, using numbers, but this procedure was not used and instead the following message was sent:

> Have presented the Foreign Minister at 05:20 German time with our demands in firm, insisting manner and explained the reasons for them as well as handed the memorandum to him. The Minister withdrew for consultations with the Government [...] After a few minutes he returned with the answer: We do not willingly give in; the war has already started. [37]

Meanwhile, in Britain Sir John Colville scribbled a few lines in his diary. His words succinctly define the situation.[38]

> 'The Germans have scored a considerable success by seizing the Norwegian ports despite our command of the sea, and we, who started the whole business, seem to have lost the initiative...'

Colville, perhaps hinting at the *Altmark* affair and the laying of mines, was not wrong.[39]

The President of the Storting, Carl Johan Hambro, having risen from his bed now took a firm hand on matters. Hambro knew that if the King and government were captured early on then Norway would be lost in a matter of hours. Hambro rightly considered it a matter of urgency to evacuate the King and the government away from Oslo and sought to get procedures in place as soon as possible. The fight could continue away from the capital. Hamar seemed the best choice and so a train was made ready: the Norwegians moved quickly and just before 07:30 the train departed with King Haakon, various ministers, Members of Parliament and assorted officials on board. '*Dies irae*' – '*The Day of Wrath*' had truly arrived.

Dormer urgently despatched a second telegram, which was received in London during the late afternoon of April 9th. The wording, dramatic and to the point, must have seriously worried the recipients in London.

Meanwhile, in Oslo the usual measures of destroying documents and important papers and codebooks began in earnest. Officials at the British Embassy were also taking similar measures. When all was done the

```
              SPECIAL DISTRIBUTION AND WAR CABINET
                        FROM NORWAY.
Decypher. Sir C. Dormer (Oslo).
                        9th April, 1940.
      D.  (by Wireless)   9th April, 1940
      R.   4.25.pm.  9th April, 1940.

No. 2.

              """"""""""""""""""""""""""""""""""""


      Oslo has capitulated.  Government are at Hamar fifteen kilo-
metres north of which I and several members of staff are staying,
[Grp.undec:] telegraphing names.  United States Legation have taken
charge of His Majesty's Legation.
      Reported one German ship sunk by fire from Droebak, Tönsberg,
Bergen, Trondhjem, Narvik occupied.  Two German planes shot down at
Kjeller aerodrome.  Lillestrom bombed and in flames.
      French Minister and I would be grateful for any reassuring news
as Government anxious and are subject to strong pressure to declare a
war on His Majesty's Government.  But see my telegram No. 1.
```

Author archive

SPECIAL DISTRIBUTION AND WAR CABINET
TO NORWAY.

Cypher telegram to Sir C. Dormer (Oslo).

Foreign Office. 9th April, 1940. 12.55 p.m.

No. 125.

MOST IMMEDIATE

Your telegrams of this morning.

You should at once assure the Norwegian Government that in view of the German invasion of their country, His Majesty's Government have decided forthwith to extend their full aid to Norway and will fight the war in full association with them

2. You should at the same time inform the Norwegian Government that His Majesty's Government are taking immediate measures to deal with the German occupation of Bergen and Trondjem, since they consider that at this stage this will be the most useful way to help the Norwegian Government in resisting the invasion of their country.

3. His Majesty's Government hope that they can count on the active co-operation of the Norwegian Government and people, and they will be glad to learn as soon as possible what the Norwegian Government's own plans are, so that subsequent British dispositions may be in conformity with them.

4. His Majesty's Government would meanwhile suggest that the Norwegian Government should if possible destroy the Stavanger aerodrome should they be unable to hold it.

Repeated to Paris No. 64 and Stockholm No. 142.

In London, the Foreign Office replied quickly to Dormer's early telegram: Author archive

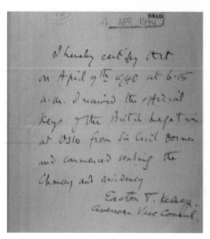

Author archive

building was locked up and the keys to the Embassy handed over to the Americans. The scribbled note (left) from the Americans gives some indication about the hurried nature of the affair.

The sinking of the *Blücher* had bought valuable time and now the flight from Oslo of the Royal Family, government, officials and gold bullion began in earnest. To facilitate the escape and for various officials, military and civilian to communicate with each other without alerting the enemy a very simplistic code was drawn up:

King Haakon – *'The Boss'*; Crown Prince Olav – *'Assistant Boss'* and both collectively known as *'The Office'*. The Norwegian Government – *'The Co-op'*; Prime Minister Nygaardsvold – *'The Old Man'*; Halvdan Koht – *'Philosopher'*; Colonel Ljunberg – *'No 63'*; Frihagen – *'The Bank'*; Finance Minister Torp – *'Oscar'* and Trygve Lie – *'Dannemann'*.

It would seem that the code was not the most imaginative, but under the circumstances that prevailed it appears to have been successful.[40]

With the King, his entourage and leading members of the government having secretly fled, widespread panic began to emerge amongst some of the city dwellers of Oslo. The British reporter, W. F. Hartin, of The *Daily Mail*, had only hours earlier crossed the border into Norway from Sweden sensing that something was going to happen. He was right. Hartin later filed the following report, which was published in a weekly war journal.[41]

> With German bombers wheeling overhead like birds of prey, the rattle of machine-gun fire on the outskirts of the town, and the heavy thud of bombs echoing down the fjord, I stood in one of the main streets of Oslo on April 9 with the capital's bewildered crowds, who were sheltering in the doorways and flattening themselves against the walls
>
> With a piercing crescendo of noise a great four-engined machine dived right over the housetops and streaked skywards again, her tail gun covering the length of the street.
>
> I had crossed the frontier from Sweden only 20 hours previously on my way to Oslo. It was then that I got the first hint of what was happening.
>
> The Norwegian guard came to me saying: "Had you not better leave the train, sir?'
>
> He told me that the Germans had landed at Moss, 20 miles from Oslo on the east side of the fjord, and that their ships were in the fjord and that their 'planes had bombed the airport.
> Everyone in the train was awake. "That cannot be true," they all said, "where are the British?"
>
> At Fetsund, 20 miles from Oslo, there was no more doubt about it. The train was halted. As we stepped on to the little wayside

platform we could see the German bombers wheeling over the long wooded ridge, diving behind it.

Black puffs of anti-aircraft fire pitted the sky for the whole length of the ridge. The thud of bombs, the rattle of machine-guns echoed back to us from far away.

They were bombing Kjeller, the Norwegian military air base. Suddenly, her engines screaming, a Dornier "Flying Pencil" whisked just over the station to have a good look at us.

Everyone instinctively scattered. Only the perplexed guard of the train kept on at his task of trying to find out why we were unable to move.

The minutes dragged into hours. He came back from the telegraph office looking like a man who had heard himself sentenced to death.

"Oslo is being evacuated," he said. "General mobilization has been ordered. The Germans are marching on the town. They have captured some outer batteries on the fjord, but fighting is still going on near the city."

We ran down to the little wayside petrol station and questioned every car driver who came tearing out of Oslo down the long, winding hill.

From these people we learned that the Government and the Royal Family had moved to Hamar, that the Bank of Norway had hurriedly evacuated their gold to the interior, and that all the Government departments were leaving the capital.

It was in this atmosphere, with German bombers never out of sight that we pulled out of Fetsund.

As we approached Oslo train after train crammed with women and children passed us going the other way.

On some of the hills outside the town we could see the anti-aircraft guns, searchlights, and sound detection apparatus being hurriedly mounted.

Hastily commandeered lorries were racing crazily to the capital packed with Norwegian troops and equipment.

Oslo central station was like Victoria or Waterloo in the first days of September. But now I seem to have seen so many crowds and crying children with the red-eyed mothers clutching pathetic bundles of belongings that I am incapable of receiving further impressions. There they were, the inevitable flotsam of human misery, urged hither and thither on a remorseless tide of war.

With Desmond Tighe, of Reuters, we pushed through this crowd and hurried to our hotel in the centre of the town.

There everything was in the same turmoil. People were hurriedly packing their bags and clearing out. Everyone was advising us "Get out while you can. The Germans are not three miles away."

We learned that the British Legation had early that morning burned their papers and left for Hamar.

British nationals were cared for by the American Legation. We had heard that the Germans were already in the suburb where the legations are situated, but Tighe and I decided to make our way there on foot.

By the quieter streets we finally came on to one of the main roads leading out of town. Huge crowds lined it – sullen, laughterless crowds of young Norwegian men and girls.

Where they began to thin out we suddenly halted. Headed by four Norwegian policemen in steel helmets, a column of field-grey troops were trampling along the cobbles.

As they marched not a yard from where I stood I had every chance of examining them.

Their general physique was anything but good. Their equipment was formidable. Every fifth man carried a machine gun, every third man a sub-machine gun.

Others were bent double with the exhaustion of carrying heavy batteries for portable filed radios. Others sweated under precision instruments in big leather cases. Rank upon rank trudged by until I judged at least 1,000 had passed me.

As we walked the sky was still filled with German bombers, some wheeling only just over the housetops. Others were patrolling further out along the line of the fjord.

At the United States Legation about dusk they wished Tighe and myself well, and we got back to the town by bus.

There at the entrance to the station were the same tired-looking youngsters in their field-grey. Two guarded the entrance, two others stood beside a machine-gun in the hall. As we stood interminably for the train in a queue with men and women, many of whom had infants in their arms, a section of these troops marched through on to the platform.

They were getting ready to search the trains, or, as they put it euphemistically, "to exercise military control." Fortunately for us, their organisation was not yet equal to dealing with every train in and out of Oslo, and we got under way without any visit from them.

(*The War Illustrated*)

Taking into account journalistic licence, Hartin's description of events is a sobering one. Additionally, newsreels taken at the time of invasion in Oslo give the impression of people resigned to accepting their fate. Throngs of Norwegians gathered to line the streets mesmerized by the marching Germans and their military bands. Some continued with their day-to-day business whilst others stopped to chat and laugh with the Germans. Just hours later as rumours spread of an imminent British bombing attack on Oslo, people began to leave the city in droves.

Desmond Tighe, Reuter's special correspondent in Oslo, filed a similar report to Hartin, adding that the Germans had begun to bomb the city, witnessing an explosion a mere 200 yards from where he was standing.[42]

3

The Bank and the Bullion

Meanwhile, as Hartin of the *Daily Mail* was witnessing events at first hand with the Germans marching up Karl Johans Gate, a nation's wealth in gold bullion was being whisked away to safety. But for the vision of one man, Nicolai Rygg, Director of Norges Bank, the Germans may well have captured it, and it would have been more than enough to boost the German war machine. With commendable foresight Rygg and Minister of Finance, Oscar Torp, had jointly made arrangements prior to the invasion that if Norway should fall or a crisis erupt then an immediate evacuation of the gold reserves and valuables would begin. And when indeed the call came Rygg rose to the occasion.

Norges Bank, from its establishment in 1816, had been placed directly under the auspices of the Storting (Norwegian parliament). But the Norwegian Government had no ultimate control or influence, and the

Norges Bank, Oslo in 1922. Picture credit: Norges Bank

bank's leadership was free to act in what it considered to be the best fiscal interests of the country. In 1893, Karl Gether Bomhoff was appointed as the first chairman of Norges bank and during World War I he helped to steer the bank through difficult times whilst Norway remained neutral. But the war still affected Norway and with the country heavily reliant on foreign trade, the Norwegian merchant fleet became victims to submarine warfare. Losses also mounted up due to the mining of Norwegian waters and as a result of these catastrophic losses inflation rose sharply and the Norwegian monetary system suffered substantially. Economic deterioration had set in.

In January 1916 Eric Hambro, of CJ Hambro & Son, was instructed to act as an agent for the British Government to purchase considerable sums of Krone. The figures involved ran into millions. Hambro's reputation with the financial world, and particularly in Scandinavia, was considerable and therefore he was deemed as the natural choice by HM Government to secure Norwegian currency, with the proviso to be careful not to draw the attention of the markets to his actions. An account was set up with Norges Bank using the name of CJ Hambro & Son. Purchasing began soon after and on at least one occasion gold was purchased from Argentina and used to secure Krone. Britain also traded heavily with Norway purchasing fish and raw materials thus gaining favourable transacting conditions with the Norwegians and denying the Germans a valuable resource, although being neutral Norway naturally traded with Germany also. In 1917 the British Government changed tack and borrowed Kr. 140,000,000, deferring payment for two years with the option of paying back in currency or gold. It was a calculated gamble as the British Government were hoping for far more favourable conditions when payment was due. By the end of the war though, Norway, like many other countries, was heading for depression. The final paragraph in a letter sent from Hambros Bank to the Treasury in Whitehall and dated 23rd January 1918, gives a small insight on the prevailing conditions.[43]

> Meanwhile whole Norway is longing for an arrangement with London and New York. The country will be in a few days time in some respects be on more severe rations than the people in Germany. Norway is, however, keeping the Flag flying as best it can and we are not downhearted, even if we shall have to suffer severely.

The involvement of a member of the Hambro family in the financial affairs of Norway was not the first, nor would it be the last. Bomhoff held the post of Chairman of Norges Bank until 1920 whereupon he resigned his duties. Unfortunately for the next incumbent a worldwide depression had started and Norway did not escape its grip. The next leader of the bank was Nicolai Theodorius Nilssen Rygg.[44]

It was a difficult time for all as currency issues, shipping and trading concerns as well as bank crashes only served to intensify the work of Rygg, who had set a priority of restoring the gold value of the Krone to its pre-war value. This was achieved in the spring of 1928, but by 1931 Norway had followed Britain and abandoned the gold standard. It was a judicious financial repositioning and by 1932 the economic issues had eased considerably. Rygg then focused his attentions elsewhere.

Still standing today, from the outside the bank's imposing grey stone architecture appears somewhat unfeeling and functional. The interior, by contrast, is opulent with a striking black and white marbled hall entrance with curved elevated archways. The high walls are adorned with the inscribed motifs of past grandeur and lead to a grand staircase flooded with light that long ago echoed to the footsteps and dignified discussions of the banking and business fraternity. It was in this ordered environment that past incumbents went about their day-to-day banking tasks, unhurried and precise. Rygg's domain afforded him excellent opportunities to plan, but even he as a visionary would have struggled to envisage what was about to befall Norway. The dark, ominous clouds of war were once again looming on the horizon and Rygg, along with other far-sighted members of the world's financial and political institutions, took steps to preserve and protect the long-term prospects of his country's

Norges Bank interior, 1906. Picture credit: Norges Bank

Nicolai Rygg
in 1939. Picture
credit: Norges
Bank

gold reserves. Norway was neutral; Norway was safe…for now. Rygg
though, decided to take no chances.

Two years prior to the invasion Rygg sat in his spacious office with its
vast windows exploiting the daylight that flooded the stark, high ceilinged
square room. Undisturbed and unhindered, he began planning for the
removal of Norway's gold reserves. As with other countries carrying out
similar acts of safeguarding their bullion interests, secrecy was of the
utmost importance and Rygg ensured that no undue publicity would
surround his carefully crafted plans. For Rygg, it really was a case of
in pace, ut sapiens, aptarit idonea bello – in peace, like a wise man, he
appropriately prepares for war.

Early in the New Year volunteers were called for and the packing of the
gold began in earnest. The vault, with its vast, solid, dark door studded
with brass rivets stood sentinel in front of two very robust, heavy-duty
wheeled vertical bar gates; access to the inner vault was via lock and dial.
Over the course of several days white painted boxes were filled with bars
of gold and sealed with an iron band; smaller kegs were packed with
bags of coins. Movement of the gold began, but transporting the heavy
crates through the narrow passageways was difficult and cumbersome.
Fortunately, there was just sufficient space to shift and slide the sealed
bullion cargo through the heavy wooden doors of the bank to the waiting

lorries. The gold inside the vault of the Bank of Norway at that time was around some 421 million Krone (Kr). However, a significant amount of the gold was left undisturbed in the vault because under Norwegian law not all the gold could be removed from the country at once; a percentage had to remain and thus a total of 300 million Kr was shipped to the USA leaving behind around 120 million Krone.[45]

Ironically, the movement of some of the gold reserves out of Norway came to the attention of the British, in particular the Ministry of Economic Warfare. Norwegian merchant ships, along with other non-belligerent nations' ships were victims of the stop and search routines of the Royal Navy. On February 5th 1940 the Treasury received the following message:[46]

Ministry of Economic Warfare
February 5th, 1940

My Dear Waley,

The naval report of a Norwegian ship, Randsfjord, which was examined at sea by the Northern Patrol, was found to be carrying gold marks to the value of 4 million dollars. The gold is stated to have been with the National Bank of Denmark since 1919 and was consigned by the Norges Bank for the account of National Bank of Denmark to the Federal Reserve Bank of New York.

It was signed by an enigmatic figure known only as 'BOBBIE': it would seem that the British were keeping a careful watch on what was going on in the northern waters.

Later, with over 300 million Kr safely in the USA, Nicolai Rygg turned his attentions to another urgent matter…that of paper money not in circulation. Rygg contacted the Norwegian Finance Minister Oscar Torp, requesting that with Europe at war and the newspapers full of alarming news, paper money should be sent out of the country to a safe place. A speedy decision was required, but Rygg's request fell upon deaf ears. The Norwegian Government, perhaps absorbed in maintaining the country's neutral status hesitated in their answer, perhaps understandably as the war seemed far away from their shores. Nevertheless, their prevarication and, some would argue, their blindness to international developments, caused avoidable delay.

During the early hours of April 9th, Rygg's concern rapidly mounted with the desperately worrying news that a force of German warships was steaming up Oslo Fjord. Knowing that not all the bullion had been removed and that the Germans would welcome a golden windfall to finance their war machine, coupled with the frustration that the decision he had so wanted had not been forthcoming, Rygg immediately sought contact with the Commander-in-Chief of military forces, General Laake, suggesting that the

Gold bars in the vault in Oslo. Picture credit: Norges Bank

bullion be moved as soon as possible. Laake agreed and ordered Rygg to commence the evacuation of the gold at once to Lillehammer as the bank there had a brand new vault where the gold could be stored. The pace of events rapidly increased when just moments later Oscar Torp telephoned Rygg confirming to him that Norway had indeed been invaded and the Germans were already occupying the major cities, although they had not yet reached Oslo.

Rygg immediately set about contacting various bank officials to help organise the urgent evacuation of the remaining gold bullion. The race was on to move the bullion out before the Germans could get their hands on it. It must have been clear to all that but for Rygg's prudence and persistence in moving the major part of the Norwegian gold reserves to America prior to the invasion, the task that faced the bank workers would have been insurmountable. As it was, the job in hand would be demanding enough. Arrangements were hastily made for the removal of the bullion by truck. The race had begun, but the Germans were not yet quite at the start line.

4

Flight to Lillehammer
April 9–10th

At 7am Rygg telephoned Andreas Lund, the bank manager of Norges Bank at Lillehammer, to warn him of the disaster that had befallen Norway and instructing him to prepare immediately for the arrival of gold bullion now being evacuated out of the city. Rygg declared that the new vaults at the bank would be ideal for the bullion and that it would be brought over on a couple of trucks. Rygg though, had been somewhat conservative in his calculations for exactly how much transport was needed and eventually 26 lorries were required to haul the precious cargo 115 miles over snow laden roads to Lillehammer. For Lund, and many others an adventure was about to begin. The amounts of gold packed were:

818 large crates @ 40kg each
685 smaller crates @ 25kg
39 kegs @ 80kg – filled with bags of coins equating to 1000 coins per bag with 5 bags per keg. The total weight of the cargo was 53 tons, but the weight of the bullion alone was approximately 49 tons. It was valued at 120 million Krone.

The lorries needed to haul the bullion were chartered from local merchants in Oslo, with the majority of the trucks being hired from the Christiana Coal & Firewood Company. The truck drivers, with no idea as to the nature of their load and journey, were directed to the side entrance of the bank where loading of the gold began in earnest.

Snow was still lying on the ground and it made for hazardous driving conditions. The cab comforts of the lorries were extremely basic and conditions cold and bleak.

The drivers looked on quietly as the bank employees loaded the heavy boxes and kegs on to the load-beds of the trucks with Rygg carefully noting and recording each box and barrel in his register.

Rygg and his bank officials decided that security would be best served by placing bank guards at strategic points close to the bank to ward off prying eyes whilst still maintaining control over the area. The military, although aware of the operation, were not used as it was considered too great a risk of drawing unnecessary attention to what was happening and besides it was thought that their services were needed elsewhere in defence of the country.

The bank employees worked hard at their task loading the bullion, growing weary as the hours wore on, but they toiled on relentlessly until all the lorries were fully stowed with the precious metal. As each lorry was loaded and secured it was immediately driven away; there really was no time to lose.

Onboard escorting the driver and cargo were two armed bank guards.[47] Rygg's tactics of sending each lorry off in turn so that a significant distance was kept between each vehicle was inspired. A convoy of lorries would have surely aroused the Luftwaffe's suspicions exposing the convoy to possible attack and the chances of getting through would have been seriously reduced. A single lorry though, would not attract much attention.

The first truck was recorded as leaving at 08:15 on April 9th with the last driving away from the bank just before 13:30 – exactly the same time that the Germans were marching their way down Karl Johan Gate – the main street in Oslo that leads from the King's Palace. Indeed at 14:00 that day the Commander of Oslo garrison at Akershus Fort, Colonel Hans Petter Schnitler, declared the surrender of Oslo to the Germans at the fort. The location of the bank is only a couple of hundred yards away from the Akershus Fort, but with German attentions focused elsewhere in the city the gold transport had slipped away unnoticed. It had been a narrow, if fortuitous escape made possible only by the actions of Colonel Eriksen at Oscarsborg Fort, the sinking of the *Blücher*, Rygg's prudent planning and the gargantuan effort of the bank employees.

Refugees flooded out from the capital. Pedestrian and vehicle traffic hindered the progress of the lorries as the evacuees sought refuge away from Oslo. People became angry at not being given help by the bullion trucks as they trundled past, but of course the trucks could not stop for anyone, whatever their needs. At one point some of the lorries were apprehended by a Norwegian military detachment, but once it was hastily explained that the mission was vital to Norway the lorries were allowed to continue their journey. The exodus of evacuees also caused a shortage of food as many of the shops had quickly sold out of provisions with the refugees buying all they could afford. As a result the unfortunate lorry drivers were only able to consume coffee, if they were lucky, at hotels along the route. Nonetheless, despite the grim conditions all the lorries successfully completed their journeys to Lillehammer. The final truck arrived that same night at 20:00. It could only have been a very cold and miserable experience for the bank guards sitting at the back of a covered truck with little to do except stare at boxes and kegs.

The drivers and guards, totally exhausted by the journey, wearily made their way to various hotels for rest and some food. Ragnar Groth Nilsen, a bank employee later recounted in the bank's in-house magazine, 'Orienteering'.[48]

> I sat at the back of the truck (No 14) all the way to Lillehammer. A younger guy from the Mint was in the lorry with the driver, but I didn't know either of them. Those who worked in the bank security should have been trained in small arms with at least 20 shots per year. I had been at Akershus, but it was more fun than serious training.

Nilsen's shelter for that night was at the Grand Hotel in Lillehammer and he returned to Oslo the next day. Knut Romdahl, another Norges Bank employee detailed to be a guard duly took up the position on Lorry No 17, a small grocery truck. However, because of the load layout of the truck there was only space for 18–20 kegs, which were loaded correctly at the sides of the load-bed. The two guards then sat between the kegs in the gangway doing their utmost to keep warm. For Romdahl the mission to take the gold to Lillehammer would be straightforward, but matters were a little different on his return to Oslo. Romdahl takes up the story.[49]

> Everything was fine until we reached a roadblock manned by two Germans. Two Norwegians were arrested, but they were later released without charge. We eventually walked home alone along dark and deserted Oslo streets.

Meanwhile, in Lillehammer, Lund had been busy preparing his bank for the nation's wealth. Staff were briefed on events and space made in readiness for the gold. Later that day, the lorries began to arrive and unloading began in earnest. However, work could only take place when the Luftwaffe was not flying overhead – the bank staff did not want to draw unwarranted attention to their endeavours and so it was a very careful, if somewhat drawn out process. Passers-by had earlier watched as the lorries trundled into Lillehammer towards the bank, but that was the least of the concerns of the armed and alert bank officials as the event had not gone unnoticed by the media and soon there were reports on Norwegian radio of lorry loads of gold arriving in Lillehammer. There were also reports of the shipment in a Trondheim newspaper, but incredibly the messages did not reach the straining ears of the Germans, who by now must have furious that their much sought after war booty had disappeared, along with the Royal Family and the Norwegian Government.

By nightfall, the last of the 26 lorries had its valuable load deposited in the vaults of the Lillehammer Bank. The bullion had been moved out just in time and the Germans had missed their prize by a whisker. It had been a very close run thing, but the Norwegians now had the upper hand.

At the bank in Lillehammer, Andreas Lund personally counted the bullion boxes and casks: 818 large cases, 685 smaller cases and 39 casks. The figures tallied exactly with Rygg's account. The bullion was safely locked away and the bank manager from Lillehammer was breathing a little easier by nightfall. The Germans had not the slightest inkling where the bullion was despite the Norwegian media's very best efforts, albeit unintentionally, to inform them. If the Germans had been more observant of the media then matters may well have been different. Fortune was smiling on the gold smugglers.

Lillehammer Bank

Rygg arrived at Lillehammer Bank later that evening of the 9th April to check all was well and that the bullion was secure in the vaults. The locks to the vaults were activated and Rygg ordered that in the event of the Germans taking the bank they were only to be shown the upper vaults, not the lower vault where the gold was kept. It is difficult to imagine the Germans not carrying out a thorough check of the bank and only being satisfied with the meagre contents of the upper vaults, such was the innocence of the Norwegians.

Later that evening, Rygg was notified that King Haakon and the Norwegian Government were now safe having left Oslo early in the morning by train. Their journey away from the capital had been perilous and fraught with danger. As the party attempted to make good their escape the train happened to trundle past the airfield of Kjeller just as a battle was raging overhead. German bombs rained down close to the train bringing it to a shuddering and sudden halt. The passengers quickly disembarked the train and ran to seek shelter in a nearby subway horrified at what was happening. The bombing intensified and it was decided to move away from the subway as there was no point in waiting for a direct hit to land on them. The Germans wanted to smash the airfield and were not searching for a small, seemingly harmless passenger train. The escapees climbed back on to the train and carried on with their journey. Later, that morning, and without further incident, the party arrived safely at Hamar. Rygg joined them there after visiting the gold at Lillehammer, although strangely he did not meet up with Torp, but rather Halvdan Koht, the Norwegian Foreign Minister. Hurried discussions took place with various officials as the government attempted to make sense of the situation they found themselves in. As a result of his talks with Koht, Rygg was requested to return to Oslo, but strangely it wasn't to be until April 15th that he duly arrived back in the capital after taking a rather circuitous route including a return to Lillehammer to ensure all was well. There is no record of why Rygg took so long to return to Oslo.

Rest and recuperation for the assembled throng at Hamar was out of the question as grave military debates and sombre political discussions took place with those members of the government that had travelled in the train. Anxious Norwegian eyes looked skyward as German bombers passed overhead, but no bombs were dropped and the discussions continued.

King Haakon and the Royal party sought refuge in a house outside of Hamar whilst the members of the Government assembled in a local meeting hall. Storting President Hambro, Prime Minister Nygaardsvold and Foreign Minister Koht addressed the members and gave an account of events to date to a mute and apprehensive audience. The Prime Minister offered to resign, but Hambro and others thought it was the wrong time for major changes and that level heads were needed in desperate times. Some discussed whether it was viable to negotiate with Germany, whilst others considered it fruitless given Germany's past record in dealing with the occupants of conquered countries. The meeting broke up just after 19:30 that evening. Word had been received that German troops were on their way to Hamar by bus to capture the King and his loyal government. Hastily, but wearily, the party boarded the train once more and headed east to Elverum. King Haakon and the royal family had already left earlier for Elverum at 18:30 travelling by car.

As those chaotic scenes unfolded at Hamar, Vidkun Quisling, a name that was to become forever synonymous with the word traitor, was trying to steal a march on the elected Norwegian Government, and the Germans, by announcing on air via Oslo radio, that it was *his duty and right* to take over the government.[50] He stated that the government had failed to protest vehemently to the British after they had carried out mine laying off the Norwegian coast and that they, as a consequence of their actions, had now fled the country in utter humiliation. Quisling further announced that it would be his party, National Samling, that would now govern the people of Norway and that he, Vidkun Quisling, would be Prime Minister and Minister of Foreign Affairs. Any resistance would be futile and *'equal to criminal destruction and life'.* The German government, Quisling said, had offered *'its inoffensive assistance accompanied by a solemn assurance to respect national independence and Norwegian life and property',* in return for acceptance of the situation.[51]

The announcement stunned and shocked many Norwegians, and to some extent the Germans who were apparently unaware of Quisling's intentions. Herr Bräuer, hearing of the announcement, called Berlin to seek clarification on Quisling and his new self-found role; but Hitler, and despite the diplomatic remonstrations of Bräuer, allowed Quisling to govern, for the time being at least. Hitler had made a serious mistake with lasting consequences. Together with Quisling, he had unwittingly sown the first seeds of Norwegian resistance.

Elverum meanwhile, was becoming a very busy place as foreign embassy personnel arrived in various states of dress seeking shelter. With the government back in session, the King in residence and foreign diplomatic staff in attendance Elverum had, for all intents and purposes, become the capital of Norway and the focal point for the media as the press sought answers to the world's questions. It was at Elverum that Storting President Carl J Hambro put forward the following motion:

> …[to] give the Government an all embracing authority to guard the interests of the kingdom, and, on behalf of the Storting and the Government, to take all the measures that might be found necessary for the security and the future of the country, such authority to be valid until the Government and the Presidential Board agreed to call the Storting to session again.[52]

By now the Germans, having occupied Oslo, had found to their dismay that their intended prize of King, Government and bullion had already fled the capital. Frantic searching was followed by hurried discussions to try to work out where their prey had flown. They soon formed a plan.

Directed by their Air Attaché, Hauptmann Eberhardt Spiller, who was apparently acting on his own initiative (as later stated by von Falkenhorst in an inquiry held after the war), commandeered a small fleet of buses, cars and a lorry and had set off with some 90 heavily armed parachute troops (fallschirmjägers) possibly in order to make a name for himself in the eyes of his superiors by capturing the Norwegian Government and the Royal party in one lightening attack. The armed convoy made their way slowly north out of Oslo amid a confusion of military and civilian traffic. The Germans were well trained, battle-ready soldiers ably commanded by Hauptmann Erich Walther. Their objective demanded stringent tactics and when the opportunity arose during their journey northwards they captured stray Norwegian officers at gunpoint forcing them to act as guides. Their aggressive activities did not go unnoticed by others who wisely kept their distance and immediately informed their superiors that an armed German column made up of commandeered vehicles was heading north with Norwegian captives onboard. Those at Elverum were notified and warned.

Spiller's gamble though, did not taken into account the resourcefulness of the Norwegians who were equally determined to stop the Germans in their tracks. Two roadblocks were constructed; one at Midtskogen, a small village mid-way between Hamar and Elverum, and another 3 km further back. The Norwegian barricade was a hurried, improvised affair constructed of timber and motor vehicles requisitioned for the cause. The officer-in-charge, Major Olav Helset had orders to halt the German's encroachment and come what may the Germans were not to advance beyond his barricade. In the worst case scenario the barricade further back could also be brought in to use.

The Norwegians made the best use of the wooded terrain and set up a field of fire that would be difficult to penetrate, but they were also few in number and were forced to seek volunteers from the local rifle-club to bolster the defences. The Norwegian force then consisted of a mix of Royal Guard regulars, volunteers and recruits supported by officers and NCOs from a winter training school. A regular officer, Kaptein Johan Ingebrigt Rognes manned the main roadblock in the centre of the pincer. At that time Rognes was a small arms instructor and his advice and training to the recruits, some of whom had never fired a shot, was to prove invaluable.[53]

At around 01:30 on April 10th the German paratroopers and their irregular vehicle convoy suddenly came under sustained fire from two heavy Norwegian machine guns. The paratroopers quickly de-bussed and at once returned fire, but it was clear that the Germans were at a disadvantage. The battle raged to and fro, but the Norwegians held the high ground and the upper hand. The German's rate of fire was impressive, but above the heads of the defending Norwegians. With the Norwegians retaining their advantage the Germans could see that the engagement was faltering. They were already taking casualties, some of them serious. The attackers reassessed the situation and then tried to close in on one of the Norwegian machine-guns that had been in difficulties, but the strategy failed as soon as it had started. The fire from the Norwegians was relentless and withering. Matters suddenly came to a swift conclusion when Hauptmann Spiller took a bullet and fell, mortally wounded. The battle was over. The Germans knew there was no way forward and with Spiller seriously wounded they sought the only solution possible – to promptly withdraw.

Two pictures depicting Captain John Rognes (later Lieutenant Colonel): on the left is a drawing by Andreas Hauge, whilst the on the right is a drawing by Lieutenant Øyen. Both drawings are with the kind permission of the Rognes family.

At around 03:00 both sides pulled back with the Germans retreating to Oslo no doubt to answer some serious questions from their senior officers. Unfortunately for the Germans, Hauptmann Spiller succumbed to his wounds the next day in hospital. Allegedly, in one of Spiller's pockets a wallet was found and inside was a small handwritten note with the following names: *'King Haakon, Nygaardsvold, Sundby, and Hambro'*.[54] If this was the case we can clearly deduce from this that Spiller had his objectives, perhaps with orders from above, and that he was determined to achieve and execute them, despite the post-war denials of von Falkenhorst. If Spiller and his paratroopers had managed to accomplish their purpose then the whole course of the Norwegian Campaign may well have taken a different direction and perhaps Nicolai Rygg and his gold bullion would have been under new management. But the assorted motley crew of fighting Norwegians had secured more time for their Government, the Royal Party and nearly 50 tons of gold bullion to continue their escape.

The respite was only temporary however, as the Germans, determined to secure the whole country as quickly as they could, thrust home their superior military advantage in all directions.

The bullion remained in the Lillehammer vaults for ten days. Understandably, the bank staff became extremely anxious that the secret would leak out and that the Germans would just come along and help themselves. The bullion had to be moved again, but it had to be at the right moment and it couldn't just be moved with nowhere to take it to. Meanwhile, to safeguard the bullion from unwanted attention it was decided to hire marksmen from the Lillehammer Rifle Club. If the bank used soldiers then their very presence could arouse suspicion and highlight the fact that something unusual was going on; it was a clever move.

On April 10th, Rygg returned in haste to Lillehammer to warn Lund that the Germans were closing in on Lillehammer. The bank staff were aghast – would all their hard work go to waste and would the Germans be able to break in to the vaults? Would the Germans use force against the staff to get the gold? There was little they could do except wait for the inevitable. The minutes passed and nothing happened…no Germans, no bombs, no shouting, no guns, no violence, nothing. It became clear after a few anxious hours that the rumour was just that, a rumour, and Rygg realising he had been misled, immediately sent away all descriptions of the vault lock. He also asked Lund to memorise the numbers to the lock. As a further precaution he divided the two keys between two members of the bank staff, Messrs.' Julius Pettersen and Hans Olsen Skurdal. [55] If the Germans came, then they would have to work hard to get the vault open and it wouldn't be easy for them. Meanwhile, news of the non-arrival of the Germans spread quickly and a palpable feeling of relief filtered amongst the bank staff. Equally they all knew that it would only be a matter of time before rumour would become a reality and none more so than Rygg and Lund.

5

Allied Help Arrives

The invasion was now in full swing and the Germans were making good progress against the small and under equipped Norwegian forces. A cry for help had gone out to Britain and she was responding as fast as she could, but not fast enough. Confusion reigned supreme as the British, caught out by the German invasion, hurriedly assembled troops and equipment and it wasn't until April 17th (22:00) that the British first set foot on Norwegian soil in large numbers at the ports of Harstad ('*Rupertforce*'), Namsos ('*Mauriceforce*'), Åndalsnes ('*Sickleforce*') and Namsos (24th Guards Brigade, 146th, 148th and 15th Brigades respectively).[56]

The landings were not without problems. Equipment had not arrived or had been placed in the wrong ships in the wrong order – it was a logistical disaster of enormous proportions from the outset. Range finders for the AA guns were missing; there was an inadequate supply of field glasses (binoculars) to go round; base plates for the 3inch mortars were missing, rendering the mortars useless. The few mortars that were operational had only smoke shells to fire and not the conventional exploding shell needed to stop the enemy; plus being of the 3inch type they only had a range of 1600 yards. Radio equipment was almost non-existent and therefore runners had to be used to pass messages and to top it all the soldiers had only been issued with a handful of ammunition for their rifles. The soldiers, many of them territorial and without experience of any sort of combat, let alone winter combat, managed to organise themselves into some sort of fighting force and under the command of their officers made the best of an extremely bad situation.

Brigadier Harald de Reimer Morgan, commanding officer of '*Sickleforce*', had been given orders to occupy Dombås and then move on to Trondheim, but because of the fluid nature of the British landing and the rapid progress of the Germans the orders changed so many times as to become virtually useless in the almost hourly shifting situation in Norway.

General Ruge, recently appointed Commander-in-Chief of Norwegian forces, having replaced General Laake, was defending the area south of Lillehammer. Requesting British assistance he dispatched two British officers, Lieutenant Colonel E. J. C. King-Salter (British Military Attaché to the Norwegian Government and recently returned from Finland) and Captain Francis Foley (British Intelligence) to make contact with Morgan at Dombås. They duly obliged and having travelled to Dombås convinced Morgan that taking Trondheim would be disastrous. If the Norwegian line broke at Lillehammer the Germans would then be free to progress almost unopposed up the Gudbrandsdal valley. Morgan agreed with Ruge's advice, stating to the Norwegian Commander that he had been sent to help Norway – Trondheim would have to wait.

Back at Lillehammer Bank, the staff were kept busy as military personnel and civilians requested money and securities for various reasons; the demands were great on all. Bombing raids were frequent and the staff had to contend with closing the bank and then re-opening as soon as the last planes had disappeared into the distance. Lund realised that the unique and dire circumstances they were living under could not be endured much longer and that soon the Germans would over-run the country and that would almost certainly include helping themselves to the contents of the bank. The British were poorly equipped and though like the Norwegians they fought hard and tenaciously, it was not enough, not nearly enough. Lund knew that the gold would have to be moved again, but it could only be under orders from Norges Bank.

Late one evening on April 13th, the bank received an unusual request. A Norwegian naval officer, Lieutenant Diesen called the bank and made arrangements for Andreas Lund to meet Commanding Admiral Henry Diesen at the Grande Hotel in Lillehammer.[57] Lund was suspicious and quite rightly saw this as an unusual demand. He sought the advice of the Lillehammer Chief of Police to see if Admiral Diesen was who he said he was and if he was actually in Lillehammer. After all, the Commanding Admiral was geographically very far away from the sea and what was his interest in the bullion? During those dark days rumours of *Fifth columnists* and Quislings were reverberating around Norway and risks could not be taken on the say-so of a junior officer. The police later confirmed Admiral Diesen's identity and presence in the town. This assurance satisfied Lund that all was well and he agreed to meet.

At an arranged time, Andreas Lund and Julius Pettersen met with the Commanding Admiral at the Grande Hotel. Diesen requested Lund move the bullion as soon as possible because the Germans were not far away. Lund listened intently to the demands of Diesen, but disagreed with the idea and insisted that it was Norges Bank who was the authority in this case and that he would wait for orders from the Bank before proceeding. Diesen protested forcefully but Lund again remained steadfast in his position and insisted that he could only operate under the auspices of Norges Bank. The meeting concluded with Lund and Pettersen re-iterating that they had no authority to move the gold despite the protestations of the Admiral. However Lund and Pettersen left the hotel concerned that Diesen was perhaps correct that the bullion should be transported somewhere away from the front line. Lund's mind was in turmoil. The situation was becoming perilous and he thought that it would not be long before the German troops would arrive and close in on their quarry. What Lund did not know at that time was that the Germans still had no clear idea where the gold was and that their primary target was the King and the Norwegian Government.

The Germans for their part realised that Dombås and its rail junction was a major strategic position and that if they could capture it quickly with a detachment of Fallschirmjägers (parachute troops), secure the junction and destroy railway lines from Åndalsnes, then British troops being transported out of the west coast port rail towards the Gudbrandsdal region in support of Norwegian troops, would be halted. Without British support the Norwegian resistance would collapse allowing German troops to push up from the south to Dombås.

There is no evidence of operational orders being issued to the German paratroopers to capture the King or the gold. Nonetheless, the German High Command must have been aware that securing the Dombås railhead could also net them further prizes.

At approximately 17:00 on the evening of April 14th, fifteen Ju 52 transport aircraft from 1./FJR1, each loaded with approximately twelve lightly armed Fallschirmjägers, lumbered slowly into the air from Fornebu airdrome, Oslo.[58] En route, one aircraft was lost to Norwegian ground fire near Lillehammer, but the others successfully reached Dombås. Arriving over the target area at about 18:30, streams of German paratroops left their aircraft. The drop, though, was not particularly successful and paratroops were scattered over a wide area. One aircraft was shot down over Dombås, whilst the Norwegians shot some of the troops as they parachuted down. The defenders quickly captured a few Germans who had fallen away from the target area. Nevertheless, the Fallschirmjägers, although lightly equipped, were a potent force and clearly this was a very dangerous development for the Norwegians. Drastic action had to be taken to eliminate the problem.

The German paratroopers fought tenaciously against the Norwegians, but took casualties quickly. Mortars and heavy machine guns were brought up to try and remove the stubborn resistance.

Officer of Marines, Lieutenant Colonel Simpson later described the situation is his report to the Admiralty:[59]

> German parachute troops were reported near Dovre and a few others near Lesja to the Northwest of Dombås. I had dispatched by train one 3.7" Howitzer under the command of a sub Lieutenant D.C. Salter, R.N. to Dombås in order to assist in clearing out the German parachute troops reported in that area… We had a conference in my H.Q. during which I explained the situation as I knew it, and I got through on the telephone to the Military Attaché, Lieutenant Colonel King-Slater at G.H.Q., who said that the situation in front of Lillehammer was critical and unless reinforcements came within 24 hours it was possible that a debacle would ensue…Brigadier Morgan then decided himself to go forward to Dombås to clear up the situation there, and to return to Åndalsnes as soon as possible to make his final plan. He left at about 0100 hours on 19/4 and was back again by about 0900 hours the same morning, having given orders for the mopping up of the German parachutists.

It had taken five days to clear the German parachutists, although the situation could well have radically altered had the Germans reinforced the landing with further troops. It had been a close-run thing, but with the Germans in the area either killed or captured, there was now a window of opportunity to get the bullion railed out of Lillehammer.

With Norwegian forces back in control of Dombås and the surrounding area by April 19th, the railway lines to the north and the west coast remained free for the transportation of allied troops.

Torp shared Lund's worries and knew that the safekeeping of gold at the Lillehammer bank was no longer an option. The bullion had to be moved and it had to happen quickly. Torp needed someone with sound leadership qualities to take on the immense task of seeing the gold removed to safety and considered that Fredrik Haslund, Secretary of the Labour Party, was the man to do it. Haslund was well qualified to handle the situation as he had already engineered the safe movement of the Royal Family and Members of Parliament from Hamar to Elverum. Earlier, Haslund had followed the Royal party and Norwegian government out of Oslo, becoming a driver and messenger for the King during the journey. Torp had identified Haslund as a man who he could trust and who possessed an organisational aptitude and an ability to be a decision maker without recourse to others; all essential qualities for what Torp had in mind and as such no one else was considered for the job.

Haslund was not too surprised at such a request as only three days earlier his name had been linked with the movement of the gold from Lillehammer, but the German parachutists arriving in the Dombås area on April 14th curtailed any such movement. Haslund duly met with Torp at the Grand Hotel interested to know what the Minister of Finance had planned for him. He listened attentively as the plans were presented to him – to lead the gold transport out of Lillehammer to the port of Åndalsnes and away to safety via the Royal Navy. He was also advised to report to a Colonel David Thue at the port from whom he would receive further instructions.[60] Haslund understood the full weight of this responsibility and promised Torp he would execute his duties to the best of his ability. Torp, of course, expected nothing less.

The next day, Haslund immediately set about organising transport out of Lillehammer. A *mixed traffic* train was required – goods wagons as well as a passenger car or two. Secondly, the route had to be prearranged so that Haslund's train could travel through Otta, Dombås and on to Åndalsnes unhindered. NSB, the railway company got to work straight away to ensure that Haslund's needs were met. Papers of citation were required to ensure confirmation of Haslund's authority over the bullion and these were coordinated via the local military commanders, Colonel Finn Fougner and Major Arentz who obtained signed papers from General Ruge of Army HQ. Another officer, Colonel Ole Broch then made further arrangements for Haslund to meet up with General Ruge at a small village called Tretten; arriving there without incident, Haslund discussed with Ruge how the bullion could be transported out of Lillehammer. In turn, Ruge offered a military escort, which Haslund gladly accepted, but warned him that the transport could not move until the German parachutists in the Dombås area had been fully dealt with.

Meanwhile, in London on April 16th, Parliament was in session and unbeknown to the Norwegians and the British military authorities questions were already being raised in the House of Commons. Member of Parliament for Kingswinford, Mr Arthur Henderson asked the Chancellor of the Exchequer, Sir John Simon whether he had any information regarding the value of the Norwegian gold reserves and if the Germans had seized any of it during their invasion? Sir Simon rose from his seat and replied that the gold holdings of the Norwegian banks amounted to some *'£18,000,000 or £19,000,000.'* He further stated that he had no other exact information on what amounts were being held outside the country. Sir Simon understandably was also unable to answer the second part of the question as to whether the Germans had captured any of the gold. At that precise moment in time, and apparently unknown to the British and the Germans for that matter, the bullion was still in Lillehammer.[61]

Haslund now returned to Lillehammer and immediately sought out the Fylkesmann (County Governor) as well as the Chief of Police for the Lillehammer area to finalise arrangements for the transport. Secrecy was to be paramount if they were to succeed. On April 17th Torp arrived in Lillehammer to join in the preparations and warned Haslund that the gold would have to be moved at very short notice. Lists were drawn up and a further detailed inventory made of the gold boxes and their contents. It would seem that even when at war one still needs an accountant.

In Dombås, a few scattered German parachutists remained in the area, although these were being successfully engaged in an effort to clear the area. As soon as the area was deemed safe Haslund would need to move quickly. By April 18th plans were well in hand and volunteers were being sought in preparation to move the gold with the arrangements being implemented by the police chief. The assembled volunteers, around thirty in number, were ordered to meet at a secret location at 22:00 and to arm themselves with spades and shovels. This was to give passers-by the impression that the men were off to dig trenches, but the reality was far from the case.

The men were quietly transported to Norges Bank without fuss and setting aside their digging tools, immediately began the arduous task of loading the trucks in preparation for the short journey to the railway station. The plan was to move the gold the following day. Security was naturally of the highest order with roadblocks and guards put in place to ensure that no unauthorised persons came anywhere near the bullion.

Meanwhile, the soldiers were being assembled at Jøstadmoen military camp.[62] The guards were chosen hurriedly and were made up of men of all ages and from varying units. Initially, mobilisation of Norwegian forces had been confused and shambolic. Orders and counter orders had been issued, but outside the German controlled areas mobilisation had been more organised. Men unable to attend their assigned camp instead (certainly in the case of soldiers in the Lillehammer area) made for the camp at Jørstadmoen instead. One of those men who had joined the camp was Nordahl Grieg.

Grieg, a Norwegian poet and playwright, was staying at the Continental Hotel – perhaps better known as the Theatre Café – in Oslo with his fiancé, Gerd Egede-Nissen when hostilities broke out. At first Grieg disbelieved the rumours that the Germans were invading thinking that it was the Germans and British naval forces playing out a sea battle in retaliation to the British having just laid mines off Norway. These illusions were shattered when on the morning of April 9th, whilst at breakfast, Grieg witnessed a German officer in uniform dashing into the hall of the hotel and demanding to see Mr Quisling and failing him, Mr Hagelin, a Norwegian businessman.[63] The officer quickly disappeared into the hotel lift to seek out his man.

Rumours circulated rapidly that mobilisation orders were being announced via Norwegian radio. Grieg dashed out of the hotel and made his way to a nearby Norwegian military establishment only to be told to go home, as the situation was useless. Grieg, devastated, was witnessing at first hand the sudden and shocking manifestation of armed Germans wandering the streets of Oslo, and he was convinced that his beloved Kingdom of Norway was yielding swiftly to the German invaders.

Overwhelmed by hopelessness and brimming with contempt for the traitor Quisling, he decided against returning to his hotel. Realising that he had to get away from the capital, Grieg telephoned Gerd and told her to get out of Oslo, promising that he would somehow find a way of rejoining her when he could.

Later, that evening, Grieg found himself listening intently to a radio for any update in the news, enraged as the broadcasts from Quisling's Government continuously announced that resistance to the Germans would be futile and be met with severe penalties. The broadcasts were accompanied with supposed inspiring national music; Grieg despaired.

The following morning the poet travelled by train and bus until he eventually reached Hønefoss. There were no Germans there and for a while he felt safe. But no matter what military establishment Grieg reported to the only advice that he received was to go home, such was the confusion in the Norwegian mobilisation. Undeterred, Grieg made his way to the Gudbrandsdal valley where he chanced upon the Jørstadmoen military camp and it was here he was accepted into the local force. In the ensuing patriotic but uncoordinated melee to resist the Germans, Grieg managed to obtain a Krag rifle along with a few rounds and some remnants of a uniform and then spent the next few hours dashing around in a car looking for German patrols. Fortunately for the keen recruits the Germans were still some way off and so no shots were fired in either direction.

Just days later Grieg, along with others, was ordered to Lillehammer to occupy the railway station. Once assembled, they were informed that the Germans were rapidly approaching and that Lillehammer was to be defended at all costs. At that point in time, Grieg had absolutely no idea about the military objective that had been bestowed upon them and guarding a nation's wealth would have been very low on his and his comrade's list of guesses, but arriving quietly and taking up his duties on the station, Grieg witnessed workmen loading an infinite amount of white boxes, some large, some small into railway trucks. He also noticed some very heavy kegs and these appeared to be sealed with red wax; everything was marked with two black letters...NB – Norges Bank. Watching the comings and goings of the bullion loaders matters soon became clear and it didn't take the soldiers long to realise that the whole of the gold holding of Norges Bank was being loaded aboard the trucks. A short time later, during the early hours of the following morning, orders were issued that the train was to have a military escort and that the soldiers currently guarding the station would be that escort. Grieg clambered aboard not realising the unrelenting seven weeks that was about to ensue.

Grieg, who had trained as a neutrality guard some years prior to the invasion, was later quoted.[64]

> We were turned into some kind of soldiers within 5 minutes. No one asked for names or numbers and nothing was written down. We were allowed in to peoples' homes to take whatever we wanted such as guns and uniforms. We stayed in farmhouses overnight. Next morning there was a full alarm…the German parachutists were supposed to be in the area. We jumped into cars and were told to load our guns, but it was a false alarm and no parachutists were found. April 18th and 30 men from this unit were ordered to be ready for a special mission at short notice The next evening (19th), we were told to bring provisions for two days and 100 rounds each. In the moonlight we drove towards Lillehammer with the Germans known to be approaching. With us we brought two recently arrived cadets, sergeants in rank. These two sergeants were given command of 15 men each plus we had a commanding officer, a Major. We stopped at Lillehammer and were ordered to secure the railway station.

From Jørstadmoen military camp 30 Norwegian rank and file soldiers were tasked to guard the gold. One officer, Major Bjorn Sunde was appointed the leader of the men; two non-commissioned officers, Sergeant Alf Pahlow Andresen and Sergeant Pettersen, in turn supported him.

Bjorn Sunde was a civilian engineer by trade prior to the invasion, but had reported to Jørstadmoen camp when war broke out. A few days later, and without any pre-planning whatsoever, he was ordered to take charge of 30 soldiers and 2 NCOs for a special assignment. Whether he knew what he was letting himself in for is not recorded, but he did not hesitate.

The soldiers detailed to guard the gold were a composite group of vastly differing ages, abilities and backgrounds. Some were of a professional standing such as teachers whilst others were equally diverse in livelihood being farmers, labourers, and a poet who had all come together in some

German infantry pushing up through the Gudbransdal Valley. Picture credit: Tore G Eggen.

desperate attempt to repel the invaders. Their concerns and anxieties for what lay ahead were not incongruent, but Sunde and his two NCOs saw to it that minds were focused – the safe transport of a nation's wealth rested firmly with them.

6

Move the Bullion!

Andreas Lund, who had been anxious about his role in the safe-keeping of the gold at Lillehammer, attended a meeting with Haslund on the afternoon of April 18th whereupon he quietly, and perhaps with some discomfiture, revealed to him that in 1933/34 he had been a member of Vidkun Quisling's Party – *National Samling*, but had left in 1934 after being threatened with exclusion.[65] Lund wanted Haslund to be aware of his political connections but Haslund had other priorities and showed no real concerns regarding this revelation. Further meetings commenced with Finance Minister Torp, Haslund, Lund and a local army officer, Colonel Finn Fougner and with Dombås now clear of parachute troops the decision was taken to move the gold. Lund, having been previously ordered by Rygg to send away all descriptions of the vault locks was requested to open them – the time was now close to midnight. Julius Pettersen and Hans Olsen Skurdal also attended as they had the keys to the main door. Lund later wrote:

> At last orders came and we went down to the vault to open the door. It was impossible to get the code in the right order. It continuously slipped out of my hand. The knowledge of what this was about started to wear on my nerves, it was no simple affair to blow up the modern armoured door with dynamite and now time was literally money…gold money. I worked for ½ an hour to open the door; it was the longest ½ hour I have experienced to this day.

Concerns were quickly raised when it was realised that Lund could not open the vault. Frantic calls were made to the Finance Minister Oscar Torp to warn him that the vault could not be opened. In desperation the idea of using dynamite was considered, but by whom has never been made clear, although Haslund would have been quite within his rights to demand this if the vault could not be opened. Norway's national poet, Nordahl Grieg later wrote about the debacle, although somewhat romantically.[66]

> When the Germans were approaching, Torp, after consultation with the government, gave Haslund the most extensive authority to get the gold out of the way. The whole affair was however locked up in the Lillehammer branch of Norges Bank, and the iron door was closed with a complicated lock, the secret of which was only known in Oslo. Haslund was just on the point of sending for dynamite when one of the bank employees drew him aside [*Lund*]. The man wanted to say that he had belonged to the Quisling Party, National Samling; he was not pleased about this, and might he be allowed to try his hand with the lock? He had once seen it opened and he had a good memory. He threw off his coat and struggled with the lock for two hours, with the sweat pouring down his face, it was as if he was fighting with Quisling, and he won. The door sprang open, and the 1503 boxes were taken out and transported down to the station to be loaded up.

After the war several people criticised Lund for his *forgetfulness* and blamed him for attempting to delay the release of the gold from the vaults, but this is a very harsh viewpoint and there is absolutely no proof whatsoever to support this claim. What does come across is a man who was heavy with fear and anxiety with his responsibility to safeguard the nation's wealth. It is also worth pointing out that the vault was brand new, had been opened only once previously and had never been used operationally until the gold arrived. Taking into account his anxious state, surrounded by others whilst he worked out the combination in his head and the fact that he had only seen the combination once before, it was an accomplishment that Lund managed to get the vault opened at all.

Just after 01:00 Lund was successful with the code, the vault doors swung open and the backbreaking business of loading the gold on to the trucks began. Haslund, in one of his later radio broadcasts from Boston, in the USA, describes the scene in the town at that particular moment, but like Grieg he couldn't resist a little romanticism in his description.[67]

> Lillehammer was asleep; there was no sound, no lights showing, and an insidious darkness that filled every doorway, every window with its inky stain.'

Haslund likened Lillehammer to being like 'the bottom of a deep grave'.

The bank officials and Haslund anxiously awaited the arrival of the lorries that would help to transport the gold and although it was dark the unspoken thoughts were that the Germans would suddenly arrive and take their prize without so much as a fight from the inhabitants. Then away in the distance a slight rumbling could be heard, then drawing nearer and louder…it was the lorries approaching slowly and cautiously. No sooner had the vehicles stopped in front of the bank than orders were issued and the loading of the gold onto the small lorries began in earnest.

Haslund anxiously looked to the sky scanning for any signs of dawn, which would herald the return in mass of German bombers, but the veil of darkness was still in place.

Haslund, always mindful of security, had the centre of the town cordoned off by armed police. The crews of the lorries, some of them brought in from the surrounding districts, worked long and hard loading the gold stopping only for the briefest of pauses to regain their breath. With impressive haste the lorries were fully loaded. Haslund sensed that this was only the beginning and that much work still lay ahead, but exactly what he had no real idea.

As soon as the lorries were loaded they made the very short journey to Lillehammer Railway Station where the arduous task of unloading the lorries one by one, and then re-loading the railcars began. [68] The men worked mainly in the dark, occasionally relieved by dim, shielded torches, but these were required mainly for the controllers from the bank as they inspected the metal bounded boxes and made a cursory inventory check of their contents.

With the loading complete, Haslund clambered aboard the train signaling its departure from Lillehammer. On board with Haslund were Julius Pettersen and Andreas Lund of Norges Bank who had volunteered to accompany the transport.

The wooden railcars, creaking and straining, moved slowly away from the platform as the train, with considerable effort, pulled its valuable load away.

As the train pulled out of Lillehammer Station the guard soldiers suddenly realised that they were heading north and not south. The relief must have been immense knowing they were heading away and not towards the German lines.

The train should have departed at 01:00, but actually left at 04:00. Haslund omitted to state in his report why this was, but it would seem that the holdup in getting the vaults open would have been a significant factor.

Essential precautionary measures featured clearly in Haslund's thinking. He wanted to factor in a degree of safety and warning so he ordered two men, Hans Kristiansen and Øivind Schou, to drive ahead and reconnoitre the way ahead for the train checking for damaged rail tracks and anything else that could hinder their journey.[69] The idea was to use a standard red signal lamp to stop the train if they encountered any problems. The two men, who had transported part of the gold from Oslo to Lillehammer, were ideal for the adventure. Fortunately there were no problems save from being stopped by Norwegian patrols and having to show their papers to the soldiers. The train proceeded to Otta with headlights dimmed hoping to avoid unwanted attention from any marauding Luftwaffe aircraft. Haslund also warned his soldier guards to be very alert with rifles placed strategically at the ready. A disciplined silence permeated through the cool spring air; their position and presence was not to be surrendered to carelessness.

Using the cover of darkness the train made as much progress as it could, but with dawn now pushing aside the obscurity and safety of the

Lillehammer Railway Station seen from trackside. Picture credit: unknown.

night the bullion train sought the relative safety of a siding at Otta to hide from German bombers. The guards though hidden, remained alert to any danger. Haslund knew he could not risk making a run for the coast during daylight hours as at any moment a well-aimed bomb could wreck the whole operation. He had also been made aware of German paratroopers further up the Gudbrandsdal Valley, which again presented issues for the transport, despite Norwegian troops and snipers from the local rifle clubs having dealt with the majority of them. The source of real unease though was that isolated elements of the paratroopers ahead of them could set explosives across the line to wreck the train and then ambush any survivors. With the Germans searching for the King and perhaps knowing he was on a train, Haslund could not risk the chance of the Germans mistaking his train for that of the Royal entourage. Capture of the gold would be seen as a massive coup for the Germans.

Later on the 19th Haslund, together with Lund and Pettersen, managed to secure a car and journeyed carefully up the Ottadalen to rendezvous with ministers Torp, Lie and Koht, as well as MPs Colbjørnsen and Størstad and other assorted officials at a small hotel. The purpose of the meeting was for Haslund to hand over to Torp the complete inventory list of the bullion confirming that all the gold was now in transit and under the guard of the Norwegian Army. Lund also secured the approval of Torp to add two large crates of cash from Norges Bank at Gjøvik, which amounted to nearly 10 million Krone. The evacuation of Lillehammer Bank was also advised and that the bank staff should remove all local valuables as they departed. This was agreed. The same day two lorries and two cars departed from Lillehammer with cash, valuables and as many bank employees they could squeeze in travelling to Hundorp, some 70km north of Lillehammer.

A false sense of optimism permeated its way through the Norwegians: the British were coming, the Norwegian Army was holding the Germans …and soon the Allies would be kicking the Germans out of Norway and the war would be over. Nordahl Grieg also experienced that sense of shared optimism amongst the guard and later wrote perhaps with some naivety:[70]

> At Otta we waited for 24 hours while the railway line over the Dovrefjeld was being cleared of parachutists. About 200 Germans

had come down; the majority were killed in the air, but a few had entrenched themselves in the farms. Major Arne Sunde (brother of Major Bjorn Sunde – leader of the military on the gold train) commanded the 'mopping up' of the Germans across the mountain. The line was now free and the first of the trains from the north came trundling in to Otta Station. There were three carriages chock full of British soldiers. They had their thumbs in the air, and we thought that help was now arriving and that this was only the beginning. We talked of being sure to celebrate May 17th in Oslo, and while we were running by night across the mountain down towards Romsdal, sentiment got the better of us, and we felt almost sorry for the Germans who were caught in the south as in a trap with the Skagerrak (Sea) blocked from the outside. Some of us considered that, to save a senseless slaughter of human beings, we ought to be able to give these unfortunates a chance of getting back to Germany across the sea with some kind of safe conduct. The night passed in thoughts like these, and we reached Åndalsnes in the morning…

Darkness once again draped its protective cloak over Norway, but more importantly over the train affording it the much-needed cover to move out of Otta. With the boiler fired and ready the train pulled slowly out of the station. It was 22:00. Trygve Sørlie takes up the story.[71]

> The train left Otta round 10pm. I was curious and excited and looked through the window for traffic from the road. White spookily dressed Norwegian soldiers manned the station at Dovre and on the level crossing towards Dombås in the cold spring night. We continued through Lesja towards Romsdal. At Bjorli we left 5 empty trucks and these were checked by Haslund and Sunde. They had to be sure that the right trucks were left behind. These trucks were to be used for military transport. The train arrived at Åndalsnes approximately 04:30. Also, between Otta and Åndalsnes the drivers Kristiansen and Schou were driving ahead of the train in a car along the road to check ahead that the railroad was clear. This part of the transport went quite smoothly with no accidents and no enemy attacks.

7

Åndalsnes

During the late evening of the 8th and early hours of the 9th April, and certainly by April 10th, it had dawned on the British that the German invasion of Norway was in full progress and that they, the British, had been well and truly out-foxed. Churchill stated:[72] *'We have been completely outwitted'.* What was even more galling for those in the War Office was that there was no reliable and accurate information coming out of Norway. Indeed, contact had been temporarily lost with Sir Cecil Dormer, the British Minister to Norway as well as with the Norwegian Government. London had absolutely no idea what was happening and who was where; communication via telephone was non-existent. This dire situation however, was remedied on April 12th when Captain (later Major and CMG) Francis (Frank) Foley, a so-called Passport Control Officer of the British Legation in Oslo, but in reality an officer with MI6 (Military Intelligence), reached the port of Åndalsnes and made contact via a transmitter to London.[73] Foley was later instructed to give the Commanding General Otto Ruge his every assistance. Foley did not disappoint and was to prove a very decisive and valuable link between Norway and London.[74]

The War Cabinet in Britain was now in a state of flux as it desperately began planning for a counter-invasion. The Chiefs of Staff, absolutely stunned by the latest events in Norway, met at 06:30 at the War Cabinet Offices on April 9th. General Ismay, having been woken by the Duty War Cabinet Officer, was later quoted as saying.[75] *'As I hurried into my clothes, I realised, for the first time in my life, the devastating and demoralizing effect of surprise.'* One by one, amidst a tense and sombre atmosphere the Chiefs of Staff took their places to discuss the latest events and to fathom out some sort of military response, but it was to be a few days

```
                SPECIAL DISTRIBUTION AND WAR CABINET
                          FROM NORWAY.

Telegram from Passport Control Officer (Norway).
                          14th April, 1940.
        D.     2 p.m.    14th April, 1940
        R.                14th April, 1940

No.

              """"""""""""""""""""""

(Sent with reference to Passport Control Department
telegram no. 9 - which conveyed the Prime Minister's
message to the Norwegian Commander-in-Chief).

      "Commander-in-Chief thanks.  He told me this morning
he had conference yesterday his staff and officers who
know England will come and help, but they quote Poland
etc., and fears he will be too late.  Morale is low
                  (more follows).
MESSAGES FROM NORWEGIAN COMMANDER-IN-CHIEF TO HIS
MAJESTY'S GOVERNMENT THROUGH PASSPORT CONTROL OFFICER
        5.45 p.m.       14th April, 1940
              """"""""""""""""""""""
      1.  British action in some form is necessary both to
make further resistance possible and to make the Norwegian
people and army understand that England really means
business.
      2.  The critical point is E (? Eastern) part of Norway
North of Oslo, wheere Norwegian army is trying to rally
pressed by German forces.  We cannot hold on many days without
help, which must be given by bombing Fornebo.
      3.  Trondheim must be taken at a time when I am able
to help you and I shall not be able to do so unless you
attack at once.
(Copies sent direct to Service Departments by Passport
Control Department.)
```

National Archives: WO 106/191. Picture credit: author

before something tangible in the way of a full counter-attack could be implemented.

Meanwhile, the Norwegians would have to fight on virtually alone until the Allies could muster an invasion force. Norway, with increasing regularity and alarm, was desperately calling for Allied assistance in some form, any form.

Prior to the German invasion of Norway the British and French Chiefs of Staff had drawn up *'Plan R 4'*, the allied invasion of Narvik, albeit a limited one – to cut off the iron-ore traffic coming out of Norway via Sweden. Plans also included simultaneous invasions of strategic Norwegian ports. Troops of the 24th Guards Brigade had been embarked at Clyde, Scotland in preparation for Narvik. Another battalion, 146th Infantry Brigade was bound for Trondheim with other battalions planned for Bergen; two battalions of the 148th Brigade were destined for Stavanger. However, with the German invasion of Norway 'Plan R4' was thrown into complete and utter disarray and troops were hastily disembarked whilst their cruisers headed out to sea in a sorry attempt to thwart the Germans. In the confusion and hurry to leave port, crucial war material and kit was taken off, placed on the wrong ship, accidentally remained onboard after the disembarkation of troops in Norway or inadvertently stowed incorrectly with essential parts missing. Food was mixed with ammunition, tools mixed with medical equipment. Mortar range finders and associated ordnance, communication equipment, vehicles and maps for the wrong areas had either been left behind dockside or were in the wrong ship. It was a nightmare scenario and certainly not the ideal preparation for war. It would take days to sort out under normal conditions, but these were not normal conditions and it was whilst the force was at sea that it was realised that the chaotic inventory mess was nothing but a logistical disaster of immense magnitude.

Eventually, a force was cobbled together with two battalions of trained regular soldiers from the 24th and 15th Brigades and five battalions of Territorial soldiers from the 146th and 148th Brigades. The Territorials, proud, wholehearted soldiers, had not been trained with Norway in mind; indeed, they had only received between two and seven months training prior to Norway.[76] Ten *'Independent Companies'* (forerunners of the commandos) were also sent, but again these were made up of men from the Territorials, albeit specially selected. They were certainly to prove their worth in Norway, but it really was a case of too little too late. French *'Chasseurs Alpin'* and a Polish Brigade made up the allied force.

By April 14th the matter of where to invade Norway was becoming a little clearer for the British although as the following plan will show the fog of confusion was slow to lift:

1. A small 'reconnaissance' force of 300 men would land at Namsos – a town some 80 miles from Trondheim. The code name for this operation was *'Operation Henry'*.
2. A 'diversionary' force of 600 plus men under the name of

'Operation Primrose' would be landed at Åndalsnes – some 150 miles south of Trondheim – and led by Colonel Simpson.

3. A force of 5000 men to be landed at Namsos – *'Operation Maurice'* – who would then march on to Trondheim.

4. *Sickleforce* – to land at Åndalsnes under the command of Brigadier Morgan.

Unfortunately, 146th Territorial Brigade, which was originally destined for Narvik, was diverted when at sea to support *'Operation Maurice'*.

The allied counter-invasion was hardly a surprise to the Germans as since April 10th the British newspapers had been falling over themselves to announce an imminent invasion at Ålesund, Åndalsnes, Molde, Namsos, Narvik and Trondheim.

On April 17th, British forces landed at Åndalsnes (*'Operation Primrose'*). Originally destined for Ålesund their destination was changed at the request of the Norwegians. Numbering 680 Royal Marines and seamen led by 45 officers, they would become the guard for the British base. Brigadier Morgan, who arrived with *'Sickleforce'* on the 18th April, had been tasked with landing at Åndalsnes. He was subsequently issued with the following order:

```
Small force British guerrillas operating your right
flank. About 600 sailors landing Åndalsnes night 17/18.
Their role after landing will be communicated to you
later.

3. Your role to land Åndalsnes area secure Dombås then
operate northwards and take offensive action against
Germans in Trondheim area. Not intended that you should
land in face of opposition... However, these orders
were changed whilst the task force was at sea to, '…
when you have secured Dombås you are to prevent Germans
using railway to reinforce Trondheim: am sending small
demolition party. Secondly, you should make touch with
Norwegian G.H.Q., believed to be in area Lillehammer, and
avoid isolating Norwegian forces operating towards Oslo.'
```

The securing of Åndalsnes was good news for the Norwegians involved with the gold transport. With the area around Dombås being cleared of German paratroops the railway line would soon be free for operational use. The single railway line from Dombås follows through the Romsdal valley to Åndalsnes, which is at the head of the fjord.[77] A small jetty of some 150 feet in length serviced the harbour permitting a ship to tie up alongside, with the lower water level at the port's termination being approximately 18 ft in depth. A 5-ton electric crane serviced the quay, but it was of little use to the Allies as the power from the town to the quay had been severed. To the west of the port was a small wooden quay of some 60 ft. in length. The railway station, which is situated only a matter of metres from the quay, provided relatively easy access for goods and passengers, but it was only possible to run one train each night as movement during the daytime was impossible due to the German air activity. There was however a reasonable amount of rolling stock for the defending forces to make use of. A major restriction in the use of the trains was that the gradients were severe and trains of sizeable length required two or more engines.

The Allies noted that it was relatively easy for the Luftwaffe to put a halt to rail traffic by merely bombing the single line and several bridges to achieve their goal of cutting off Åndalsnes. The road that serviced Åndalsnes was formed from rock covered with a sandy soil; when wet the sand would freeze thus permitting a reasonable surface, but the surface was also prone to rutting badly and with the thaw well in progress the road became virtually impassable at times.

Communication with Molde was via various W/T sets as well as with ship's radio. There was also a telephone line, although this was thought infiltrated by Norwegians with pro-German sympathies. The strikingly picturesque mountains that stand watch over Åndalsnes offered some protection from attacking aircraft that had to be almost overhead before they could bomb. Nevertheless, for the 2,000 or so townspeople of Åndalsnes, the Norwegian forces and the allied military, the mountains would not be enough to stop the onslaught that was to come. Åndalsnes was unsecured against air attack and this really was the crux of the problem for the defending forces. The only solution of sorts was the use of Royal Navy anti-aircraft cruisers in the fjord.

The Germans, quickly assessing that Åndalsnes was of major strategic importance, and acutely aware that the Allies had made landfall, unleashed the might of the Luftwaffe upon the town on April 20th. Sergeant Alf Pahlow Andresen, an NCO (non-commissioned officer) on the gold transport, later wrote about what happened:[78]

It was a beautiful, sunny day when we rolled in to Åndalsnes early morning on the 20th April. There was no sign of the Germans bombing anywhere. The British we met were confident even if they knew that a lot of war material had been lost in the transfer from Britain to Norway and laid at the bottom of the ocean after German bombers had sunk some of the transport.

A few Bofors guns were in position outside the railway station. We were curious as they were manned by reservists. They had been given three weeks training in using anti-aircraft firing. We thought about our own training.

Around 9am the first Heinkel 111 roared overhead. The British destroyers in the harbour immediately left towards the mouth of the fjord firing every gun they had. Where I was hiding behind some railway sleepers near the station and some carriages I could hear the howling of the first bombs and I did not feel happy about it. I felt less than helpless. Splinters were howling through the windows of the coaches. The four or five of the German aircraft were totally dominating the scene.

Air attacks increased dramatically and life at Åndalsnes was continually disrupted. Men fought hard against the odds to keep the port open, but losses mounted steadily. The British employed two anti-aircraft cruisers, HMS *Cairo (D87)* and HMS *Curacoa (D41)* in an attempt to provide some form of aerial explosive umbrella of protection for the port and town. Over ten days these ships expended a vast amount of ammunition in their quest to ward off the bombers, which in turn were careful how they approached their bomb run. On the 24th HMS *Curacoa* was hit and badly damaged. Other ships were drafted in to provide additional support; anti-aircraft sloops, destroyers and armed trawlers, but they were all vulnerable, though in drawing the attentions of the bombers towards the ships they managed to reduce the amount of bombs originally destined for the harbour and town. Their actions were gallant in the extreme, but without an established air defence, lack of air superiority and an inability to strike back and strike hard at the enemy, the noble cause was heading for an early curtailment.

Lieutenant (later Commander D.S.C and Bar) William Donald was No.1 to Captain A. L. Poland D.S.C on the sloop HMS *Black Swan (L57),* which was positioned in Romsdalsfjord, steaming round in the confined waters to avoid becoming a sitting duck when she came under sustained attack. Donald notes:[79]

> At first it was quite exciting. The bombs always managed to fall well clear, and no harm was done. It seemed more like a game than anything serious, and on the second morning I was quite sure we had shot at least one aircraft down, if not two.
>
> But then things began to change; the same afternoon one stick of bombs fell mighty close, and, due to an error on my part, the guns failed to open fire and the plane flew away unscathed. Not anticipating such an extensive period of firing, we blazed away merrily even at extreme ranges, and it became increasingly clear that we were going to run short of ammunition…It began to dawn on everyone that the whole Norwegian campaign was not going as well as might be expected…Events were moving so fast ashore on the overall picture that by the time any signal had been written out, enciphered and transmitted, the situation had completely changed.

Donald could see from the many signals that were flooding in *that the campaign was rapidly getting out of hand.*[80] But there were lighter moments and after the bombers had left the Chief Boatswain's Mate requested permission to lower the whaler to so that he could collect the dead fish that lay on the surface and organise the ship's company's tea. Permission was granted, but as the Chief was going about his business the whaler was requested to collect the Admiral, who at that time was aboard HMS *Carlisle (D67).*[81] The Admiral was duly collected, but unfortunately was forced to share his trip to shore-side with a load of dead codfish. It was noted that the Admiral was not impressed.[82]

An unnamed British Sergeant at Åndalsnes who was working transport between Åndalsnes and Dombås was quoted as saying:[83]

> German bombers raided the troops every day from 7am to 5pm. There was never a break in the attacks" he said. "I never thought even Germany possessed so many bombs. At Åndalsnes they dropped at least a thousand in a couple of days. Their objective was the landing field, but on the day we left the only part of Åndalsnes they had missed was the jetty. Our chief trouble was that we were smashing hard at something with really nothing. If we had tanks and fighter aircraft we could have done really good work.

Andreas Lund's experiences of his time at Åndalsnes are worth noting as they give a graphic account of the horrendous conditions prevailing at that time, although one may consider his thoughts classically understated:[84]

> We were all dead tired on our arrival and we checked in at the Grand Hotel. Here, there was a multitude of British officers and Petersen and I were given a room on the third floor. We just fell straight on to the bed with our clothes and shoes on and went to sleep immediately.
>
> After a few hours' sleep we went downstairs to have something to eat. Just after that we met Haslund and told him we would go down to the train to check the seals on the coaches and to ensure they were not damaged. Shortly after we had come down to the railway station the first air-raid alarm sounded. I went down into a shelter in a sandy hill with Major Sunde and some soldiers. It was a very primitive hollow and not very comfortable. Major Sunde shouted a warning and we could hear the howling of the bombs and shortly after they exploded around 50 metres away. At the same time three warships in the harbour opened fire and the British anti-aircraft guns also started to fire. Sand was coming down from the roof on to my head and I had a desperate wish just to get out of the cave, which had only one entrance and no other exits. After a while the bombing ceased and we could leave the cavern.
>
> We went back to the hotel, but before we got there more aircraft arrived overhead and we had to go down into the hotel basement where there were a lot of people. One bomb fell near the hotel and made a huge crater. The sound of the anti-aircraft guns mixed with the howl of the fire sirens was indescribable, but eventually the noise died away. I met again with Pettersen and Haslund, who had sought refuge in the station area and it was Haslund who suggested we drive out of town to get some rest. Together, we drove a little way up the valley where we found a farm. They were willing to sell us food and we rested a little before we returned to Åndalsnes that evening. It snowed upon our return and we used our car headlamps to see our way. Some Norwegian guards stopped us and said that they could see us from some distance. Also, two of our drivers, Schou and Kristiansen, had been arrested, but released when they said whom they were working for.
>
> Haslund was not happy about the gold train remaining at the station whilst we were waiting for a ship to transport the gold onwards. He therefore made contact with Station Master Frydenberg

to make arrangements for a safe place for the train. It was quite uncomfortable and miserable at Åndalsnes Station that night. The Station Master had placed his bed in the office because his home had an explosive device lodged in the wall. I also recall him warning against spies as he said that he had heard a noise outside his office, but when he tore open the door a man disappeared into the night.

Meanwhile Trygve Sørlie, having previously overseen the train onto a siding and out of harm's way at Åndalsnes Station, took his rest at one of the railway houses, but no sooner had he settled than he was awakened abruptly by the bombs falling on to the town coupled with the anti-aircraft fire from the ships in the harbour. Sørlie quickly realised that this was not the place to be and gathering his personal belongings made his way to the station. As he approached he noticed a small commotion and could see some captured German paratroopers in a car complaining bitterly that they should be treated with respect under the Geneva Convention and that as prisoners of war they should be moved immediately away from the area because of the bombing. The irony of the situation did not pass him by.

Haslund meanwhile was busy considering his route to the port at Åndalsnes where he hoped that the gold could be taken off by a warship. To his dismay the port had become the main target for the Luftwaffe. The British had made the town one of their points of entry into Norway in the vain hope of re-capturing Norway from the Germans. Åndalsnes had therefore become a must destroy target for the Germans. Haslund knew it was suicide to wait there for a British warship and so with the support of the Finance Minister, Oscar Torp, Haslund gave orders for the train and its guards to move back a few kilometers to Romsdalhorn and a precious siding. Romsdalhorn was an ideal location to hide a train. The towering mountains that loomed over the tiny station would make it extremely difficult, perhaps nigh on impossible, for an enemy bomber to swoop down a sheer sided, almost crevice like valley and drop its deadly load on a stationary train. The likely outcome for any large bomber attempting the feat would have been disastrous. Haslund and his crew had chosen wisely, although it would have only taken one renegade pilot risking all in an attempt to bomb the train.

The raids continued unabated on Åndalsnes. The Germans were focusing on the destruction of all transport routes. Railway engineers worked flat out to keep the rail lines open between raids, but again and again the bombers returned to drop their bombs onto the town below. Frydenberg moved some of his staff to Romsdalhorn Station from where they began 12 hour maintenance shifts. Trains were halted whilst a posse of rail-men commenced repair work. As soon the lines were clear the trains were running again.

At around 11pm on April 20th railwayman Leif Evensen answered the phone. He was ordered to ensure a train, currently on its way from Åndalsnes, was placed on a siding. He was also ordered not to officially record the train movement. Although puzzled, Evensen did not question the order but immediately set to work and in due course the gold train arrived at the station and was parked on the siding, well away from curious eyes and onlookers.

One of the soldiers chosen to escort the bullion, Ove Voldsrud, has spoken about his time as a soldier guarding the gold. He gives an intriguing if a little understated insight into events.

On April 17th Ove Voldsrud reported for duty at Jørstadmoen military camp, near Lillehammer, to take part in the fight against the Germans. For Ove, the war could not have come at a worse time. He was 33 years old, a family man and had just become a father for the third time. Although Ove was a devoted father and husband, his sense of duty to his country prevailed and with his new-born daughter barely 6 hours old he left his wife, children and the family home to report for duty. It was a difficult farewell. Ove takes up the story:[85]

> At Jørstadmoen [camp] we got uniforms, guns and ammunition, and [*that night*] we slept in a barn. The next night we were ordered to meet by the road. We were picked up by trucks and were driven to Lillehammer railway station. We were ordered to protect the station and the train at the station. Various people were loading a lot of cases into the train, and we were told that we should join the train as guards. At that time we didn't know where the train was going to.
>
> The next morning we travelled to Otta. German parachutists had taken shelter in the basement of a barn and they used the farmers as shield. After some time they [*the Germans*] were waving with a white flag, and the Germans surrendered without a fight. That evening we left Otta and headed for Åndalsnes. We arrived next morning. In Åndalsnes we were met by German bombers, who tried to bomb

British warships in the fjord. The streets of Åndalsnes were crowded with British soldiers. Men and boats were probably the target, but we were not in a good position. Sverre J. Borgedahl and I were guarding the train, when Fredrik Haslund and two men came and opened one of the trucks, which was sealed. We thought we recognised the Prime Minister Nygaardsvold and the Foreign Minister Koht with Haslund. Suddenly there was a warning of air attack and the three men ran for cover. Because Sverre and I were on guard we couldn't leave the post. We approached the open wagon carefully and with curiosity getting the better of us we took a look inside the truck. We thought it was full of explosives. When we saw the cases with the letters NB Norges Bank, we then knew that the cases contained gold. Then suddenly we heard the whistling sound of a bomb falling, and in the next moment the bomb went off 20–30 metres away. I got a splinter in the wrist and was bleeding a little, and Sverre got a cut by the ear. We were lucky. The bombing continued during the day. By the time Fredrik Haslund returned we had locked the truck.

Romsdalhorn Station had a direct telephone line to Åndalsnes and Haslund ordered that the telephone be constantly manned so that in the event of a British warship entering the harbour arrangements could be quickly made to move the gold down the railway line to the harbour. The soldiers took it in turns to man the telephone, although it was not a popular task. The gold train was held at Romsdalhorn sidings for a few days whilst plans were made for transporting the gold to the quay and onto a British warship in the quickest time possible. Whilst this was going on the soldiers watched as the Luftwaffe made every attempt to bomb Åndalsnes out of existence. The bombers would swoop down, often diving through the low cloud that surrounded the mountaintops and into the valley. Haslund later described it as a cauldron. The Norwegians watched and hoped that the German fliers would crash their machines into the mountains, but the Luftwaffe pilots, ever alert to the dangers, skillfully guided their planes away from the unforgiving mountains and on to their chosen target.[86]

In a heart-stopping moment, two bombers audaciously dived down into the valley and attempted to bomb the railway line. Ten bombs were dropped but fortunately only one hit the railway line blowing a hole approximately 3 metres deep and 6 metres wide. The line, although broken was repaired within three hours by a railwayman and a squad of soldiers. Haslund remained confident that he and his men could deliver the gold; the British could also transport their soldiers out of Åndalsnes and towards the front lines. Special praise should go to the Norwegian railway workers who defied the odds and the Germans to make their line passable. It would not be the first or last time that the railway workers would surpass all expectations.

The Germans were relentless in their attempts to disrupt and bomb the military traffic from the port of Åndalsnes, but their aim was often poor and they found it difficult to eliminate selected targets. Civilian targets were not so lucky. The Germans bombed the towns unremittingly and at times completely obliterated their chosen objectives. Haslund knew that this intensely intolerable situation could not last and that if plans were not in place sometime soon the chances of getting the bullion away to safety would be virtually non-existent. Meetings were held to discuss what was to be done next. Various suggestions were proffered but it was agreed that contact be made at once with British naval forces to see if they could assist. Norwegian naval forces were also contacted to see if they could aid in any way possible. A hastily arranged conference of Norwegian ministers and authorities took place at the Grand Hotel Bellevue in Åndalsnes where it was discussed whether the Norwegian torpedo boat 'Trygg' could take the bullion in one lift, but it was argued by the skipper of the 'Trygg', Lt Munster, that the ship was not sufficient in size and that the only realistic option was to make a formal request to the Admiralty to send a ship or ships to rescue the bullion, or to evenly distribute the gold between several small ships. But whatever the decision the bullion had to be taken to the UK.[87]

The conference came to a sudden and violent end when the Germans began their bombing once again and a near miss blew out the doors, windows and part of the roof of the hotel. It was only by sheer good fortune that the Germans, unaware of the importance of the conference, missed with their indiscriminate bombing.

On April 20th, Torp made contact with the British, and according to Haslund, plans were set in motion for a Royal Navy cruiser to steam into Åndalsnes and embark at least some of the gold. The following signal from the navy confirms that contact:[88]

```
FROM: C.S.20        MESSAGE           RECEIVED
                    2143/20TH APRIL   20.4.40
                                      DATE
                                      2206
                                      TIME
                NAVAL CYPHER (D) by W/T

ADDRESSED: ADMIRALTY

                    IMPORTANT.

   At Cabinet Meeting here Government requested
immediate transfer 50 tons gold at Åndalsnes to
England.
   It is desired to divide it between 3 ships either
warships or merchant ships.
   Request very early information when this consignment
can be embarked.

                    2143/20
```

At that time the naval authority in Norway was Admiral Sir John Guy Protheroe Vivian RN. In Maurice Michael's book, *'Haakon King of Norway'* he writes:[89]

> …some members of the Norwegian Government got through to Åndalsnes and were taken to see Admiral Sir Philip Vian [sic] to discuss two rather important matters: the Norwegian merchant fleet and the Bank of Norway's gold…and she [*Norway*] wanted transport to England for 320 million Crowns' worth of gold, which at that moment was stored in a tunnel [*sic*] at Åndalsnes railway station. As Admiral Vian told his visitors, that must have been the first time a British Admiral had been roused in the middle of the night to be offered a thousand ships and £16 million worth of gold 'on a plate'.
>
> (Author's note: Captain Vian was made a Rear Admiral in July 1941 and was not at Åndalsnes during that particular period. Trygve Lie, in his book, *'Kampen For Norges Frihet'*, page 114, makes a similar mistake referring to Admiral Vian as being part of the meeting where the discussion of the movement for the gold took place. In fact it was Admiral Vivian).

Although the signal to the Admiralty originated from Admiral Vivian, the responsibility of the actual organisation of transport for the bullion out of Norway fell to a Royal Navy officer of immense talent, the formidable and gifted Captain Michael M Denny RN – the Royal Naval Officer-in-Charge of Åndalsnes and Molde.[90]

The Norwegians found Denny to be immensely helpful and he went to extraordinary lengths to ensure that he and his men did their best under the most awful conditions. Denny was later to be instrumental in the allied evacuation.

In Denny's report, which was compiled upon his return to England he comments, albeit again in a typically understated way, on the appalling conditions that prevailed at that time.[91]

> From my arrival at Åndalsnes at midnight, on 17th April, to my departure from Molde at midnight, 30th April, the base organisation at Åndalsnes and Molde lacked the necessary staff and communications essential for efficient functioning. For the first five days I was virtually single-handed, and the base naval reinforcements and equipment then were duly lost in the bombing...'

Denny also commented on the lack of wireless telegraphy (W/T) between Åndalsnes and Molde, which hampered matters further and that movement in and out of the waterways was continually disrupted by bombing attacks. He also writes that from April 26th the situation deteriorated dramatically.[92]

> At the Base the incessant German air activity caused more and more dislocation. With all wooden quays destroyed, the area surrounding the single concrete quay devastated by fire, the roads pitted by bomb craters disintegrated due to the combined effect of heavy traffic and melting snow, the recurrent damage to the railway, the machine gunning of road traffic...

Denny could see that Åndalsnes couldn't take much more before it would be rendered totally untenable as a port and town. All port work had to be carried out between the hours of 22:00 and 06:00 to stand any chance of avoiding the attentions of the bombers.

Denny's work also took him to Molde (he travelled by motor boat) and he states that the port had, up to that point, not received the same attentions from the Luftwaffe as Åndalsnes, although his motor boat transport was attacked and strafed en route to Molde.

Whilst at Molde, Denny was informed of the whereabouts of the gold bullion and was asked if he could assist in any way its safe conduct to the UK. Denny readily agreed and upon his return to Åndalsnes he immediately set about contacting the Admiralty. His report, written up on May 7th in conjunction with his war diary, has an entry dated the afternoon of April 24th, which is somewhat at odds with the date given by the Admiralty of the 20th. His entry states the following:[93]

> …was informed in strict secrecy of the whereabouts of the Norwegian gold bullion, by the Minister of Defence [*Colonel Ljunberg*] and made provisional plans for its transfer to the UK.

His efficiency in making provisional plans for the evacuation of the bullion was exemplary as later on the evening of April 24th HMS *Galatea* docked at Åndalsnes. Meanwhile, the Germans had started to increase their attacks, particularly on marine craft used for the transportation of troops. Denny noted that three of his ferries had either been sunk or badly damaged, he had also lost his motor boats to bombing and therefore transport across the fjords was now out of the question, at least during daylight hours. To add to Denny's woes he was informed that the local telephone system had been totally compromised. On April 26th Denny noted.[94]

> Owing to failure of batteries, Molde W/T set became inoperative. Communication with the Admiralty was maintained via Ålesund, receiving by broadcast. Both Molde and Åndalsnes were bombed throughout the day, the latter particularly, and had to be evacuated. During the day all wooden quays at Åndalsnes were completely destroyed by fire and the whole of the town in the region of the quay was burnt to the ground. At Molde the majority of bombs were incendiary and on this occasion were of Czech manufacture and so were happily blind, but the town water supply was cut by H.E. (High Explosive) bombs and some difficulty was experienced in controlling the fires with the inadequate labour supply available.

Whilst in Molde, Denny was assisted by Captain A. O. Douglas RN (Retired). He accompanied Denny to Molde on April 17th. In his report he writes:[95]

> Molde had been bombed the preceding Sunday, 14th, the objective being the quays, and although some damage had been effected, it had not interfered with any of the quays…Captain Denny had

requested me to organise the civil population for A.R.P. (Air Raid Precaution) and working parties. This I proceeded to do and on the morning of our arrival…and all the first day I was busy collecting my working party. This party consisted of 40 men divided into four parties of ten with a leader who could understand English. Three lorries were requisitioned…and the whole party was under the direct control of Mr Hustmark who served me most loyally. Besides the working party I also procured the services of young men on bicycles whom I asked the Chief of police to send out on the roads, which guarded the approaches of the town; they were to make themselves inconspicuous and report back anything they saw. Needless to say we had several false alarms, one of which was the approach of German soldiers in three lorries, the soldiers dressed in Norwegian uniforms. They eventually proved to be good Norwegians.

On Thursday, 25th April, the working party went on strike for pay, but I arranged with the Norwegian Naval Authorities that they should be paid by the week every Saturday, and furthermore that Mr Hustmark should be given official standing of some description; thus the difficulty was overcome.

That same afternoon the town was bombed and one house started to burn furiously. An efficient water supply was at this time available and the fire was prevented from spreading to the next house by the untiring effort of the working party and the local fire brigade. This house was a sort of general store and contained cloth goods and bicycle tyres. I told the working party to get what they could out of the house to prevent it catching fire, and one young man offered me a warm bag containing 100 number 6 sporting cartridges. I was glad to see them thrown in to the sea. One young man, who with sublime contempt for the enemy continued to man the hose whilst the street was subjected to machine gun fire, was some minutes later instantly killed by the side of the house collapsing outwards into the street. Although the house was of wood and we were able to lift the side up almost at once it was obvious that nothing further could be done.

Meanwhile, Haslund had been busy. Arrangements had been put in place for an assistant and liaison officer to be taken on to help him after Andreas Lund and Julius Pettersen had been relieved of their duties on April 21st. The two bankers had been advised to make contact with their banks again and early that morning the duo began preparations to return

Dombås Railway Station prior to the invasion. The photo is taken atop of the tunnel.

Dombås Railway Station after it had been bombed.

The tunnel at Dombås; little has changed since the dark days of 1940. Photo credit: author.

home. Their journey back was treacherous and not without incident. The train the men were travelling in reached Dombås around midday, but an air raid was in progress. The travellers ran for the shelter of the tunnel, but just as they entered it there was a direct hit on the station. Lund was sent flying by the blast; but the gentleman beside him was killed. Passengers screamed and cried; dust and debris filled the tunnel. It had been a close run thing for the bankers and their two accompanying drivers, Kristiansen and Schou. In the early hours of the following morning, totally exhausted, Lund, Pettersen, and the two drivers finally reached their respective families.

With Lund gone, the man now sought out to assist Haslund was Kristian Gleditsch, his brother-in-law. Gleditsch's wife, Nini, also joined him. Gleditsch was a geographical engineer prior to the invasion and had been appointed to the Head of Information Office by General Ruge when the Germans invaded and so was considered reliable and a safe pair of hands.[96]

Whilst in Åndalsnes, the Gleditsch's took refuge in the Grand Hotel, Bellevue, a magnificent 19th century wooden building with a distinctive tower. It was here that the Gleditschs met up with Lieutenant Martin Linge, an officer who would later feature prominently in Norwegian history.[97] General Ruge was also at the hotel along with senior Norwegian and British officers working out various plans and strategies. Kristian and Nini Gleditsch soon got to work by helping to produce a Norwegian/ English newspaper, titled the *Åndalsnes Avis*. The edition coincided with British soldiers landing at Åndalsnes and soon sold out. Meanwhile, Norwegian ministers Torp, Frihagen, Lie and Ljunberg met to decide whether it was safe for the King and government to move to Romsdalen; their discussions must have been serious, sombre and sullen.

The situation in Åndalsnes was deteriorating fast. The British forces command, fearing for their own safety, moved out of their hotel. The Gleditsch's managed to secure a car, which they shared with Martin Linge – later to achieve fame as head of Norwegian special forces – journeying to Romsdalhorn. Meanwhile, the British forces command installed themselves at a farmhouse outside the centre of Åndalsnes and Nini Gleditsch managed to establish contact with them before they evacuated themselves to Romsdalhorn.

For the Gleditsch's the situation was really no better at Romsdalhorn. The Germans continued to bomb railway lines knowing full well it would halt the advance of the British. They literally were stuck between a rock and a hard place.

Did the Germans know that the Norwegian gold bullion was there? The answer in short was no. If they had known then surely a different approach would have been taken. Germany was desperate for gold and it would have made no sense to attempt to bomb it into oblivion.[98]

At Romsdalhorn there was a surprise waiting for the Gleditsch's in the form of Nordahl Grieg. Their last meeting was in Spain when Grieg was fighting with the International Brigade against General Franco's forces in the Spanish Civil War. The three friends, who regarded each other like close family, joked and swapped stories of their experiences of the invasion and subsequent battles.[99]

Meanwhile, at Romsdalhorn Station, the soldiers continued to guard the gold. The engine had been released for other duties; there was a dire need for transport to and from Åndalsnes and it was a case of priorities. Haslund's determination to move the gold was undimmed though. He took advantage of Nordahl Grieg's knowledge of English and tasked him with the duties as a liaison officer. Communication with the British was absolutely essential and Grieg was the ideal man for the job, in fact it was Grieg who ensured that the telephone link with the British was firmly established after he had visited the emergency telephone exchange at a small place called Hagan, just outside Åndalsnes.

During interview, Ove Voldsrud spoke very highly of Nordahl Grieg and was glowing in his praise for the manner in which Grieg dealt with people from all ranks and upbringings. Ove described Grieg as a honourable man who could make you feel completely at ease whatever your status in life. Praise indeed.

Ove also recounted a story, almost as an afterthought, about an incident, which appears to have never been formally recorded by officials and historians, although a similar story appears in Dorothy Baden-Powell's book, 'Pimpernel Gold', albeit more dramatic. Ove stated that whilst they were at Romsdalhorn Station a stranger appeared. The man, purportedly a Norwegian, was dressed in a windcheater jacket, which Ove thought at the time was strange. He noted that the man was wearing a patriotic

Ove Voldsrud pictured on duty at Horten in 1926. Picture credit: Voldsrud family.

Norwegian armband and appeared to have something concealed under his jacket. The man initially just stood and watched what was going on from a distance. He quietly disappeared but then returned twice more, attempting at one point to strike up a conversation with Ove, who ignored him. On the third occasion the man was arrested and taken away. However, Ove says that a battery like object was removed from the man before he was hauled off. Subsequent investigations have proved fruitless despite extensive searching of official records. It is possible that the man who was arrested was just curious to what was happening at the station and that after his 'arrest' he was released without charge. However, in Baden-Powell's book, *'Pimpernel Gold'* she makes reference to a spy in the Romsdalhorn area attempting to make contact with a lone German Luftwaffe aircraft, but was caught in the act by loyal Norwegian soldiers and shot dead. Are the stories linked? Possibly, but one must be cautious about spy stories and the urge to draw hasty conclusions. What is clear is that some sort of incident happened and perhaps the truth will emerge in the future. Author's note: an expert from the Royal Corp of Signals stated that at the time the Germans had the technology to communicate from ground level to aircraft above, but that the aircraft would need to be very close to the radio operator or directly overhead. In the mountainous region of Romsdalen the aircraft would almost certainly need to be overhead before a signal could be sent or received.

On April 24th there was a temporary lull in the bombing. Under cover of darkness Haslund ordered the gold train down into Åndalsnes and onto the quay. The British cruiser, HMS *Galatea,* commanded by Captain Schofield RN, had docked and was disgorging British soldiers and equipment.[100]

Time was of the essence and without hesitation the Norwegian soldiers, including Ove Voldsrud, toiled hard loading 200 boxes of gold from truck No 8138 onto the deck of HMS *Galatea.* The loading was anything but easy, but the soldiers stuck to their job. Box by box, barrel by barrel they completed the task. Major Sunde took up a post of patrolling the area with an unnamed British officer, whilst Haslund oversaw the loading of the gold.

With the fast approaching dawn heralding the imminent return of the bombers, the order was given to cast off and *Galatea* slipped her moorings and made her way down the fjord and into the open sea. Forever in the true traditions of accountancy, *Galatea's* Paymaster Commander signed for the gold consignment. The captain then gave the order to set a course for

Romsdalhorn Railway Station. Picture credit: author.

Rosyth, Scotland. On board *Galatea* were Norwegian officials tasked to ensure that Norwegian interests were met in England and that the gold be safely transferred to the Bank of England.[101] When the first consignment of the bullion was at sea the Military Branch of the Admiralty thought it wise to let the Bank of England in on the story.[102]

```
                              Military Branch
                              Admiralty
                              SW1
                              25th April 1940
```

```
                    SECRET

Dear Waley,
  You will probably wish to know about Norwegian gold
so far as we know the story.
  A telegram was received from a naval authority
in Norway on 20th April saying that the Norwegian
Government had asked for 50 tons of gold to be shipped
to England, to be sent over in three lots.
  We heard last night that 16 tons was on its way, and
I arranged with Bolton of the Bank of England that is
should be turned over to the Royal Bank of Scotland at
Edinburgh on arrival. This was done this afternoon and
I believe it is now en route to London.
  We can't tell yet when and how the remainder will
arrive but I will let Bolton know as soon as news is
received.
                    Yours sincerely,

                    P H Jones (for S Gilmour)

  S.D.Waley, Esq., C.B., M.C.,
  H.M.Treasury,
  S.W.1.
```

Haslund felt somewhat relieved to see the cruiser sail away with the boxes of gold, but the job was only partly complete. It was hoped that other warships would come in to collect the remainder of the gold, but these hopes were soon dashed as the intensity of the bombing increased. Haslund knew that the gold could not wait at Åndalsnes as he had received a message from General Ruge, the commanding general of Norwegian

Åndalsnes in Flames.
Picture credit: Tor
Christian Jevanord

forces, stating that the Germans were close to breaking through. His thoughts turned to Molde, a small town and port only a short distance away, which had not yet received the full attention of the Luftwaffe. The beauty of the snow-covered mountains caught Haslund's attention for a few seconds as he *'glimpsed the jewel-like encrusted peaks shimmering in the transparent spring night.'* The Germans, though, had no such poetic thoughts and within a few days they had laid waste to Åndalsnes, the quay and the rail lines despite the very best efforts of the Norwegians to repair the infrastructure between bombing raids. The first shipment had left just in time.

8

HMS *Galatea*

The British cruiser HMS *Galatea* was the first to be assigned the mission of embarking the Norwegian gold bullion. Designed and constructed in the Arethusa Class, she was laid down at Scotts Yard in June 1933, launched in August 1934 and completed in August 1935. She displaced 5,220 tons and was armed with six 6-inch guns in twin turrets with a secondary armament of four single 4-inch guns, although twin 4-inch guns replaced these prior to the start of war. Two triple banks of 21-inch torpedo tubes and two quadruple .5-inch machine guns completed the armament for the cruiser. An aircraft catapult was fitted to the ship and an Osprey seaplane issued, but by the time of the Norwegian Campaign this had been replaced by a two-seater reconnaissance Fairey Seafox.

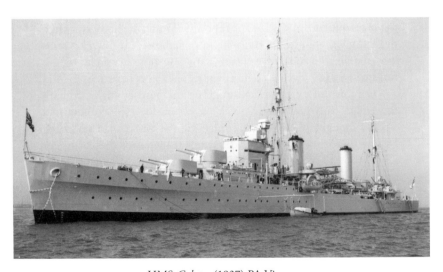

HMS *Galatea* (1937) PA Vicary.

As part of the 2nd Cruiser Squadron, HMS *Galatea*, along with HMS *Arethusa* and 11 destroyers, left Rosyth on April 8th to take up positions some 80 miles off the coast of Stavanger. Ronald 'Peddlar' Palmer RN was an experienced Petty Officer and was certainly well qualified to handle whatever challenges the Admiralty had in store for HMS *Galatea*.[103] The following is an abridged account taken from a statement kindly given by Ronald's family. His words are classically understated, but nonetheless poignant:

> Reinforcements were sent from home to bring ships up to their full war complement. Most of these replacements were Royal Naval Volunteers, those weekend sailors who during those dark years proved their worth and their courage on so many occasions. In two weeks we were ready for sea again so we went west going up the Irish Sea and on to Scapa Flow to join the fleet there and from then on life was very hectic. We were to spend most of our time at sea during the next months; first, on convoy duty, then on various patrols until 8th April when Germany invaded Norway. During the next month we did two trips to Norway going up a fjord to Åndalsnes taking British troops and their equipment over and a third trip to bring some of them back during the withdrawal. It was a risky business. German aircraft occupied shore bases and seemed to take a liking to us. They would appear two or three times a day, always at meal times. I remember the Chief Torpedo Gunners Mate coming into the mess one teatime, he had just poured himself a cup of tea when the alarm was sounded 'Enemy aircraft overhead'. He flung his arms into the air and looking up said "can't you b****'s wait until I've finished eating?" Even in danger funny incidents occurred.
>
> On our third visit we had to go up the fjord by night, embark the troops and get out as quick as we could. Two cruisers had already 'bought it' doing the similar run. It was a mad stampede getting the Army on board and during all the chaos the Paymaster sent for me to meet him on deck. He said "we have to get that lot on board" – a pile of small wooden boxes. I said, "but that's stores Sir – the stores chief should be doing it". His reply shook me, "that's not stores its gold! Seven million pounds of it, to be taken to the United Kingdom for safe keeping for the Norwegian Government." We did a very careful check as it was piled into a cubby hole in the deck structure with both of us doing the same method of 'fives' and comparing results later – they were correct. All the time the hustle was progressing getting the troops in.

At last we were ready to sail again but dawn had arrived. We reached Molde where the fjord widened into a large bay and there were the German planes awaiting us. Fortunately we had a good Captain – his idea was to steer to where the last bomb dropped – nothing hits the same place twice!! More by good luck we were not hit and after a running battle of nearly five hours we got away. We only had eighteen high angle shells left so I was told.

There is no record in the log book of *Galatea* detailing even the slightest hint of her special cargo, but on April 24th at 02:30 *Galatea* unobtrusively slipped her moorings and departed Åndalsnes with 200 boxes of gold bullion; her destination was the safe haven of Rosyth, Scotland. The log records the journey to the UK as uneventful until 17:50 on the 24th when two enemy aircraft attacked *Galatea*, with no hits recorded. There were no further attacks and on the 26th *Galatea* docked, securing alongside the north wall. The gold was promptly unloaded and the responsibility was handed over to the Royal Bank of Scotland Inspectors Messrs Small and Sutherland, who escorted it to London on the London, Midland & Southern Railway. Upon arrival in London the Chief Cashier of the Bank of England valued the first consignment at £2 million Pounds Sterling.[104]

A document in the Bank of England states the following:

```
                    Bill Of Lading
                    ----------------


Received from Commanding officer, HMS Galatea the following
parcels containing Gold Bars and/or Gold Coins:


        200 cases marked N.B.


All cases and casks of wood with iron hoops and sealed
- except for Box No 551 unsealed.


To be forwarded to the Bank of England for the Norwegian
Government in the care of Mr. Øyvind Lorentzen together
with the Norwegian Minister in London.
```

On April 24th a message was sent from the Admiralty to the C-in-C Rosyth informing him that the Bank of Scotland would be taking charge of the first consignment on the instructions of the Bank of England. It was signed 'For the Head of M'. It would appear that Rear Admiral John Godfrey, Director of Naval Intelligence (DNI) from the Naval Intelligence Department (NID) and known as 'M', was taking a close interest in matters and with his close connections to the Bank of England and Sir Montagu Norman, Governor of the Bank of England, it was understandable. Interestingly, Godfrey's city 'connections' included Sir Edward Peacock, Chairman of Barings Bank, as well as Olaf Hambro, Chairman of Hambros Bank. It was this bank in particular that later played a part in the transport of Norwegian bullion as well as supporting the Norwegians with their merchant marine.[105]

The first consignment was now safe in the UK. Thanks to Haslund and his men, Captain Denny and the Royal Navy, 200 boxes of bullion had been rescued. Back in Norway though, the task of moving the remaining bullion out had already begun...

9

The Road to Molde
April 24th–29th

News of German advances came with alarming frequency. The latest reports were of a major battle taking place at Kvam on April 24th (NB the town is on the main road from Lillehammer to Åndalsnes and is approximately 35 miles north of Lillehammer). Norwegian and British forces were heavily engaged with the Germans. The fighting was bitter and desperate and losses were heavy. General Paget's 15th Brigade had embedded themselves around the village of Kvam and across the main road thereby blocking the German advance. The plan was to halt the German advance thereby allowing Norwegian forces to fall back and reorganise themselves in the Romsdal region. General Paget knew that the Brigade's situation was dire as his force of around 3000 men, supported by Norwegian ski troops, attempted to thwart the onslaught of 8,500 well-equipped Germans. Paget's forces were badly hamstrung with no air cover, no ground to air defence, no artillery and virtually no transport against the Germans with their tanks, artillery and supreme air power, and the latter supported by dive-bombers. Paget was further hampered by a threat to his left flank as well as bomb damage to the railway line to Åndalsnes. He could see that the outlook was bleak, but nonetheless his men fought hard and for two days they kept the Germans at bay. Eventually the odds were overwhelming and on the 26th Paget decided to begin a withdrawal; it was to be a chaotic affair.

A line was later drawn at Otta and once again the men of the 15th Brigade played out a similar scenario of defence.

Meanwhile, German bombers were laying waste to Åndalsnes and with the unstoppable onslaught of the German forces the only outcome for the British forces and their Allies was the evacuation of southern Norway. Although probably not appreciated at the time the dogged rearguard action of the Allies was buying valuable time for the Norwegians intent on moving the gold transport to safety and away from the Germans, but of course it would only take one sharp-eyed Luftwaffe pilot to dramatically swing the odds in favour of the invaders.

It was absolutely essential that Haslund, perhaps now bordering on desperation, move the gold away from Åndalsnes with the utmost urgency. The inevitable threat of bombing remained extremely high and staying where they were in the hope that another warship would come in to collect the remainder of the gold was not an option. Åndalsnes was a scene of utter chaos as the Germans continued to blitz the port and British troops tried to embark their ships to evacuate. There was just not enough room for any more gold to be taken off and it was too dangerous to remain in the area: Molde, a nearby port town, was now the chosen destination.

Prior to leaving Åndalsnes, and with considerable foresight, Haslund asked Kristian and Nini Gleditsch to drive to Molde ahead of the transport taking with them two boxes of valuables that were to be handed over to Finance Minister Torp. Haslund also wanted them to make contact with Norwegian authorities to see where the bullion could be stored as well as liaise with the British naval authorities to arrange transportation. Haslund did not have to reiterate the urgency and they didn't need reminding. Southern Norway was falling and time was of the utmost essence.

Haslund made arrangements to secure a vehicle for the Gleditschs, but the only one on offer was a fish van! On April 24th the van duly arrived complete with driver. A rail truck was opened (No 2950) and two boxes transferred to the fish van, with the operation carefully watched by Haslund, Sunde and Gleditsch[106]. Five soldiers were assigned to guard the van as it transported the boxes to Molde but with explicit orders to return once their mission was accomplished. This particular operation was to be known as 'the light luggage'. Kristian Gleditsch reports:[107]

> We drove swiftly through Åndalsnes, which was a miserable sight. We took a ferry and continued on the endless road around Fannefjord. The roads at this time were horrible with the thaw, combined with heavy military transport, and only a trained eye would recognise something resembling a road. At one place a row of cars were stuck

fast up to their axles and when we arrived there were just sufficient men to pull the cars free and out of our way. In the Molde area there were several guard posts controlling the road and harbour area and there was a small civilian force of the 'Molde Guard' to assist the local military.

Because of the rumours sweeping the area about German paratroopers and spies operating in the Molde area, Gleditsch and his small guard attracted a lot of suspicion. Stopping close to a farm for the men to answer the call of nature the guard soldiers were observed by some of the local inhabitants and to all intents and purposes the soldiers appeared to be loitering in the woods. The fish van, painted white and very conspicuous was duly noted by the watchers and the local military informed.

Upon arrival at the first guard post at Fannestranda the unlikeliest of financial security transit vehicles was treated with distrust and incredulity.[108] Gleditsch was questioned closely, and although the military were suspicious they were satisfied enough to allow the fish van and its occupants to continue into Molde. However, their journey into town was cut short once again as a Norwegian naval guard apprehended them. This time the officer in charge of the guard, a young naval Sub Lieutenant, was not convinced by the authorised note that Gleditsch was carrying that was supposedly signed by Secretary Haslund. Furthermore, the officer was of the opinion that the Norwegian guard soldiers were really Germans in uniform; such was the level of hysteria during that dark period.

The naval guard stood poised with their weapons cocked and pointed at the soldiers…the situation was very tense. Searching questions as to the intention and identity of the party continued unabated, but it was probably the local dialect of the soldiers that ultimately saved the day and convinced the naval guard that the purpose of the soldiers was genuine. Eventually, Kristian and Nini Gleditsch and the soldiers, along with the fish van, were permitted to pass and enter Molde where the Gleditschs sought out Fylkesmann Trygve Utheim. Even this official was not at first convinced of their intentions, but after much discussion with Kristian Gleditsch the situation was resolved and the two boxes carefully placed under lock and key within the town.

Utheim, now feeling more comfortable with his guests, invited them over to the Hotel Knausen, which at that time was housing several members of the government. It was against this background of unforeseen circumstances that the town of Molde had now become the capital of Norway. Although her reign would be short it was nonetheless a very important one.

Minister Trygve Lie met with the Gleditschs at the hotel and immediately made arrangements for them to stop over at a farm known as 'Retiro'. The five guard soldiers were dismissed and ordered to return to Romsdalhorn Station to await further orders.

Almost at once, intense discussions began amongst the various officials on the best place to secure the gold whilst in Molde. Various suggestions were put forward, but it was the proposal by Per Mordal, a bank manager at the Romsdals Fellesbank, that was accepted as the best solution. Mordal's submission was to make use of the basement at the Confectionsfabriken (clothing factory). This basement, he argued, was about the largest and safest place in Molde, and it was close enough to the quay to transfer the bullion to a ship if need be. No one could better the proposal and so arrangements were immediately put in place to prepare for the arrival of the bullion. Molde was not only the capital of Norway, but it was also about to become the bank of the nation's wealth. Unfortunately for Molde and her townspeople they would pay a heavy price for this responsibility.

Whilst arrangements for the safe keeping of the gold were being made, the five guard soldiers who had returned to Romsdalhorn Station found that preparations were already in hand to move the rest of the gold. Haslund had conversed with Colonel Ernst David Thue and Captain Rohde of Infantry Regiment 11 (IR11) about the possibility of moving the gold out of Romsdalhorn by lorries. The three men were minded to move the bullion with the utmost urgency. The next day, April 25th, Haslund received a sobering note from Thue stating that he and his men could no longer guarantee the safety of the bullion and its guard soldiers as the Germans were getting closer and in his opinion would be coming down the valley at any time now. The gold transport team had just hours to get away. The Minister of Finance, Oscar Torp, was informed of the situation and he gave his blessing for the bullion to be moved; the alternative was not up for consideration.

In the interim, Utheim was using his influence to ensure that the ferries at Åfarnes were kept operational and available for the gold transport as and when required. Captain Rohde managed to obtain 25 lorries for Haslund. He also provided drivers. Two hours of hard, backbreaking work commenced as the soldiers and railway staff carried the remaining 1303 boxes and barrels of gold bullion from the railway trucks to the lorries.

The soldiers climbed aboard their assigned lorries and slowly moved out and away from the station. Haslund, installing himself on the lead lorry with Nordahl Grieg, instructed the drivers to remain a reasonable distant apart from each other to avoid attracting the interest of the Luftwaffe. Sergeant Pettersen manned the second lorry, whilst somewhat unusually Major Sunde manned the third lorry with Sergeant Pahlow-Andresen.

Difficulties lay ahead in the form of poorly tarmacked roads, many of which were little more than trackways covered in snow and mud and with the thaw well under way the driving conditions were grim at best. There were also fjords to cross and the only way was by ferry. This would be long and laborious; at that time in Norway there were few bridges with the ferries being the main method of travel between communities. Haslund was not sure if these ferries were running – some may have been put out of action by bombing he considered, but his mind was made up to move out and if the ferries weren't running then an alternative would have to be found.

With the lorries loaded and crews duly aboard the convoy moved out of town. To their horror within a short time of the convoy starting the Luftwaffe returned and this time the target was the convoy. Lining up astern, four lumbering bombers closed in on the convoy and made straight for a line of sitting ducks.

For the Germans any form of transport was seen as fair game and a legitimate target, irrespective of whether it was civilian or military. Steadying their aim, the bombers, Heinkel 111s, came in to attack, flying low to increase their chances of hitting their victims. Lookouts onboard the lorries watched the bombers avidly, scanning desperately for the moment of attack. Then they came, four bombers taking it in turns to strafe the lorries and anyone who happened to get in the way.

A sharp knock on the cab roofs of the lorries by the lookouts in the back of the trucks warned the drivers who forced their vehicles to a crashing stop into the cover of bushes and trees by the roadside. The crews jumped out and dived for what little cover existed whilst others sought shelter under the lorries. White hot, metallic splinters from the strafing rained violently through the air as the bombers roared overhead. Miraculously, once again fortune favoured the Norwegians and no one was injured or killed. The bombers' aim had been providentially poor.

With the aircraft swinging away down the valley, the soldiers grabbed the opportunity to seek more substantial shelter by running and taking refuge in a large house beside the road. The house was full of British soldiers taking cover from the air raid, their helmets covering the back of their heads. Haslund, searching frantically for something to cover his head, found an old washing bowl and covered his head with it, which gave rise to much laughter and merriment. The attack lasted approximately three quarters of an hour. Haslund concluded that the Germans were poor at hitting individual targets and preferred large targets such as towns and quays. His mood rallied as he realised that the chances of the convoy being hit by bombers were second-rate at best, barring plain bad luck.

The crews remounted their trucks and once again set off towards Molde. The bombers returned again, but on this occasion the convoy bravely increased speed and continued on their way without stopping. Just in front of them a house took a direct hit and blew up, but the convoy found just enough of a gap amongst the debris on the road to squeeze through. The convoy toiled along the treacherous roads eventually reaching the ferry crossing at Åfarnes. There were no ferries there and a message came through to Haslund announcing that one of the ferries was out of service and being repaired after being bombed. It mattered little as Haslund knew it would be suicidal to embark a ferry during daylight hours for fear of being an easy target. There was little to do except wait for darkness and the remaining ferry to arrive so Haslund took the opportunity to get the lorries under cover where possible, camouflaging the others with bushes and branches and ordering the exhausted crews to rest; it wasn't a difficult order to obey.

Sergeant Andresen later commented that trying to find a suitable crossing was difficult and that wherever they went they were treated with suspicion by their own. Evacuated Norwegians that occupied the farms thought the trucks were filled with ammunition and, understandably, they did not want the soldiers and their cargo anywhere near them for fear of death and injury.

Later that night the ferry arrived safely but it could only take two lorries at a time and six long hours were to pass before all the lorries were safely across. That was just the beginning for once across the other side of the fjord the long incline that leads away from the quay was difficult for the overladen lorries to climb and coupled with the slushy snow, mud and poorly made road it didn't take long for one of the trucks to shudder to a halt, beyond repair. There was no choice in the matter: the gold had to be removed from the lorry and redistributed amongst the remaining trucks. The trucks were originally designed to carry 1.5 tons, but their loads with the bullion were in excess of 3 tons and to travel as far as they had was indeed a remarkable feat. But for the men the problems did not end with the mechanical limitations of their transport. As mentioned earlier the road was in a terrible state and with the spring thaw set in snow and thick mud spewed in all directions. The winter had once again eroded what resembled an apology for a road with deep ruts and potholes cratering the surface. In some places the road conditions were so bad the crews set about repairing the road themselves just so the convoy could safely pass. Along other stretches of the road repair gangs set to work to keep the road open having been informed that an important convoy had to pass unhindered. It was a very long night; four of the lorries broke down, but Haslund managed to secure three more vehicles to take their place. Time and time again the gold had to be un-loaded and re-loaded leaving the crews exhausted to the point where they could barely move.

Locals also helped where they could to ensure that the lorries continued with their journey. Mr Asbjørn Nakken was one of those that assisted without hesitation:[109]

> Late in the night of April 28th two men knocked on our outer door. They asked for help to drag a lorry out of a ditch and onto the road again. I was a 15 yr old boy at the time. On the farm we had two strong horses and enough equipment. So my father and I went together down to the vehicles. Each of the lorries did not weigh more than approx. 3 tons, so it was an easy job to get the lorry out of the ditch. The roads in this district were so narrow that it was impossible for one vehicle to pass another on the road. We did not talk much to the people and they did not utter much.

> We did not ask what sort of transport this was, but later we got
> some information of a transport of gold through the district, so we
> understood that was part of the national gold holding we had been
> dragging out of the ditch.

Progress was painfully slow, but eventually the convoy crawled into
the relative safety of the port of Molde. Seeking out officials to assist,
Haslund was informed that the Norwegian Government had taken
office at the Hotel Knausen and that King Haakon and Crown Prince
Olav were also in residence along with Norges Bank thus effectively
making Molde the capital of Norway.[110] Haslund halted the trucks at
a place called Fannestranda, just a kilometre or two east of the town
centre and he immediately set about enquiring as the whereabouts of
the Finance Minister, Oscar Torp. The gold had to be unloaded and
placed in safe storage and Haslund wasn't prepared to release the bullion
until he was happy with the arrangements. Torp was soon located, and
he briefed Haslund about the Confectionsfabriken building. Haslund,
satisfied, ordered his men to drive to the building, unload and stow
the bullion in the basement. The townsfolk welcomed Haslund and
his crews and after pleasantries were exchanged they once again set to
work unloading the heavy boxes and casks into the basement of the
factory with the help from Molde citizens as well as governmental
civil servants who arrived from their temporary accommodation at a
nearby farm. The long work quickly became a tiring affair, but women
volunteers ensured that the guard soldiers were kept fed and watered.
It was a very welcome gesture.

The setting of the factory was perfect: a large vault with an extremely
thick and weighty door providing the final barrier to any opportunist.
As an added precaution guards were posted
at various points. The vault, despite being
cleared of various items, was not quite big
enough and so the task of enlarging the
safe area was entrusted to local carpenter,
Erik Berg.

Nordahl Grieg later described the
stowing of the gold with glowing praise
for Molde and her people.[111]

Confectionsfabriken building –
Molde. Photo credit: E Birke.

Towards the morning we arrived in Molde where we carried the boxes in to the basement of the Confection factory. How well everything was organised in this town! Eager women volunteers and nurses ran around, along with volunteers with armbands patrolling the street. The anti-aircraft gun crews were very alert with the sirens going off as soon as a plane approached. A few days later, though, everything was burnt down and not a single life was left in the ruins. Later when I heard the air defence alarm for other small Norwegian towns, I felt poignant and sad, it was a pathetic signal…

The residents of Molde played an active role in the defence of the town and were keen to do all that they could and it wasn't just to help with the loading of the gold bullion. The locals, at the bequest of the Chief of Police and the editor of a local newspaper, had set up a quasi-armed militia and these people patrolled the streets and crossroads, guarded various buildings and generally quelled any problems with traffic and possible looting. Captain Denny, the Royal Naval officer-in-charge of the British forces at Molde and Åndalsnes, who had arrived on April 17th, further refined this by requesting that the men lay down their arms, and instead patrol nominated areas and report back as required. Denny later reported that this was largely successful. Other townsfolk acted as aircraft spotters and would set off the air-raid alarms as soon as an aircraft was spotted, thus giving the locals time to escape and make for the woods behind the town.

Haslund meanwhile sought out the Norwegian military authorities and requested that his crews be rested for a day. He could see that his men were exhausted to the point of collapse and that they needed to rest, but the military, bereft of transport for their beleaguered army, ordered Haslund to relinquish his transport and crews and for them to return from whence they came. Haslund trudged back to his men; he did not enjoy being the harbinger of bad news. Without fuss they once more clambered back into their tired steeds, started the engines and headed back.

10

Molde – Capital of Norway

The city of Molde played a unique role during that dark time in Norwegian history. Through tragic circumstances it had become the capital of Norway for a short period. The Norwegian Government, along with the Royal party of King Haakon and Crown Prince Olav had sought shelter in Molde after they had been forced to run from the invaders pursued by German bombers and paratroops with strong rumours surfacing of Quislings and so called *Fifth columnists* charting the King's every move and reporting it back to the Germans. For a while the townsfolk of Molde would shelter and care for them, but without adequate air defence, and the Germans likely to hear of their presence, it would only be a matter of time before the town was bombed. How right the prophecies were of those who predicted an onslaught. The bombers duly arrived overhead and unmolested they dropped their deadly cargo. Time and time again the bombers returned until the bombing was such that the town succumbed to a combination of bombs, incendiaries and the inevitable conflagrations that engulfed and overwhelmed the close-set wooden houses. The local fire brigade, brave as they were in the face of massive and insurmountable adversities, just could not cope.

Whilst the King was in residence in Molde a remarkable incident occurred whereby a photographer captured the King and his son on film standing by a young silver birch tree just moments after the Royals and their entourage had run for cover from another air-raid. That photograph went on to become a symbolic image for the Norwegian struggle against tyranny as it was flashed across the free world.

It was on April 23rd that the King, Crown Prince and the rest of the government arrived in Molde. They had travelled by ferry from Åfarnes with the help of the local Fylkesmann Trygve Utheim, arriving at Molde around 03:00, filthy dirty from their travels. They settled for the night at a small hotel, but having rested they later moved on to Glomstua, a farm northwest of the town. It was here that the world famous image of the King and the Crown Prince flanking a silver birch tree was taken.

Per Bratland, journalist and photographer spoke about the background of these pictures in an interview he originally gave in the early 1980s. A lengthier version appears in his book – *Are We Like That? – Er vi slik?* (1971).[112]

Bratland at the time was working for the Norwegian Foreign Affairs press office. It was late in the evening of April 25th when he arrived in Molde with a message only for the ears of Finance Minister Oscar Torp. Having found Torp, he informed him that the gold transport was en route from Åndalsnes. This was welcome news for Torp who had feared for the safety of the men and the gold. But Bratland knew there was an even bigger story and so approached Halvdan Koht at the Retiro asking if he could photograph and interview the King. Koht must have been surprised as he had thought that only a few people knew where the King was. Bratland reasoned that the value of the interview would be immense if the world could know that the King was alive and well and still in Norway despite the German invasion. Koht could see the potency of his argument and agreed to Bratland's request, but there would be restrictions, which Bratland had to agree to.

Bratland was duly blindfolded and placed in a car at the house of Utheim, which was then driven around the town for a while in an effort to disorientate him. Bratland later admitted that he had no idea where he was, but that he was some time in the car. He thought the date was Saturday April 27th. Arriving at Glomstua, Bratland was told to wait outside the house, although after a short while he was invited in. Just at the moment he was taken inside the farmhouse an air-raid siren sounded and the King and Crown Prince came out of the house and walked quickly up the sloping hill towards the woods that backed on to the house. It was considered safer to be in the woods rather than in the house.[113]

The bombs began to fall, but the King and his son didn't flinch and sensing his moment Bratland began taking photos. Bratland did not possess the luxury of a telephoto lens so just kept moving forward brazenly snapping away until only their Royal faces filled the lens. The initial images were distant, but it was the close-ups that Bratland was after. Bratland spoke to the King and Crown Prince asking them to move nearer to the birch tree; the snapping continued with Bratland edging ever closer. No photographer had got this close before when suddenly the King called a halt to the filming with Bratland having managed to fire off 36 pictures. Of those pictures, 20 went around the world.

With the bombing over the King and Crown Prince moved off towards Glomstua without a word spoken between them. Bratland had earlier been offered the opportunity to interview the King, but it was clear to him that it wasn't going to happen. Bratland had his pictures and for that he was thankful.

The photos depicting the King and his son standing by the birch tree were not made public until some weeks later due in part to Bratland having to dodge the oncoming Germans. Towards the end of April Bratland was staying in Ålesund, along with other members of his profession. On May 1st the journalist community moved northwards in a small fishing boat towards Bodø and then travelled on towards the Swedish border, which they crossed without too many problems. Bratland then made his way to Sweden's capital, Stockholm, making it his personal mission to get to the Norwegian consulate where he could show his photographs. The consulate, sensing that that there was significant propaganda value

King Haakon & Crown Prince Olav beside the Silver Birch in Molde. Photo credit: Per Bratland

Picture postcard of Molde prior to World War 2 by HG Dahl. The church can clearly be seen against the backdrop of the fjord. The church and surrounding houses were subsequently lost to the fires started by the Luftwaffe using incendiary bombs.

Picture postcard of Molde as seen from the fjord. The date and photographer are unknown, but the photo was taken prior to World War 2. Again, the church stands prominent against the houses and merchant buildings.

in the photos, called a press conference and the photographs were shown to interested parties. It was Elsa Nyblom, editor of the newspaper, *'Vecko Journalen'*, a weekly journal, that later wrote a substantial article about Norway and included Bratland's photos.[114] Other newspapers followed up including the world famous American *'Life'* magazine. Photos also appeared in British newspapers and journals and the free world, hungry for information about the war, could see for themselves what had happened to Norway. More than anything else at that time Bratland's pictures captured the public's imagination and his hurriedly taken photos suddenly became iconic.[115]

It didn't take long for word to pass around Molde that the King and the Royal party were in residence somewhere close to the town. Rumours later circulated that someone had passed on information to the Germans and that they in turn attempted to bomb various houses, but it has not been possible to find substance to this story. What is certain, however, is that the King on several occasions took shelter in the woods that backed on to Glomstua farm – just above Molde. The guard soldiers were billeted nearby and also took shelter in the same woods when the bombs fell, but although often tempted to do so the soldiers never fired their Krag rifles at the aircraft for fear of revealing their positions. Their discipline was admirable under such dire and frightening conditions. It wasn't just bombs that fell on Molde, but also incendiaries starting fires that quickly became conflagrations and overwhelmed Molde's fire brigade. The small wooden buildings stood little chance against such a bombardment of airborne arson.[116]

On April 26th there was a welcome respite from the incessant bombing. The residents of Molde, at least those who had remained in the town, took the opportunity to reorganise themselves as best they could. Government ministers, fearful that they might all perish due to a direct hit, moved out of their hotel and dispersed to nearby farms; Hotel Knausen, though remained in use as a venue for conferences. The Norwegian forces also took advantage of the lull in bombing to take stock of their situation and attempt some forward planning. During the respite there was much discussion about the future of Norges Bank and a decision was made that the existing bank management should be relieved of their duties.

Dr Arnold Ræstad was asked to step forward and take the position of Chairman.[117] A conference was called at the farm where Ræstad was quartered and numerous interested parties met up to discuss an assortment of administration matters concerning the bank's future. The farm, Bjørsito, was situated just a couple of miles west of Molde.

Rather than be penned in and cramped inside the farm a decision was made to sit outside to take advantage of the fresh air and sunshine. Unfortunately, the Luftwaffe had also decided to bomb Molde again and so the conference hastily reconvened in the farm's cellar. It was a wise move, as any significant gathering of people outside would have certainly gained the attention of an astute pilot.

Ræstad's inaugural conference at the farm saw various Norges Bank employees arrive from outposts such as Gjørvik, Hamar and Lillehammer to attend their first meeting with the reconstituted Norges Bank, now free to operate in the non-occupied zones. The men from these outposts also brought with them several boxes and bags of cash amounting to several million Norwegian Krone, which were stored initially in a bank in Molde. The Bank of England was informed of Norges Bank's decision via telegram, which has since been transcribed by persons unknown:[118]

```
                        BANK OF ENGLAND

        Copy of telegram received from -

        MINISTRY OF FINANCE          AALESUND

        DESPATCHED: 8.30 p.m.        SUNDAY, 28TH APRIL 1940

        RECEIVED: 3.00 p.m.          MONDAY, 29TH ARIL 1940
```

In pursuance provisional decree of 22nd April, 1940, the King [Haakon] has the same date discharged the members of The Board of Directors functioning until 9th April from their duties and has appointed as the Board charged with governing the Bank until further notice Dr. Arnold Raestad [sic] Chief Director and Chairman Mr. Jens Noervie and Vice Chairman Mr. Ole Calbjaernsen [sic] Dr. Wilhelm Keilhau and Oscar Hansen Molde [sic]. Copy and translation the above mentioned provisional decree will be sent you by letter. The new Board has taken over the direction of the Bank on April 26th the address of the Head Office of the Bank is Molde.

```
                        LIMITED DISTRIBUTION.
Decypher.   Mr. Mallet (Stockholm).
                              29th April, 1940.

    D.   12.35 a.m.        30th April, 1940.

    R.    3.10 a.m.        30th April, 1940.

No. 429 Dipp.
                        hhh
IMPORTANT.
SECRET.
     Please inform the Treasury that the Bank of Norway
have now moved officially to Molde and the new board
of directors has been appointed under a new ordinance:
     Chairman, Doctor Rastad, former Minister for Foreign
Affairs, Vice-Chairman, Jens [?Nortve] members,
[?Colbnelrnsen] Oscar Hansen, Professor Keilhau.
     They are considering issue of new notes, and have
asked the Norwegian President of the Storting here for
his suggestions which are being sent tonight after
consultation with Mr. Charles Hambro.
     We are impressing on them the importance of taking
no action before consulting the Bank of England.
     The location of the Bank and the fact that it has
gold and bank-notes safe with it must be kept absolutely
secret.
```

Photo credit: author.

Further confirmations were sent to the UK from the British Legation in Stockholm, but despite these telegrams and wireless messages laying out the new Board of Norges Bank there would later be some doubt about the authenticity of the Norwegians involved and some months would pass before Norges Bank was not seen as an *'Enemy Bank'*. However, as can be seen from the document above the Norwegians had the support of Sir Charles Hambro – Director of the Bank of England and Hambros Bank. Sir Charles also worked for the Ministry of Economic Warfare (MEW) and was in Oslo when the invasion began. Having promptly escaped to Sweden he met up with his cousin, Stortingpresident Carl J. Hambro. It was after this meeting that the financial arrangements were put into place to support NOTRASHIP utilising Sir Charles' Bank – Norway now had a very able and valuable ally.[119]

Meanwhile, in Molde, the bank employees were quartered in an assortment of places in and around the town including initially the Confection building, where they had to sleep on the floor. Later, they sought shelter in private dwellings and a school, which provided some comforts.

During this time Molde continued to be the target of the Luftwaffe, intent on flattening the wooden city, and the woods behind Molde became blessed sanctuary for many during such occasions. An RAF signal, dated 28th April and sent at 21:45 to the Air Ministry in London gives an idea of the precarious situation at Molde, although The Air Ministry only received the message during the early hours of April 29th. It states the following:[120]

> Situation 2100 hours ANDASNES [sic] and MOLDE bombed throughout day. Petrol and oil unloaded at Molde early hours this destroyed…Food situation here difficult must have further rations by 2nd May.

It is difficult to imagine the sheer terror as well as the debilitating exhaustion of the townsfolk and enforced guests who inhabited Molde during that period, but despite the continued onslaught of the invaders there were still groups of people who volunteered their services. One such group was known as 'lotte' (volunteer women) who worked and liaised closely with the Red Cross and other organisations.[121] These women improvised as best they could under such harrowing conditions, but they managed to keep the guard soldiers fed and watered and provided comfort where they could. Even these women had to succumb to the Luftwaffe when their kitchen was eventually bombed out, fortunately without loss of life.

Molde was now being bombed remorselessly; the Luftwaffe were determined to rid Norway of her King and leave no hiding place for the sovereign and his entourage. The town suffered appallingly. Captain A. O. Douglas noted in his report to the Admiralty:[122]

> During the day, Sunday, April 28th, bombing became general and low flying bombers machine-gunned the streets and appeared to single out the church for special attack. Our trawlers were being attacked as soon as they arrived, and it became increasingly obvious that, owing to the enemy being in complete control of the air,

our position was rapidly becoming untenable. On Monday, 29th, Captain Denny informed me that the expeditionary force was to be evacuated that night and asked me to arrange lorries etc. However, the Germans had got the information and all that day the town and quays were subjected to intensive bombing with high explosive and incendiary bombs and by 1800 the lower part of the town was burning fiercely and the fire creeping upwards towards the pinewoods.

With the Luftwaffe overhead, the soldiers guarding the gold in the Confection building sought the shelter of the cellar in a desperate bid to get away from the bombs, but it was a terrifying experience as ordnance exploded around them shaking the factory to its very foundations. The men knew that it would only be a matter of time before their time was up; the law of averages would surely prove deadly in the end.

Fires raged across the helpless town as the wooden buildings succumbed to the incendiaries that rained down relentlessly. Molde was in chaos and the townsfolk, unable to quell the flames, departed the town in droves taking with them what few possessions they could. The fire brigade was completely overwhelmed. They fought the fires as best they could but the task was just too great. Molde was now a raging conflagration.

Amidst the utter chaos and disarray that had engulfed the town a further blow was delivered...this time from their British Allies who announced to the Norwegian High Command their intention to withdraw and evacuate from Norway. It was devastating news. General Ruge, who had arrived in Molde on the 29th, sought to galvanise his troops as best he could in the face of such despair. The British offered to transport King Haakon and Crown Prince Olav as well as members of the Norwegian Government to whichever destination they wished. Sanctuary in the UK was also on offer and Ruge advised the Royal entourage and government to accept the British offer immediately. For the Norwegians it must have been a moment of utter hopelessness.

That night in Molde a final meeting took place at the Hotel Knausen between the King, Crown Prince and members of the government. It was a very sad and dour affair and the atmosphere was as heavy as their hearts. Norway was close to capitulation. King Haakon, not wanting to forsake his people, was wracked with indecision. Britain would offer him, his family and the Norwegian government sanctuary, but what of the people of Norway…his people? The King had been in Molde for six days and during that time the Luftwaffe had come hunting for him. The King had pointedly refused to be intimidated by their pursuit, in particular taking breakfast earlier every day so that the bombing would not determine when he would finish. When the bombers came he and his entourage headed for the woods for shelter, sometimes for hours on end; somewhat remarkable for a King approaching his seventieth birthday.

On April 28th King Haakon was informed that the German Government had announced that the Third Reich was at war with Norway – some news! The Norwegian reply was swift…they had known that fact since April 9th when the Germans had attacked without declaration. Later, there was another announcement from the Germans stating that King Haakon was wanted *'dead or alive'*. The next day the Luftwaffe came again and showed their intent by bombing Molde with an unsurpassed ferocity.[123]

Whilst Molde was being bombed and burnt, Haslund and some volunteers bravely set out to rescue some valuables that were being stored at Spare Bank in Storgata – situated in the centre of town but close to the waterfront. Haslund, Ole Colbjørnsen (Member of Parliament), along with Sergeant Pettersen and a handful of soldiers defied the flames, debris and rubble and rescued what they could leaving behind only a few coins of little value. The boxes were then transported to the Confection factory to be stored with the gold bullion. Later that day Haslund met with Torp and Supply Minister Trygve Lie at the Hotel Knausen to discuss how best to evacuate the gold out of the factory. The hurried conference had been informed that a Royal Navy cruiser was on its way in to Molde and they were to be ready to embark as soon as it docked. The ship would be coming in under the cover of darkness, although with the town in flames it appeared to be almost daylight. Concerns were expressed that a large British cruiser would be unable to dock and that smaller boats would be needed to transfer the gold so contingency plans were drawn up. Two ships, D/S *Driva* and M/S *Rovdehorn* were placed on standby.

Haslund had to plan how they would move the gold from the factory to the warship. Molde was an inferno with roads virtually impassable so his plans would have to be fluid and subject to change on the spot. The biggest problem was trying to secure enough lorries that were serviceable and undamaged. Haslund asked two local men, Aksel and Trygve Melsæter

Molde burns. Picture credit: Romsdalsmuseet, N-6413 Molde, Norway.

to assist after he saw them filling up their truck with petrol. Twice they crammed their truck with bullion and each time transported it to a quay and a waiting ship, the 'Legona'. On the third occasion the brothers loaded their lorry and then were instructed to take their consignment to another part of town where they met up with a brewery lorry. This vehicle attempted to drive down the centre of Molde towards the quay, but due to the bombing, flames and debris it was forced to turn back. The Melsæter brothers didn't have much luck either and encountered similar problems. It seemed like there was just no way through. Miraculously other trucks acquired by Haslund, did make it through, despite the horrendous fire storms and chaos that was engulfing the town and lighting up the night sky. The trucks, the exact number of which is unknown, were at the quayside as HMS *Glasgow* docked alongside. It was a timely moment.

There was also the matter of the King: Captain Denny, the Royal Navy's Senior Naval Officer at Åndalsnes and Molde, was informed on the evening of the 28th that His Majesty King Haakon was in residence near Molde and from that point onwards Denny remained in contact with Sir Cecil Dormer, the British Minister accompanying the royal entourage. Denny reported the following in his proceedings:[124]

> Moved British and Norwegian Headquarters at Molde to upper part of town. Molde raided continuously with low level dive-bombing and machine-gunning from 06:00 until 19:30 and my previous headquarters were burnt to the ground. In the first attack of the day, the well-hidden aviation spirit dump was completely destroyed by incendiary machine gun attack. The town was soon in flames and continued to burn furiously all day. The mixture of H.E. and incendiary bombs used by the Germans was most effective against the town which was almost 100% wood built.

During the day, Denny received a British coded signal stating what really was the inevitable to all at Molde...evacuate. Preparations were immediately put in place in readiness for the next course of action and on the 29th Denny reported the following:[125]

> Åndalsnes Harbour front and adjacent hills were ablaze from incendiary bombs. 04:30 Commander Johnston returned from Åndalsnes and brought the Admiralty messages ordering the evacuation of H.M King of Norway.

Picture credits:
Romsdalsmuseet, N-6413
Molde, Norway.

Denny stated that he then requested *'every assistance for evacuation'*. He continues.

> Bombing continued intermittently all the forenoon and by mid-day the whole of the lower town of Molde was on fire and had to be completely evacuated. During the afternoon, I organised evacuation arrangements for the following parties:-
>
> H.M the King of Norway with entourage.
>
> The British Minister and such parties of other nationalities as he thought fit to conduct.

Molde in ruins. Picture credits: Romsdalsmuseet, N-6413 Molde, Norway.

The Norwegian gold

British wounded from the Norwegian hospital and all British personnel in Molde.

R.V.Zs [*rendezvous*] were fixed for 21:15, though I had no idea what ship would be coming in or when. During the afternoon received W/T [*wireless telegraphy*] message from Admiralty directing me to cease transmission of secret messages by radio.

Unhappily, at 21:10, German aircraft carried out an incendiary raid around the quay area, and the sole surviving structures caught fire, apparently blocking all ingress by land to the quay.

The Confection building lies in ruins. Picture credit: Unknown.

By dawn, Captain Denny his W/T set and his naval personnel had retired to the hills above Molde, as had the Base personnel at Åndalsnes. The hills and woods were now the only safe place to be. Denny, utterly exhausted, took the opportunity to inform the Norwegian authorities that the evacuation of armed forces from Åndalsnes had begun; it must have been a hugely difficult moment for him and a grave disappointment to the Norwegians. However, Denny's report goes on to mention the contribution of the Norwegians and the part they played in assisting the Allies, particularly the nurses and volunteers, but he was also suspicious of a few whose intentions he deemed dubious at best. *'Molde contained a number of Norwegians of doubtful sympathies, and there is no doubt espionage existed and that the state telephone system was tapped...'*[126]

The Allies were leaving; they had failed in their attempt to rout the German invasion, although not through lack of bravery, but rather through a dearth of leadership and decisiveness from the British Government and Chiefs of Staff High Command. It had been a miserable experience for all concerned and now Norway was to be fully occupied by an uninvited force for five long years.

Captain Denny was finally evacuated on April 30th by the *Ulster Prince,* along with significant others such as Captain Frank Foley and Admiral Diesen. Without doubt, Captain Denny had been exemplary; a job well done under the most exhausting circumstances.

11

A Daring Rescue
April 29th

HMS *Glasgow* was the seventh ship to bear the name (the first was launched in 1707). She was ordered in December 1934, and first laid down in April 1935 at Scotts Engineering Company in Greenock, Scotland and launched in June 1936 as a Southampton Class Cruiser. She was commissioned in September 1937 displacing 11,540 tons. Her armament comprised of twelve 6 inch (150 mm) guns housed in triple turrets, eight 4 inch (105 mm) AA guns, eight (40.5 mm) guns, eight 0.5 inch (13 mm) machine-guns and six 21 inch (530 mm) torpedo tubes. Her crew complement was 750 men. HMS *Glasgow* also had two Supermarine Walrus aircraft on board for spotting and other duties. Her maximum speed was rated at 32 knots (59km/h).

Of the three Royal Navy cruisers involved with the gold transport, HMS *Glasgow* is probably the best known. Carrying gold bullion was nothing new to *Glasgow*. During 1939, and as part of the Royal Tour to America and Canada, the cruiser had taken part in the transfer of Britain's gold reserves to Fort Knox. On that occasion HMS *Southampton* and HMS *Repulse* accompanied her. His Majesty King George VI and Queen Elizabeth, meanwhile, sailed in the *Empress of Australia*. It was purportedly Churchill's idea that Britain's gold reserves were to be taken to a place of relative safety, although for security and morale the transfer was kept very secret.[127]

During the so called *'Phoney War' Glasgow*, part of the 2nd Cruiser Squadron and Northern Patrol, took the fight to Hitler and his Kriegsmarine, but the biggest fight of all was with the perilous North Sea in winter, which sided with none of the belligerents. Poor weather or not

Glasgow battled her way regularly across the North Sea on patrol, but the conditions took their toll on the cruiser and Captain Pegram was forced to dock his ship in Belfast for repairs and refit. By late March after a period of rest and relaxation for the crew HMS *Glasgow* was back at Rosyth and preparing for Norway with troops and war material hastily embarked for '*Plan R4*' – the somewhat vague military objective of taking Narvik and securing the iron ore routes with Trondheim, Bergen and Stavanger also targets for occupation. Events overtook this plan and with the sighting of German battle cruisers off Norway on April 7th, 1st Cruiser Squadron, still docked at Rosyth was ordered to disembark her troops immediately and to intercept the German battle force.

On the night of April 8/9th when Denmark and Norway were simultaneously invaded, *Glasgow,* already placed at readiness, managed to get under way sailing directly for northern waters. Intelligence stated that large German warships were in the area and attempts by *Glasgow* to engage these ships, later to be identified as *Scharnhorst* and *Gneisenau,* were to prove unsuccessful. In fact *Glasgow* was never even close to locating the two ships, but later she was attacked by German bombers and suffered near misses causing fatalities, injuries and damage to the ship. *Glasgow* returned and refuelled at Scapa Flow then recommenced patrol off the west coast of Norway with HMS *Sheffield* and a destroyer escort. Enemy ships were again ascertained to be operating in the area, but no engagements were made.

On April 13/14th *Glasgow* took part in the first operation, along with *Sheffield*, to land 350 Royal Marines and soldiers on Norwegian soil – '*Operation Henry*'. The landing at Namsos was unopposed although Captain Pegram was certain that the Germans were aware of the landing. *Glasgow* took part in further operations and patrols and came under attack again from German bombers, but their aim was poor and *Glasgow* escaped unscathed. For their part, the AA gunners on *Glasgow* managed to bring down a bomber. Later, after securing their objectives, *Glasgow's* small invasion force was taken off and relieved by 146th Brigade. Low on fuel, *Glasgow* returned to Scapa Flow in company with *Sheffield*.

The British expedition in Norway did not fare well and on April 28th 1940 Captain Pegram received orders from Commander-in-chief Home Fleet to '*proceed at best speed from Scapa Flow*' to Norway accompanied by HM Ships *Jackal* and *Javelin* as destroyer escort. Their mission was to effect the evacuation of King Haakon and members of the Royal Norwegian Government. It was not an easy passage for the Royal Navy force and, close to the Norwegian coast on the 29th at around 18:30, it was harrassed and attacked by two Heinkel 111s. Fortunately, all six bombs dropped missed their intended targets and the force continued their journey with the utmost haste. Late on the 29th and under the cover of darkness *Glasgow* entered Romsdal Fjord. Escorting destroyers *Jackal* and *Javelin* were immediately dispatched to protect the entrance against the threat of U-boats; *Glasgow* did not want to be caught unawares.

The west coast ports were crucial to the Allies firstly because they were deep-water ports where warships could dock, though it was a tight fit. Secondly, Åndalsnes' port was serviced by a crane, making it a little easier to load and unload, although only one ship at a time could tie up to disembark. Molde had a decent quayside but close by there were protruding rocks out in the fjord making it hazardous to turn large ships around. Thirdly, the Germans had not seized those two ports.

Captain Pegram, who later wrote up his proceedings for the operation, takes up the story:[128]

> On nearing the coast, one heavy pall of smoke could be observed in the Ålesund area, one apparently over Kristiansund and another over Molde. This latter died down as we approached, but on proceeding up the fjord towards Molde it was seen that German aircraft were engaged in bombing the town and extensive fires had been started.
>
> When Molde itself was sighted, it was burning fiercely. At 23:10/29, the ship went alongside the quay, the eastern end of which was already on fire. Fortunately, there was a light onshore wind, or I should not have been able to go alongside, and ship's parties were able to extinguish the fire in the vicinity of the ship.
>
> On arrival, a signal was received by lamp from ashore at a point some distance North-East of the jetty that the main body was there and that it was not possible to reach the jetty. I asked the Senior Naval Officer to come on board by puffer (small fishing boat) and when Captain Denny, RN, arrived it was at once clear that he was under a misapprehension regarding the plans for the re-embarkation of troops. Not having received the signals concerning this operation, he was under the impression the Glasgow had arrived in order to commence the re-embarkation forthwith, and the personnel of the Base Staff was ready to embark. Captain Denny made it quite

clear to me that in his view there was no question of embarking troops from Molde, for there was no road communication to the town open, the fires were still raging and all local small craft had become frightened and fled. My signals timed 22:50/29, 00:30/30 and 00:23/30 were dispatched. Captain Denny himself insisted on remaining on shore with sufficient staff to assist any further evacuation, which might take place. He had been subjected to the most constant strain without sleep under hazardous conditions for many days: he was tired out, but indomitable. It must have been a blow to him having to remain ashore after feeling that his work was completed, and I hated having to see him go. His courage and quiet composure under such an ordeal was grand to see.

His Majesty King Haakon of Norway and Crown Prince Olav embarked from a local tug at 23:38/29, and various members of the Norwegian Government were also embarked...

Besides the Norwegians, French and Danish Ministers were embarked, together with the staffs of the British and French Legations...

Also embarked were 117 survivors from six sunken trawlers, together with 17 officers and men of the Royal Artillery, and most of the base staff at Molde. Of the above 15 were wounded. A complete list of naval and military officers is given in Enclosure No4. The total number evacuated was: – civilians and officers 92, others 185.

Captain Denny remained ashore at Molde with Captain HSM Harrison-Wallace RN, the Extended Defence Officer [XDO] and 14 others to attempt to maintain communications and to assist in carrying out the re-embarkation plan (HMS Glasgow's 00:30/30) provisions for this party were landed from this ship.

Two ships were requisitioned on April 29th to carry gold freight to HMS *Glasgow*. They were D/S *Legona* and the M/S *Rovdehorn*, the latter of which had up to that point been transporting troops and war material. Captain Peter Erstad of the steamer *Rovdehorn* later spoke about his experience in a newspaper interview given after the war.[129]

I was conveniently available with Rovdehorn when I was requested to take heavy boxes cross the harbour area to [HMS] Glasgow. Legona, a smaller, private vessel was also hired to do the same job. British sailors helped us. The bombing of the harbour area made the work difficult for us. The anti-aircraft fire from the cruiser was intense and 11 bombs exploded around us.[130]

Although *Rovdehorn* and *Legona* were not the intended targets they were very fortunate not to be hit or damaged as the bombs detonated on impact with the water.

The initial thinking behind the requisitioning of the two ships was that HMS *Glasgow* would not berth alongside at Molde, but anchor in the fjord; this did not, in the event, come to pass.

Captain Erstad made two short trips with the *Rovdehorn* from the nearby 'Pharmacy Pier' carrying the precious gold to HMS *Glasgow*. With the burning town providing a very bright backlight it wasn't difficult for the *Rovdehorn* to lie up beside the cruiser on her starboard side to transfer the gold. *Glasgow* was able to use her crane to load the gold onboard and then lower it down through a mid-ships hatch way whereupon it was carefully stowed. *Legona's* consignment was also taken onboard the same way. But it soon became clear that the loading of the bullion was too slow and that an alternative method was needed to get the gold onboard. Whilst *Rovdehorn* made two trips with bullion, *Legona* made one trip with her consignment of gold and then returned to ferry assorted passengers to the cruiser.

The privately owned steamer *Legona* happened to be just west of Storkaia [the pier where *Glasgow* was moored]. The skipper and owner, Martin Legernes had arrived in Molde with his ship in order to save furniture from his newly built house. His family had evacuated the house to a nearby family farm at Daugstad. Onboard the *Legona* that night [29th] were several neighbours and relatives who had come to help evacuate the house of its contents.

It was whilst *Legona* was moored at the pier that a British officer came aboard and requested to speak to the Captain. Fortunately for the officer Captain Legernes spoke reasonable English, and the officer asked if the *Legona* could be taken over to HMS *Glasgow*, which was moored at the end of Storkaia Pier. An agreement was quickly reached and some 18–20 people were embarked, including four ladies in sporting wear. Legernes is recorded as saying:[131]

> There was a very tall man in a blue overcoat whom we reckoned to be King Haakon. When we reached [HMS] *Glasgow* a rope ladder was dropped over the side of the cruiser and I asked the passengers to walk up on top of the bridge deck and then on to a crate containing

the lifebelts and then on to *Glasgow*. That worked well and everyone was successful in getting onboard *Glasgow*.

According to Glasgow's log *Legona* pulled alongside just after 22:30. Captain Pegram's report describes the *Legona* as a small tug, although other reports described the ship as a 'puffer'. Whatever the descriptions, King Haakon was safely aboard HMS *Glasgow*.

Captain Legernes was correct in his belief that he had the King aboard his ship. Another witness, Tomas Breivik, also noted the tall, erect figure of the King embarking the *Legona*, additionally spotting that the Crown Prince was already onboard *Glasgow* and walked up to greet his father when the King embarked. Breivik notes that the two men remained on deck, despite the danger, watching the fires raging and engulfing Molde. Breivik then states that with all safely aboard HMS *Glasgow* the *Legona* returned to Reknes Pier to continue the loading of furniture from various private houses.

In a newspaper interview after the war Captain Legernes explained that the second trip with the *Legona* was to take boxes to HMS *Glasgow*. Due to the weight of the boxes and kegs, Legernes and his crew soon worked out that the cargo was gold. The captain stated that he carried 114 boxes and 25 small kegs and although they were very heavy there was plenty of help from British sailors to load the gold quickly [most probably with the use of the ship's crane] onto HMS *Glasgow*. The operation was almost certainly concluded at around 01:00 (April 30th) as Captain Legernes states that an aircraft flew over from a westerly direction and it was at this point that anti-aircraft guns on the cruiser opened up.[132]

Legona returned to her 'humanitarian' duties, but left Molde shortly after due to the amount of enemy aircraft circling overhead. *Legona* and *Rovdehorn* had done their duty.

The research of primary and secondary sources has revealed a variation in accounts with the movement of the gold to HMS *Glasgow*. Haslund's report states that 316 large crates, 440 smaller crates and 39 kegs were ferried to HMS *Glasgow* by the two small ships. However, a number of accounts from Royal Navy veterans state otherwise and that the gold was manually hauled aboard HMS *Glasgow* via gangplanks to the Quarter Deck.

Royal Navy veterans interviewed by the author in 2004 all stated

D/S *Legona*. Photo credit: E Birkeland – Molde

that they were ordered off *Glasgow* and onto the quay to manhandle the bullion back on to the ship. One naval rating clearly remembers soaping the gangplank at the edges so that the crates and kegs could be pushed up the wooden plank and on to the ship.[133]

There were also accounts of men accurately guessing the approximate weight of the cargo as they lifted the boxes and barrels. Others also complained that whilst the boxes were easy to lift with two men, only one person could lift the kegs and that this was difficult and cumbersome.

With the descriptions given by Haslund and those of *Glasgow*'s crew it would appear that some of the gold was brought onboard via the crane and lowered into the ship and that a further amount was taken onboard via manual handling from the quayside.

As the loading continued with a frenetic urgency, suddenly and without warning out of the swirling ruddy coloured smoke a German bomber appeared. No bombs were dropped and it shot across the fjord with at least one gunner on *Glasgow* opening fire. This was more than enough warning for Captain Pegram and he ordered the sailors aboard and the lines to be let go before the loading of the gold was complete. Just as *Glasgow* was about to pull away Haslund spotted a Member of the Storting, Mr Ole Colbjørnsen, hurriedly embarking *Glasgow*. He shouted to him that he would get the remainder of the gold transported north. With the King and Crown Prince safely aboard, along with members of

HMS *Glasgow* 1938. Picture credit: Maritime Picture Library.

the Norwegian Government and various other officials, she reversed out into the fjord. Some of the quay collapsed as one line was still secured there, such was the haste to depart.

HMS *Glasgow* pulled away stern first into the black abyss of the fjord and it would appear the ship maintained this position for some distance and time. Numerous *Glasgow* naval veterans have commented on this stating that they have never sailed astern for so long and for so fast. An officer in his report also made mention of this feat and it was clear that skillful use by *Glasgow's* navigation officer of a stop-watch and dead-reckoning amounted to seamanship of the highest order. Close checking of the 'Ship's Log' reveals that the ship did not alter course significantly for at least an hour turning 320° at 02:10.

Captain Pegram takes up the story once more:[134]

> At the request from His Majesty King Haakon, approximately 25 tons of gold bullion was embarked, but as the ship was sailing in formation a message was received that a certain quantity had not yet arrived down on the jetty. Tallying had proved impossible under the conditions prevailing. Whilst the ship was alongside the town of Molde was further subjected to bombing attacks and an unsuccessful attack was made on the ship...
>
> Certain members, I believe a majority, of the Norwegian Government desired His Majesty to be landed at Mosjoen. I discussed the matter with His Britannic Majesty's Minister [*Sir Cecil Dormer*]

and with His Majesty, and strongly advised his going to Tromsø, for I felt it is quite probable that the ship would be attacked by bombs before His Majesty could be landed unless we went further north. I pointed out that it was always possible for His Majesty to move south unobserved in small craft through the inner lead, should he wish to do so. His Majesty was convinced that the Germans knew of his departure and privately told me that he wished to go to Tromsø, and that I might, perhaps, tell his Government I was not prepared to take my ship elsewhere. Fortunately, after a further council meeting the government agreed to go to Tromsø.

On emerging from Romsdalsfjord at 02:25/30, I steered to the westward, in order to be well clear of the coast by daylight, and at 02:30/30 course was set for Tromsø.

On Wednesday, 1st May, after a Cabinet Meeting I was requested to make the arrival in the Tromsø area as inconspicuous as possible. His Majesty did not intend to land at or establish himself in the town itself for he felt sure that it would be bombed when his presence was known. I therefore flew off the Walrus (aircraft) at 13:00 to proceed to Tromsø and to arrange for some small local craft to meet HMS Glasgow on arrival in Malangenfjord. His Majesty, the Crown Prince and the Government were disembarked into the armed vessel Heimdal in Malangenfjord at 20:18/1 (NB Thirty five years previously King Haakon had sailed from Denmark to Norway on the Heimdal to be enthroned as the King of Norway).

Although it must seem impertinent on my part to refer to this, I am unable to refrain from remarking on the tremendous impressions made on us all by His Majesty and the Crown Prince. His Majesty had undergone the severest ordeal, he was feeling broken-hearted at the fate of his country; he had remained in his field uniform for days on end, and had been subjected to continuous bombing whilst without sleep, his embarkation and departure had taken place under most trying conditions, with night bombing occurring for the first time; under these circumstances, his quiet composure and dignity, his kindliness and thoughtfulness for others, his confident, even cheerful, bearing when in public were an inspiration to all of us and unforgettable.

During His Majesty's stay on board, I had many opportunities of private and confidential discussion with him. I believe that His Majesty spoke with complete frankness and freedom, and in confidence I am therefore forwarding by hand direct to the Admiralty a report of the impressions I gained from these conversations.

After consultation with His Britannic Majesty's Minister, I have informed Colonel Ljunberg, and the Minister of Defence, of the evacuation of Åndalsnes and Namsos. It was already known of His Majesty and the Norwegian Government that some evacuation was taking place before they embarked, and after hearing the Prime Minister's speech on the 2nd May, and the Defence Minister, who by then felt sure that both places were being evacuated, was most anxious to be told what the situation was.

I have told him that the evacuation has taken place, and that the troops are to be re-formed for further operations in Norway, but that I was not in a position to say where. I told him also the purpose of His Majesty King George's message to King Haakon, and impressed upon him that the failure to take Trondheim and the evacuation do not indicate any withdrawal from Norway on our part, and that I was sure it was our intention to do all in our power for them, though I, of course, had no idea what plan was contemplated.

I have received the impression, both from the Norwegians themselves and from His Britannic Majesty's Minister, that they have felt very much out of touch with our plans. Colonel Ljunberg made it clear to me that he felt Trondheim to be the key position, and that as we had not been able to take it the situation for this country was almost hopeless.

After the departure of His Majesty, I proceeded to fuel HMS *Jackal* in Malangenfjord; one at a time, the other ship remaining on A/S [*anti-submarine*] patrol to seaward (255 tons to HMS *Jackal*, 214 tons to HMS *Javelin*. After making the arrangements for His Majesty's disembarkation, the Walrus refueled at Tromsø and proceeded to Harstad in accordance with the Commander-in-Chief, Home Fleet's 1345/30.

Sailed from Malangenfjord for the Clyde at 0110/2, setting course well to the eastward at 1935/2, HMS *Jackal* was detached to Sullom Voe to replace Asdic Oscillator and rejoin us as soon as possible.

The conduct of all the officers and men was all that could be desired under arduous conditions. I was most impressed with the cheerful bearing under adversity of the trawler crews and base staff; they were embarked at Molde under trying conditions. They had had a bad time. Amongst the officers were several quite elderly gentleman, peers of the realm and army colonels of the last war, now Sub-Lieutenants, RNVR, whose only wish was to remain in Norway fighting, or to get back to their trawlers again as soon as possible. Captain Denny asked me especially to mention the name of Sick Berth Attendant David Wright, official number C/JX 57232, who had been in charge of the wounded, in case he should not be able to do so. This rating's cheerful bearing and quiet competence under difficult conditions were worthy of all praise.

P.H Pegram: Captain – May 1940

The following is a signal sent to the Admiralty in the early hours of the 30th April from HMS Glasgow:

```
Secret.                   Message.

From H.M.S. GLASGOW.        Date 30.4.40

NAVAL CYPHER D BY W/T

Addressed Admiralty. Repeated F.O. Narvik, C.
in C. Home Fleet.

IMPORTANT

My 0250.  Following also embarked British French and
Danish Ministers with wives and some of legation staff.
Norwegian Prime Minister, finance, defence, justice,
and other members of government. Crew of trawler sunk
(corrupt group), convoy HN17. Commodore Boase and
Captain Cecil Allen. Base staff and unit of Royal
Artillery. Also approximately 23 tons of gold bullion.
Bombing attacks while alongside and on leaving at 01:00.
No hits on ship.
```

If the Heinkel 111 flying low over her had not caught out *Glasgow* then it is difficult to say whether all the gold would have been taken off by the cruiser, but there was just too much air activity for Captain Pegram's liking and with the dawn fast approaching he was concerned that his ship would be caught like a sitting duck in the fjord in the cold light of day; events proved that his concerns were correct.

As *Glasgow* sailed for the UK from Molde, Oscar Torp, the Norwegian Finance Minister dictated a letter that was to be used as a power of attorney to nominated Norwegian officials in the UK. Torp was well

```
            Power of Attorney.


        I, Oscar Torp, Minister of Finance of Norway, hereby
authorise and empower
        Mr. Ole Colbjörnsen, Member of the Norwegian Parliament,
to act as my Representative in shipping consignments of Gold to
England and deliver same in safe custody in the Bank of England for
account of and to the order of the Royal Ministry of Finance and
myself,
        and to negotiate and transact such other business for the
Norwegian Ministry of Finnce - alone or together with other Govern-
ment Representatives in Great Britain - as instructed by me.
        I solicite all persons concerned to give mr.Colbjörnsen
every assistance asked by him in order to fulfill his duties for me
and the Ministry of Finance.

Molde 29. April 1940.                    (s) Oscar Torp.
                                         Norwegian Minister of finance.


This is to certify that Mr.Oscar Torp
Minister if Finance, has signed this
document in my presence.
Ministry for Foreign Affairs, Molde, April, 29th 1940.
                    By authorisation:
(Seal)              (s) E. Braadland
        This is to certify the authenticity of the
        foregoing two signatures.
            (s) John Lascelles.
        First Secretary of H.M.Legation in Norway
        H.M.S."Glasgow", May 1st, 1940.
```

Torp's letter. Photo credit: author

aware that difficulties could arise once the bullion was placed dockside and he needed to ensure smooth transfer to the Bank of England and that the bullion was not misused in any way.

Commander Cuthbert, later, Vice Admiral Sir John Cuthbert, was an experienced naval officer on board *Glasgow*. He later penned his thoughts about his experiences in Norway. As with Captain Pegram's account and that of the crew, his observations provide a valuable insight into the events of that dramatic night.[135]

After three strenuous weeks off the Norwegian coast, working everywhere between Bergen and Namsos during the German's initial advance the *Glasgow* slipped into Scapa Flow on Sunday 28th April

1940 to fill up once more with oil fuel. Things were not looking too good in the Trondheim area and we expected our stay to be short, so it was with some surprise that after topping up we remained at anchor, although at short notice.

In the afternoon the Admiral sent for our Captain and gave him his secret orders. These were to be passed on to no-one, but as the Captain pointed out, the odd bomb might write him off as we crossed the North Sea and the job would be left undone. It was therefore agreed that the Commander might be told that the *Glasgow*, with two destroyers as escort, was to take the King of Norway from Molde to "a place of safety".

Because of the secrecy, preparations could not be made onboard but word was passed around that as Molde had been heavily bombed it might be necessary to evacuate some civilians and the Commander's cabin was given an extra furnishing to be ready for "the Mayor" [*King Haakon*]. At the same time it was also rumoured that the Admiral might shortly transfer to the ship and so the signalmen were set to make an Admiral's flag.

At this time of the year complete darkness could not be hoped for but it was decided to close on the coast in the evening as German bomber activity usually died down after seven or eight o'clock and did not start again until six in the morning. When still a long way off, great columns of smoke could be seen rising from the burning villages, but the bombers also managed to find time to give us a bit of a welcome though they achieved nothing except a few holes in the sea. As we entered the fjord more bombers could be seen flitting around like bats in the half-light and further bursts of flame shot up into the sky from the tortured town. On turning the corner the blaze looked so intense that it seemed doubtful whether we should be able to get alongside but luckily there was a light onshore wind which gave a small working space between the edge of the pier and its burning sheds. A few men had been sent to the pier and its burning sheds... [*And others*] had been sent to the pier by boat to take our hawsers as the normal way from the town was blocked by fire.

As soon as we were secured, work was started on putting out the nearest fires, which were showing up the ship in the most unpleasant manner. In the meantime a little puffer had come alongside our starboard side and from it up the pilot ladder, clambered the tall figure of His Majesty followed by the Crown Prince [*some unconfirmed reports suggest he came earlier*]. They were both in field uniform which, indeed, they had not taken off for days and their personal luggage required no large working party for its sum total was a couple of suit cases and haversacks.

Following in the wake of the King were men and women of many nationalities and styles of dress carrying a few odd pieces of hand luggage; the obvious privations they had endured may perhaps give us some excuse for not recognising at once the Norwegian Government and the 'Corps Diplomatique'. The thoughts of everyone, from His Majesty downwards was to cause the least possible inconvenience to us and no more charming, helpful and appreciative passengers could be imagined despite the obvious discomforts of a Wardroom designed to accommodate some twenty five when it receives a further influx of ninety.

The King and Prince Olaf were escorted to the Captain's after cabin while the government parked themselves temporarily in the dining cabin.

They expressed great willingness to fall in with any plans the Captain wished to make for sailing, the destination naturally being a matter for subsequent discussion. They did however express a particular desire to be accompanied by the Norwegian Gold Reserve and to this the Captain agreed on the understanding that nothing was to prevent sailing at 01:00 in order that we might be well clear before the morning strafe.

Meanwhile, in the Commander's cabin, our Captain and various other senior officers were putting the local British Senior Naval Officer (SNO) (subsequently Admiral Sir Michael Denny) and his meagre staff into the general picture and giving him the plans for the general evacuation. Owing to the bombing of the wireless set he had had no signals for days, though judging by the number [*signals*] that were being pushed out at that time it is perhaps doubtful if he would have been much the wiser had he received them.

On deck too, things were happening. Just as we were approaching the fjord we had received a signal telling us that food might be short and we were to land as much as we could spare without delaying our departure. This we felt was a delightfully vague way of passing on the baby of ignorance.

We knew of course that the evacuation was about to begin, but nobody knew exactly when it would be complete, nor was it possible to guess how many troops would be involved. We certainly didn't want to leave food behind for the benefit of a hungry enemy.

I forget what decision was reached but before we berthed there was a substantial stack of food waiting on the quarterdeck. In the event, none was required as it was decided that there was no further chance of troops reaching Molde and that we should evacuate all who were already there with the exception of the S.N.O. and a small party who were determined to see things through until the end.

By 23:00 the fire on the pier and its vicinity had been sufficiently subdued to let an ambulance through to the ship with wounded; the gold also began to arrive by lorry and boat. Here a slight snag arose, as it was naturally foreign to the nature of any treasury official to part with unlimited quantities of gold without carrying out some check on it. A careful tallying of all the boxes was therefore started but when it was represented, somewhat forcefully, that if this done there would be time to embark only a very small proportion, the habits of a lifetime were cast aside and the sailors got down to it. Lower deck was cleared and everyone not closed up at his gun or standing by in the engine room went out on to the jetty and returned with a lifetime's pay on his shoulders – and then went back for more. As there was no time to stow it at once the quarterdeck was soon stacked high with bullion. The greater part was in cases, easily portable, but some of these had naturally suffered in their journeying and one broken case was retrieved by the Paymaster who whisked away temptation by putting it in his safe. A certain amount was also in traditional kegs, these proved more awkward as they were too heavy for one man to lift and yet too small for two to get round easily and quickly. Eventually, these were rolled and bumped up a steep gangplank some eighteen inches wide, fitted with treads but no sides. The gold was struck down into X and Y magazines where it remained until we eventually reached the UK.

For an hour and three quarters the work went on, the last load being embarked as the hands went to stand by wires – Captain Denny, in person, was letting go the shore ends. Just as we slipped an enemy bomber passed overhead so low that it seemed certain to hit our masts. There were subsequently several claims from guns' crews that it had been destroyed but these I fear were optimistic, though it is probable it didn't escape without damage. Once clear of the light from the burning town it was our policy to try to remain unseen so we held our fire, though the destroyers blazed away merrily whenever an aircraft was heard or sighted.

Half blinded by the light of the town it was no easy matter to go astern and then swing our stern between unlit reefs in order to turn. Careful forethought, a thorough knowledge of the ship, a stopwatch and a cool nerve will do much, and we were soon heading out of the fjord at high speed.

On the first morning the wife of a distinguished foreigner was wakened by a tap on her cabin door. "Steward," she demanded, "is that the Steward?" "No mum" was the reply, "It's a Royal Marine". While we were at sea His Majesty and the rest of the party took a great interest in the ship and everyone in her. There were few places that were not fully explored. We did our best to fix them up with clothing and the Purser's slop chest did a roaring trade.

One small difficulty arose in obtaining a pair of cufflinks for the King, as we knew he wouldn't accept any of ours. However, the Commander's servant was sent to the ship's bookstall to see if they had any in stock. The most expensive variety cost sixpence, but with an eye to the next audit, the custodian would not hand them over on the security of several million pounds of gold and it had to be made quite clear who was actually paying for them.

The trip north was uneventful; the only stipulation about landing the party, once the approximate locality had been agreed upon, was that it should be conducted secretly. This was to avoid drawing the enemy bombers, should the King's presence become known.

In consequence, our aircraft [Walrus] was flown into Tromso to make arrangements with the British Consul. That evening we steamed slowly into a narrow and deserted fjord. Snow was right down to the water's edge and there wasn't a breath of wind stirring. Then round the corner came a tiny tug to take off the King and a small party. Although late at night, it was quite light and with every officer and man lining the ship's side, in the silence he had specially asked for, the King returned again to share the sufferings of his country.

When the King was about to depart Glasgow Captain Pegram asked the King if the Ships Company might give him three cheers. The King replied "No Captain, it is not good for a King to break down in tears at a time like this."

Norway's Prime Minister at the time, Johan Nygaardsvold, was also in Molde on that fateful occasion and later wrote:[136]

We drove through burnt-down areas ... and through areas where houses were still on fire, where sparks were flying and the heat was almost unbearable. ... At last we reached the quays, the whole area

Picture postcard – photographer unknown. King Haakon and Crown Prince Olav aboard HMS *Glasgow* sailing north after their rescue from Molde. In the distance an escorting destroyer can be seen.

ablaze. The British cruiser "Glasgow", a big one weighing 11,000 tons, had all her fire hoses working, pouring Niagara-like cascades of water over the quays. Sheltered by these cascades we boarded the cruiser. Shortly after we had boarded, but before our luggage had been loaded, German planes appeared over Molde, heading directly toward the 'Glasgow'. We were ordered below deck, while air defence guns opened fire. The cruiser immediately cast off, heading for the open sea.

The Norwegian Foreign Secretary, Halvdan Koht had also managed to make his way to Molde and later wrote describing his experiences:[137]

> While the fire spread across the pier, the men worked hard to bring the gold from *Norges Bank* on-board *Glasgow*. At one stage, one of the small kegs containing the gold broke open and the bullions rolled across the deck. Everybody scrambled to retrieve them, but not a single krone was lost. Soon it was impossible to continue the work, and the ship had to cast off before all the gold had been taken on-board.

Many of the sailors and marines on *Glasgow* also wrote of their experiences and these stories give a vivid and striking insight on the conditions and what the men witnessed. The stories describe how the bullion was loaded onto *Glasgow* and these accounts differ in great detail from that of Fredrik Haslund, leader of the gold transport. It is worth remembering that chaos, upheaval and disorder ruled in Molde during that dramatic period and understandably accounts vary. Many of those aboard *Glasgow* were 'Boy Seamen' and Molde was their first real experience of war and its consequences. These are their stories.

Tom Morton RN had just come off watch in the engine room:[138]

> ...the ship was at 'general quarters' and you could see Molde all in flames and still being bombed. When we tied up alongside the jetty everyone that wasn't on watch or manning the guns was sent ashore to bring the King and Crown Prince and also the other people that were travelling with them. We were then busy getting the gold onboard the Germans were still bombing the town and we were very lucky not to be hit. I know we left there in a great hurry and took half of the jetty with us.

Don Edwards RN:[139]

> At the time I was at Molde I was a 16 year old 'Boy Seaman' getting my first taste of real war aboard HMS *Glasgow*. The thing I remember most is the heat from the burning town and the sad sight of the hospital near the shore with large red crosses painted on the roof a mass of flame. I was to learn later that hospitals and hospital ships were not spared. Also the incendiary bombs on the burning jetty re-ignited after being sprayed by high-pressure hoses. Buckets of sand were more effective. We landed King Haakon at Tromso [*sic*] with his government. He hoped to carry on the war from the far north.

Reg Samways RN:

> My most vivid memory was seeing the final moments of the church burning fiercely, it was such a sad sight and I watched it collapse, the memory of that has stayed with me.

John Kelleher RN:[140]

> I was a 'regular', having joined the Royal Navy at 15 (with my mother's permission) as an Artificer Apprentice. I finished my apprenticeship abruptly in September 1939 and went on to further training at HMS *Vernon*. In April 1940 I was available for sea service and drafted to HMS *Glasgow*, which was in Scapa Flow. We put to sea heading for Norway and came under attack from Heinkel bombers. A bugle call over the tannoy sent us to 'Action Stations'. My rig for 'Action Stations' was a pair of overalls, tin hat, inflatable tube (in lieu of lifejacket), a gas mask and a bag of tools. My station was beside a main dynamo in the engine room so I had little chance of witnessing the action. All I got was hearing some thumps from

time to time. It was about now at the age of twenty that it began to dawn on me that this was not some sort of game or practice. Those buggers were trying to kill me! Anyway, they missed.'

We approached Molde with our accompanying destroyer at night and saw that the town was completely engulfed in fire including the jetty. We had to put the fire out on the jetty before we could get alongside. The VIPs were some distance away to the northeast and would have to run the gauntlet of flames and constant air attack by incendiaries. Eventually, at about 9:30pm, they bundled into several cars and sped through the town. At 10:35pm King Haakon, the Crown Prince Olaf, members of the Norwegian Government, the British, Polish, Danish and French Ministers and staff embarked on HMS *Glasgow*. Also there were 117 survivors from 6 sunken trawlers, 17 officers and men from the Royal Artillery and most of the base staff at Molde, which included 18 injured. Shortly afterwards the gold arrived in the trucks and the loading on to the ship began. Captain Pegram was anxious to get his ship well clear before dawn so the slow and difficult task of loading was terminated after 23 tons had been stowed in the magazines and HMS *Glasgow* departed about 1am on April 30th. During this time there were constant air attacks by enemy aircraft and these continued on our way down the fjord. We sailed north and disembarked the 'Royals' and government inconspicuously near Tromso [*sic*].

Bill Watts RN:[141]

...on 28th April, a Sunday, we had arrived in Scapa Flow...hoping for a few days break, when we got a panic call to put to sea and head for Norway. Monday was a beautiful sunny day, ideal for German airplanes to attack, which they did almost all day, until we headed into the fjord for Molde. At this stage we knew we were on an important mission, but as sailors we had no idea what it was to be. From several miles down the fjord we could see a tremendous fire and as we approached Molde we realised virtually the whole town was burning. We went alongside a wooden jetty that was burning at one end and noted a line of trucks and cars waiting on the dockside... the trucks contained the whole of the Norwegian Treasury gold. The moment the gangway was down we started to load the gold. It was stacked everywhere, along passages and every spare space at deck level; the King and his staff were taken on board, when, whoosh, out from the flames came a German aircraft...then just as quickly he had gone over the top [*of the ship*] and disappeared. That was taken as a signal to get the hell out of there, going full astern, taking half the jetty with us, we headed back down the fjord. We then headed north...

Cyril Milner RN:[142]

I joined HMS *Glasgow* along with the rest of 46 class from HMS *Vincent* via HMS *Iron Duke* on September 6th 1938. I did a couple of weeks exercising with the Mediterranean Fleet before returning home to prepare to escort the King and Queen to Canada and America. We were allowed ashore until 10:30 pm (we were still only boys). It was a very interesting time for us, but it was a rough passage and most of were seasick. Back home, war clouds were looming, all was happening in the North Sea before and after September 3rd 1939 mainly looking and searching for the Scharnhorst and Gneisenau. Fortunately, we couldn't locate them! We docked at Rosyth and embarked the King's Own Yorkshire Light Infantry and the Sherwood Foresters, but only got under the Forth Bridge when we turned back as the Germans invaded the very ports where we were taking the army! We set sail again and I should imagine that about 75% of the ship's company was landed at Namsos – it was 20F, snowing and very chilly! Didn't stay long, thankfully and was returned to HMS *Glasgow* via HMS *Matabele*. Later, we were back in the North Sea and heading for a place called Molde, although nobody below decks knew what we were up to, but it didn't take long for us to find out as when we got to Molde the place was well on fire. We managed to get alongside and the lower deck was cleared to load the gold and silver onboard. I can still remember those boxes of gold were heavy. King Haakon, I am almost sure, was standing on the Quarter Deck. Was he encouraging us? We were all running flat out back and fore. German planes overhead, did I imagine the machine gunning? Things were heating up and with the King and the Norwegian government onboard; we proceeded stern first (no room to turn around) and out towards the North Sea transferring the King to another ship, which took him right up North Norway.

J McBride RM:[143]

It was Easter 1940 and we knew the Germans were going to attack Norway so we were spending a lot of time off the Norwegian coast. Norway was invaded on April 9th so a '*Glasgow*' marine detachment was landed and spent a couple of days in the Namsos area until the British Army arrived and relieved, whereupon they rejoined the ship. HMS *Glasgow* was then with her sister ships off the Norwegian coast in the thick of things with incessant attacks from dive-bombers. 'Glasgow' was hit with one large bomb, which damaged her severely structurally, but did not impair her fighting efficiency and speed though she had a number of casualties. 'Glasgow' returned to Scapa Flow with her casualties and to refuel and to Rosyth, Scotland to embark a battalion of soldiers for Norway. To supplement *Glasgow*'s short-range protection two Oerlikons (AA guns) were issued. These were a welcome addition to the armoury. The Oerlikons were bolted to the deck each side of the ship, just forward of 'X' Turret. Two men manned the guns…Colour Sergeant Halford manned the Starboard gun and I was fortunate enough to man the Port gun.

HMS *Glasgow* was tasked with patrolling the Norwegian coast: it was a clear day, the hills and mountains clearly visible. From one of the hills a thick column of smoke was rising very much like a volcano. From the ship's loud speakers came "Do you hear there? The Captain speaking"; the ship's company all ears. He told us that the smoking town was Molde, which had been heavily bombed for a few days. He told us that after dark *Glasgow* was to enter the long fjord by which Molde was reached and that King Haakon, Crown Prince Olaf, ladies and gentlemen of the Norwegian government and the Norwegian gold reserves were to be evacuated from Molde. It was soon dark and we entered the fjord unseen. Dark though the fjord was as we crept along there was no doubt where Molde was with the sky lit up. We reached the long, high wooden jetty of Molde. *Glasgow* already had hoses rigged as the ship went alongside slowly. The hoses were played on the burning and smouldering jetty and soon had the fires under control. As all warships did, we carried a quantity of sturdy timber planks for damage and repair purposes. These planks were run out over the port side of the ship onto the jetty and so made a number of gangways. By now on the jetty had appeared from the shadows and smoke a number of people headed by King Haakon and Crown Prince Olaf – who wore a grey uniform shorn of any trimmings now came onboard to be greeted by the Captain and officers who escorted them to the wardroom and cabins which *Glasgow* officers had vacated. Orders were given for the ship's company to fall out from action stations and for every man to make way for the improvised gangways port side. The only exception to this order was that Colour Sergeant Halford and I were to remain with the Oerlikons – Halford to Starboard and me to Port. We were told to take the magazines off and not to fire them without direct orders and so I remained a spectator.

The men were by then streaming down the gangways to the jetty, all ranks and ratings and branches. The first of them were soon making the return trip with each humping a box of bullion, some finding it easy, others making hard work of it. The boxes were quite small and white, but obviously heavy. These were dumped on *Glasgow*'s Quarter Deck. It all soon evolved as a couple of long queues one going in one returning. I had a bird's eye view of the proceedings, but could not see the gold dump, what with smoke and darkness and I never got the opportunity to step ashore and see. An hour or two later I could see the clumps on the Quarter Deck as they rose higher than the intervening gun turrets etc. I must digress a moment to give my impression of the scene.

The smoke was rising to high overhead and so left the ship clear. As it rose from the ship we could see the hill, which was Molde. I believe the town was made mostly of wood every building appeared on fire including the church, which I could clearly see ablaze. I saw the church steeple topple. Outside the little town I could see snow covered hillocks and the trees on fire, all looked very much like snow lit up by the flames.

The noise was intense. We were so near the crackle of burning and the crashes as a building fell and lit up everything around it again and again so vividly, we seemed to be in a world of our own for looking to starboard was complete darkness within a few feet. The sky above us and the town was red and fortunately, as I have said, the smoke rose high above it drifted over we felt to be in a world of our own; an eerie experience and ones thoughts were however could the Germans do this to an unarmed little town and country like Norway. Early on in the proceedings a gent spoke to me (one of those I suspected were part of the Norwegian government) a group of them had asked directions. His English appeared to be very poor, but I was struck by his appearance and personality. When he passed on I asked another of the group who he was, "who was that"? He answered. "That is Professor Koht, the Foreign Secretary".

The guests, except for one, soon settled down in their cabins and wardrooms. That one exception was King Haakon. He passed and re-passed several times and each time acknowledged me with a nod and a little smile. He was very restless and spent most of his time walking round the decks. I noticed that interspersed with the boxes were small casks, these appeared much heavier than the boxes.

Later, I was present when a discussion took place amongst some of our chaps about the weights. They came to the conclusion the boxes were approximately 80lbs and the casks 150lbs. However, the hours passed and it was now the early hours of the morning and humping had gone on without pause. Alone, I kept my vigil. Then I heard the faint noise of aircraft and started to get a little worried. It must be Germans; we didn't see British planes over there. This was obviously a bomber. I had had strict instructions not to open fire without orders and here I am with no one around to give me orders and this plane getting nearer. Well, I put the magazine on and manned the gun. I was now very worried as the plane was not very far away and heading for us. The magazine was on and I moved over to clip the harness belt on when Colour Sergeant Halford appears from nowhere and beats me to the belt and clips it on and I'm thinking you dirty lousy bastard, what's wrong with your bloody gun. Bored with standing by his gun over the Starboard side of the ship he had strayed over to the Port side somewhere to watch the goings on and had been caught napping. Well, I thought it was too late for me to go over and man his gun. Indeed, I could now see the bomber against the red and smoke of the sky, but sufficiently high to be seen to be moving slowly and ponderously towards our stern and to pass from stern to bow. I could see the swastikas plainly. Halford opened up two good bursts right into his (*the plane's*) belly. The third long burst emptied the magazine and the plane turned away to Starboard. Halford put a fresh magazine on the gun.

The bomber was by now lost in the darkness and nothing happened, yet I swear every round had been a hit. I saw the tracers going in and a little shower of sparks as the cannon shells struck. The seconds ticking away and all was quiet except for the fires there might never have been an enemy bomber around and then there was an almighty explosion and for a few seconds the fjord was lit as bright as daylight and there was just one large blaze and down it came to the water half a mile to a mile away perhaps, and the water was on fire.

Action Stations had just sounded; very obviously this was no place for *Glasgow*. The men were tumbling aboard as fast as they could and mooring lines were being slipped and engines started.

Sod our makeshift gangways; get out while the going's good, also signs of dawn breaking. I never went so fast astern in all my career when we reached the open sea we carried on full speed astern for another twenty miles before easing up to change to moving ahead.

A large party of men were now put to work to strike the mountainous stacks of bullion on the Quarter Deck and below deck while Glasgow headed directly away from Norway toward England or Scotland and we the ship's company conjectured where we were to put our guests ashore. Rosyth seemed the most likely, but it wasn't to be, King Haakon refused to leave Norway so we headed north. The large working party continued stowing the gold below.

We said our goodbyes to King Haakon and Crown Prince Olav. It was a sombre, never to be forgotten moment as the King and Crown Prince transferred to a small Norwegian vessel to go ashore. We hated to see them go. However, with all haste we turned round and made for Scotland.

Pictures taken aboard HMS *Glasgow* of Molde

Horace Grant RN: Boy Seaman[144]
Horace served in a number of ships,
including HMS *Victory* and HMS
Glorious, but was later drafted to
HMS *Glasgow*. It was whilst he was
on *Glasgow* that he helped ship some
of Britain's gold reserves to Canada
and America in 1939 whilst escorting
The King and Queen.

Horace Grant RN

Horace remembers the Norwegian
Campaign clearly with *Glasgow*
taking part in *'Operation Henry'*, but
it was at Molde that Horace played
a significant part in the rescue of
the gold bullion. Horace's action
station was one of the 6-inch gun
turrets, but with the cruiser docked
his manning of the gun was inconsequential against that of loading the
bullion and orders were issued to get it on board with all haste. Dressed
in the standard blue denim boiler suit that he had worn for several days
and nights, he got to work. Tin hats were not donned; in fact the sailors
on *Glasgow* had not been issued with them – the Royal Marines being
the only exception.

All available hands were engaged in loading the bullion onto *Glasgow*
and Horace stated that it was hard work, the boxes and barrels being heavy
and awkward. Horace then had the idea of soaping the gangway with a bar
of 'Pusser's Soap' whereupon sliding the heavy barrels and boxes up the
gangway would become a lot easier for all concerned and would reduce
the risk of loss or damage. Horace's idea was well received and put in to
practice with immediate results. However, with the sudden appearance of
a German bomber flying over *Glasgow* the remaining gold on the quayside
was hastily abandoned. Horace was one of the last onboard the cruiser
as she reversed back into the fjord in pitch darkness; the flaming town
destroying any hope of peering into the abyss of a black fjord.

Midshipman John Knox Laughton RN wrote a three-page entry in
his diary on April 29th. He describes the crowd of people on the jetty

as the *Glasgow* came alongside the burning quay. He also notes the arrival of the Royal Party and the officials. While the Royal party was being accommodated, some stores for the town had been already been disembarked as they had heard there was a shortage due to the German attack. However, it was clear that the town was just about ruined so the decision was made to re-embark as it seemed pointless to leave much needed supplies for the benefit of the Germans. The following is an extract from John Laughton's diary:

> [*the gold*] which arrived alongside the jetty in small puffers. It required all hands to get the large numbers of small heavy boxes onboard and into the magazine; all was going well and the gold, except for one heavy load, was all on board when the drone of an aeroplane overhead warned us bombers might be in the vicinity. The ship was got underway and was just moving off from the jetty when an enemy plane swooped low overhead out of the smoke of burning Molde. A heavy barrage was fired at it and it retreated.

John Laughton's account was written on the evening/early morning that it all happened. The small vessels are described as alongside the jetty, although it is highly likely whilst some of the gold – the smaller boxes – were carried by hand from the tenders, the heavier kegs may have been brought alongside via a winch lashed up as a temporary crane on the starboard quarter.[145]

Sir Cecil Dormer – His Majesty's Minister in Norway, wrote a statement whilst aboard *Glasgow* describing the events as he saw it. Whilst Sir Cecil only makes a brief reference to the gold, his account graphically illustrates the trauma of that tragic period in Norwegian history. Sir Cecil balances his observations with the calm resolve of HMS *Glasgow* and her crew.[146]

> The only accommodation we could find near Molde was in houses belonging to the lunatic asylum, but the director, although very friendly, was nervous about having us stay there fearing that we might compromise the Red Cross flag which was prominently flying. On April 27th Molde was bombed all day. We had to spend several hours in the shelter of the improvised SNO's (Senior Naval Officer) quarters, a few yards from the jetty and therefore an unhealthy spot. The bombing was continued the next day both there and at Åndalsnes, which was on fire and from which we could see clouds

of dense smoking rising over the mountain ridge. Occasionally we could hear anti-aircraft guns at work, but the German bombers were free to come and go as they liked as the two bases were virtually undefended. Molde was not just exposed from the air, but also from the sea and the land. The bombing was continuous and carried out with horrible ease and deliberation. The weather was perfect and the bombers had no need to hurry. They came from Germany and had orders to bomb among other targets clusters of small houses in the countryside, and to machine-gun roads, both of which tasks they performed as and when they pleased.

At 6pm on 28th April M [*Minister*] Koht and the Minister of Defence Ljunberg called upon me and showed me a report from General Ruge stating that orders had been sent to the British troops to evacuate the Romsdal, but that he and General Paget had telegraphed the War Office deploring on the grounds that it would enable the German forces in Trondheim to link up with those operating from Oslo. The whole of central and western Norway would thus fall into German occupation. I had already seen and heard enough to know that Molde had become untenable as a base, but I knew of no definite decision to evacuate. M Koht was very despondent and although I was unable to encourage any idea that General Ruge's information might prove to be premature I undertook to telegraph his news to the Secretary of State. In my telegram I added that if evacuation was to be undertaken then His Majesty's Government ought to send a ship to remove the King and government to some place of refuge, for at Molde they were trapped.

On April 29th at 7am the SNO sent me a message that His Majesty's Government wished me to invite King Haakon and his Government to leave by British cruiser that night either for any other Norwegian port or for England as his Majesty might later decide. I was to say nothing about the evacuation but steps were to be taken to see that the King did not fall into German hands. I was also entrusted with a message from the King [*George*] to His Majesty to be delivered when onboard. My instruction also said that my French colleague and I with our staffs were to accompany His Majesty. I went at once to see M Koht and asked him to inform King Haakon and the Government. M Koht was very upset and for a time I feared that the government might throw their hands in. Fortunately I had told Colonel Ljunberg that I was on my way to see him and when he came into the room I found him to be most helpful for we began to talk about details of the proposal, discussing the various ports which might be suitable to go and the number of persons who could be included in the party. While I was with them a Heinkel dropped a bomb near enough to make me hope it would reconcile the Government to the idea of departure. But it was only in the afternoon that they informed me that the King and they were willing to embark. By that time Molde was ablaze.

It was arranged that we should all assemble at the entrance to the town at 9:30pm. On our way there a Heinkel flew over us – an unusual hour for it to appear. It dropped a bunch of incendiary bombs, which as bad luck would have it fell right on the quay where we were to embark. The town was one vast furnace. An old church near where we were to assemble caught fire. We stood with members of the Government helplessly watching its destruction, while we waited to be told how best to reach the ship. The brilliance of the flames threw the shadows into a darker relief, and it took some time to collect the party. The King and the Crown Prince had been seen to arrive by car but it was a long time before we could find them. We had perforce to abandon our cars on the roadside as there was no other means of disposing them.

HMS *Glasgow* was lying alongside the burning quay, the ship's hoses turning the flames into smoke through which those embarking had to pass. After the Government and several wounded men from the base had been brought onboard, lorry loads of gold arrived at the quayside for shipment to England. But not more than 23 tons of it could be taken, as Captain Pegram was anxious to sail not later than 01:15am before it became light. About 35% of the gold had to be left behind, but it is hoped that it will all have been shipped the following night either by a Norwegian vessel or by one of HM Ships when the evacuation was to be completed.

As the ship was about to cast off an enemy bomber appeared from behind the screen of smoke and flame but was quickly driven off, (and perhaps shot down) by the guns of HM Ships present. Not many who saw Molde that night will soon forget the dramatic and tragic sight it presented. The town was largely destroyed, yet it is said no lives were lost, most of the population of 3000 having already fled.

Once aboard, the question to be decided was, what was to be our destination? The Government was in favour of Mosjoen, but Captain Pegram's opinion was that it was much too close to Trondheim to afford any security from bombing and that the best place was to make for Tromsø. The King preferred Tromsø too, but was unwilling to insist; and in accordance with his Majesty's invariable practice he was ready to leave the decision to the Government. I shared Captain Pegram's view and undertook to persuade the Government to acquiesce. I had no little difficulty however, with M Koht who insisted that by going as far North as Tromsø the Government would be cut off from the rest of Norway and would be accused by the people of running away. He was in a very nervous state of mind. I pointed out that it was no use going to a port which would be certain to be destroyed the following day, that Tromsø was as much part of Norway as somewhere south and that the Captain had to consider the safety of his charges. If the Government preferred some other places they could go there later, but it was best to make for Tromsø first. There would be wireless facilities there, and the Government would be as much in touch with the Norwegian people by radio through England as at any more southern point. But M Koht was past listening to me and burst from the ward room where our conversation was held exclaiming: "You are killing us, you are killing us". I quickly sought out the other members of the Government, M [Ministers] Nygaardsvold, Lie, Ljunberg and Vold. They were much more reasonable, and it was a great relief when a little later M Koht came to me and said that by a majority (of 6 to 5) the Government agreed to go to Tromsø but asked for air and gun defences against the German bombers, also the proposal that M Koht and Colonel Ljunberg should go to London in HMS *Glasgow* after the King and other members of the government had been landed.

The guard ship which took the King into Tromsø was the Heimdal, the same ship that brought him and Queen Maud to Trondheim for their coronation. The altered circumstances between now and then were present to many of our minds as His Majesty was piped down the gangway. The scene was made all the poignant and affecting by the desolate nature of the region in which he was now to seek shelter and the uncertainty of what lay in store for his country. He was as dignified and gracious as ever and I think benefited by his spending three days on a British warship. We had been refugees for three weeks, and the atmosphere of strength, efficiency and quiet confidence which all seemed so natural once one was onboard HMS *Glasgow*, the strong personality and kindness of Captain Pegram and the hospitality which he and his officers and ratings showed us were all most inspiring and gratefully received.

Cecil Dormer – May 1940

Jack Hall RN served in 'Y' Turret as a 16½ yr old at Molde. At the time of embarkation of the bullion gossip surfaced that someone had helped themselves to a few coins although Jack Hall does not recall any of the gold being stolen by either a sailor or a Royal Marine.[147]

> …however, a rumour was going around of some sort. I helped to load the gold, although we had to leave some behind and leave in a hurry. I also remembered that I was one of the last to get back onboard after letting all but one wire go, the ship was already moving out.

On May 2nd whilst at sea and having disembarked King Haakon, Captain Pegram sent a signal to the Admiralty informing them that he had between 60 and 70% of the bullion onboard and that arrangements were now in hand to ship the remainder of the metal north in local ships. Pegram gave no indication of how long this would take. His last message, dated May 3rd reads:

> IMPORTANT
>
> Expect to arrive 15:15 tomorrow Saturday HMS JACKAL and HMS JAVELIN in company. Request Gate at 16:15. have on board Norwegian Ministers for Foreign Affairs and Defence. British Minister and 15 others who wish to travel to London without delay. Also 23 officers and 179 others…Approximately 23 tons of bullion.

Daily Telegraph Reporter – *'Bombers Missed Norway's Gold.'*

The reporter and date is unknown, but possibly written in April or May 1940. Certainly it appears to have inaccuracies and therefore may well have been issued as some sort of press release from an unknown department.

> I am able today to add further dramatic details to the account given exclusively in the Daily Telegraph yesterday of the manner in which Norway's £23,000,000 Gold Reserve was saved from the Germans, and in which King Haakon escaped to find refuge in Britain.
>
> The gold, most of which was brought away in the cruiser HMS *Glasgow* was packed in 1,500 boxes. It was saved despite the most intense bombardment throughout its journey. A full account of the operation was given to me by a man who organised the transport.

He saw the whole of it. The boxes were taken from an underground cellar in a place in East Norway to begin their adventurous journey on a dark, cold night.

Not a light shone in the streets, not a beam was seen from any window, as the lorries arrived with the loading crews.

None of the crews knew the object of the mission. The men worked fast. The gold was driven to a waiting train and in the railway carriages checkers strained their eyes to note the figures. Now and again a bayonet would gleam for a moment.

German parachute troops were then at large in the valley, but these were captured. Through the train windows protruded gun muzzles of the soldiers guarding Norway's treasure. German planes flew over the valley and cut the railway line. That damage was repaired in three hours and the gold reached Åndalsnes.

It was learned that German troops would arrive at any moment, so it was decided to move the gold and silver further north. 26 lorries were obtained and set off, spread over 2 miles to avoid making easy targets. The column was bombed and machine gunned, but managed to reach a fjord taking 6 hours carrying 3 lorries at a time, arriving Molde south west of Trondheim. There followed 5 days of intense bombardment. The town was in ruins and the quay on the fire, but we managed to get alongside and loaded the gold and silver, plus the King Haakon and Crown Prince Olaf. No room to turn around so went out stern first and went to North Norway. British troops poured in hundreds with equipment needed, with boxes stored and stowed aboard. But as the days went by the position in Åndalsnes began to worsen. The Germans had the greatest difficulty in destroying the quay and railway station.

As Captain Pegram quickly backed *Glasgow* astern and away from the burning quay and town, Paymaster Commander Boutwood RN was already at work compiling a signal to be sent from one King to another. The following photographs are reproduced with the kind permission of his daughter, Miss Anne Boutwood.[148]

So completes the story of HMS *Glasgow* and her mission with King Haakon, the Royal Norwegian Government and some 23 tons of gold bullion – well, almost. Her task was accomplished with impeccable professionalism from the officers and crew of HMS *Glasgow* and it is clear from the stories recounted by the veterans that King Haakon and Crown Prince Olav were held in very high esteem by the sailors, but they

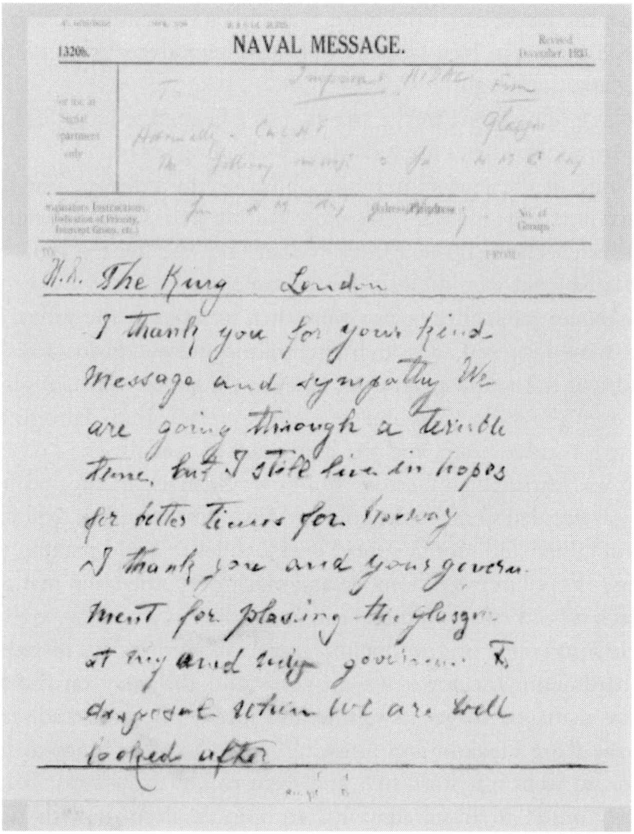
NAVAL MESSAGE.

H.M. The King London

I thank you for your kind message and sympathy We are going through a terrible time, but I still live in hopes for better times for Norway I thank you and your government for placing the Glasgow at my and my government's disposal where we are well looked after

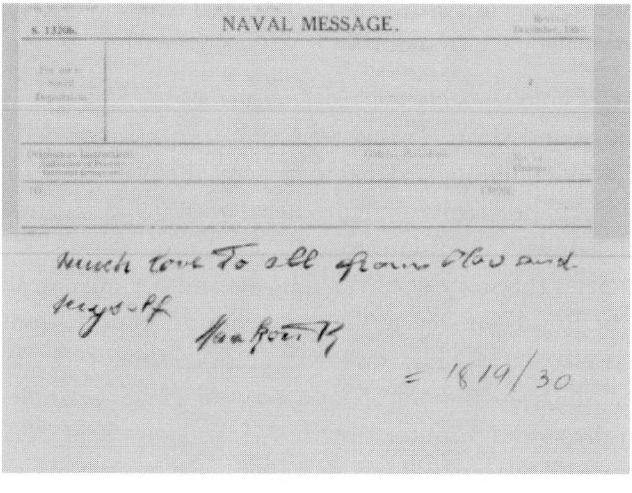
NAVAL MESSAGE.

much love to all from Olav and myself

Haakon R

= 1819/30

also felt for the townspeople of Molde who had suffered dreadfully at the terrible and devastating bombing.

In 2004 the town of Molde proudly held a commemoration ceremony for the men of HMS *Glasgow*. The town, having risen literally from the ashes after the war like a phoenix, welcomed back the British veterans and their families. There was much regaling of stories to the enthrallment of all, plus sincere and dignified medal ceremonies and church services. Amidst the celebrations I was fortunate enough to interview some of the veterans and among their discussions, memories and personal thoughts all of those that I spoke to revealed that they felt that something of themselves had been left behind in Molde during that dramatic night of 29/30th April 1940 and that they had come back to make their peace and to meet up again with a part of their soul that had been cleaved from them that night and which is now forever a part of Molde.

A small, but nonetheless very well appointed and dignified museum now exists at the Rica Hotel in Molde. Poignantly, the room where the memorabilia is held is called the *'Glasgow Salon'* and provides a fitting tribute to the Britons and Norwegians who fought valiantly to save a King, a government and a nation's wealth in gold.

12

D/S *Driva* April 30th

As *Glasgow* slipped away into the darkness, Fredrik Haslund fought down his disappointment. He still had some 18 tons plus of gold. What he did not know was that two other Royal Navy ships, the cruiser HMS *Calcutta* and the sloop HMS *Auckland* from the 18th Cruiser Squadron had been ordered in to remove the remaining bullion via HM trawlers, which would embark the gold from quayside then transfer the bullion to the ships anchored in the fjord, but the order was issued late on May 1st – much too late to be of any help to Haslund.[149]

Haslund saw the steamer *Driva* was embarking those civil servants who had been unable to secure a passage on *Glasgow*.[150] Haslund recognised this as a good opportunity to move the bullion quickly away from Molde and more importantly, away from the distinct possibility of it being lost to bombing. Haslund later stated:[151]

> …we decided to take the boxes we already had on the trucks – some 80 large boxes and 180 smaller ones – onboard Driva to be transported northwards, along with passengers.

The engineer Kristian Gleditsch was asked to take over the responsibility for this leg of the transport and was ordered to wait just outside the town until called for. Meanwhile, *Driva* had docked at the 'Pharmacy Pier', but now she too was also woefully exposed to possible air attacks so Haslund began to seek out other ships so that he could divide the cargo. It would be pointless to lose the remaining gold in one raid and splitting the load up would be the best option. Loading began at once and 8 tons were embarked on to *Driva* as well as 30 passengers. Despite the appalling conditions the loading was completed before 02:00, a remarkable achievement given that *Glasgow* had only departed an hour beforehand amidst confusion and fire.

Gleditsch, along with his wife, Nini, had been waiting at the Retiro [farm] accompanied by various officials, including those from Norges Bank. Word came for them to begin the journey through the city centre and down to the pier where *Driva* was waiting. Apprehension and fear filled the smoke laden, choking air as the officials bussed their way through the city centre in a convoy of cars heading towards the pier, dodging the debris from the bombings. For Nini Gleditsch it reminded her of her experiences during the Spanish Civil War; another experience at the hands of the Germans, this time at the opposite end of Europe.

It was just after 02:00 on April 30th that *Driva* cast off her lines and set out into the fjord, with her crew and passengers praying that their position had not been spotted by the Germans. There was so much light given off by the many fires that the slightest movement would easily be detected from the air, but so as to not make it too easy for the bombers Captain Anton M Petersen ordered that the navigational lights be kept covered.

Inevitably, the Luftwaffe returned and again the bombs fell headlong once more towards Molde and her port. One deadly load screamed towards *Driva* – the stick of bombs slamming into the water close to the ship causing her to yaw violently. Fortunately there were no injuries or damage to the vessel but it was a close run thing. *Driva's* crew, aware that providence was with them on that occasion grappled with their next problem – to head north as best as they could and to ensure that they could lay up out of sight before daybreak. It was springtime in Norway and the nights were getting shorter, dawn would soon etch her fingers across the black canvas of night.

Captain Petersen, prior to sailing, had wisely discussed the route with Haslund and Stenmarck – it was to be a team effort with many things to take into consideration. The plan was to cross an open stretch of sea and then seek shelter away from prying eyes. Crossing this area of sea was extremely hazardous as the ship would be an easy isolated target for any German bomber and there were no islands to hide in or if the worst came to the worst, to beach on. Thankfully the crossing passed without incident and *Driva* took the opportunity to shelter at Ersholmen, a small fishing village on the west coast. The first part of the journey had been successful to the huge relief of those on board as they made landfall.

Underway again and edging his way up Kornstad Fjord, Captain Petersen could see no signs of German air activity and so decided it would be wise to moor up at Ramsvika. The steamer *Kværnes* was also moored nearby and Petersen, realising that he needed more charts to navigate north and hoping he could borrow some, berthed alongside her.

It was not good for two ships to be berthed beside each other presenting themselves as one big fat target for the German bombers and so hurried discussions took place whereupon it was decided to move the *Driva* further up the coast to a more secure and secluded hiding place. *Driva* pulled away from her temporary berth and had just cleared the pier when an armed twin engine German seaplane took an unhealthy interest in affairs. The plane altered course dramatically stating its intention to attack. First Mate Emil Bergh was at the helm and he immediately turned the ship around and headed towards the shore. This was an inspired move by Bergh who realised that a direct hit on the *Driva* would send it to the bottom, but if he was close to shore she could be beached as the shore line was very flat. Bergh, with no other option, revved the engines to full speed and beached the vessel just as the plane approached her from astern. Shouted orders to clear the ship were given and the passengers frantically jumped down onto the shore and ran for their lives as the float-plane attacked again…this time strafing the panic stricken passengers. Gleditsch later described the terrifying moment:[152]

> The plane came straight down towards us…on deck we all stood with life jackets at the ready to jump ashore. Just as we slid up next to the other ship, the aircraft was right behind us. The helmsman had increased speed beaching the boat at full speed up on the shore. The bombs just missed going into the sea astern of us. So we ran across the deck over to the other boat, jumped down and ran for safety just as the plane attacked again. As we ran we scattered up a heather-clad hillside, although there were no bushes that could give us cover. We instinctively avoided the road that led up the hill from the quayside. Another bomb fell. The plane was so low down that we clearly saw the bomb coming out. We followed it down, but it moved so fast and then we heard that harsh whistle. Then came the explosions. Again, the bomb had fallen in to the sea about 30 metres away covering us with water, sand and rocks.

D/S Kværnes. Picture Credit: Fjord1 MRF AS, www.fjord1.no

Finally, the attack was over and the aircraft turned away and flew out of the fjord. Fortunately, no one was killed or seriously injured in the attack, although one of the men, Grim Skjetne, a bank employee from Lillehammer, had taken a bullet wound to his leg. Skjetne was taken in and cared for at one of the farms and later that day he was transported by car to Gjemnes and then on to Eide where he was treated for his injuries.

The passengers, weary, wet and dazed from the attack stumbled and staggered their way towards farmhouses where they were well received and cared for. Later that day another aircraft returned, panicking the *Driva* passengers into thinking they were being attacked again, but the plane on this occasion merely circled overhead and then turned away disappearing into the distance.

The mood of the *Driva* passengers at that point could only have been grim. But despite their ordeal no one spoke about the reasons why they were there even when one of the farmers became interested. Disturbingly they found out from the farmer that no aircraft had been seen in the area until they had arrived. Had a Quisling passed on their mission to the Germans? Did the Germans know they were carrying gold? Was it just an unfortunate incident and the attack a one-off? Would the Germans

D/S Driva. Picture Credit: Fjord1 MRF AS, www.fjord1.no

come hunting again? No one really knew the answers, but it was clear they couldn't stay at the farms and risk another attack. For the passengers and crew of the *Driva* April 30th had been a very long day, but they had to get back quickly to the *Driva*. It couldn't just be left beached high and dry for the Germans to help themselves. She had to be re-floated immediately. Despite the attack by the German floatplane damage to the ship was minimal, but the gold had to be moved to the rear of the ship so that they stood a better chance of sliding off the beach. Help came from the men of Visnes who stepped forward to give assistance. They didn't know what was in the boxes, and no one told them, but with the utmost urgency the boxes were stowed aft of the ship. Whilst the boxes were being re-stowed, watchers stood by scanning the sky for any signs of aircraft, but fortunately all was quiet.

High tide inched closer and *Driva's* bow started to gently rise. *Kværnes* moved out from her mooring and a line was secured from the steamer to *Driva*. The plan was to make best use of the tide as well as the pulling power of *Kværnes* to refloat the *Driva*. The moment of truth arrived. *Kværnes* took up the slack in the line and then gently increased her speed to full revs. A small pause and *Driva* gently slid off the beach and settled herself in the water. There were no leaks; no damage and all appeared well. *Driva* had been lucky, but it is clear that without the assistance of the steamer the task may just have been beyond *Driva's* crew, passengers and the farm folk of Visnes. It had been a close call.

13

The Road from Molde

Meanwhile, in Molde, Haslund, who had remained in the town had been kept aware of events at Visnes and he must have been mightily relieved when news came that *Driva* had been re-floated after the attack. But the events in Kornstad Fjord made him reconsider his plans. Orders were subsequently issued that *Driva* should move on to Gjemnes, but that the passengers could no longer be risked and that they should travel to Gjemnes by car or other means.

Haslund raised concerns that *Driva* presented herself as a substantial target for the German bombers. She would also need to be re-bunkered with coal. In his opinion, and after discussion with Stenmarck, it was thought prudent to move the remaining bullion by fishing vessels, which could steal their way around the many islands out of sight of prying German eyes. Fishing vessels would also be the perfect camouflage to carry the bullion and less suspicious than a large ship, which were still considered as 'fair game' by the Germans. Stenmarck agreed with Haslund and in turn contacted shipyard owner and engineer, Arne Grønningsæter to see if vessels could be acquired without too many questions being asked. Grønningsæter obliged and with the help of various officials five fishing vessels were dispatched to Gjemnes to be placed at Haslund's disposal.

Meanwhile, the chaos in Molde was unrelenting and it was not a healthy place to stay. Haslund and his men had been suffering a torrid time and just before the final boxes of gold were evacuated from the Confection factory due to the raging fires, a man was killed by falling debris from the factory. Sadly, Peter Rekdal was the seventh and final victim, standing absolutely no chance against the falling masonry and tiles that collapsed on top of him. Nonetheless it was a small miracle that despite the constant bombings and conflagrations the death toll in Molde was kept to single figures.

Transport was once again a priority and on this occasion a Colonel Mork commandeered four lorries to transport the gold in. The lorries also served a dual purpose and a number of officials joined the transport among them Professor Keilhau, Thore Boye and various officials from the Ministry of Justice.[153] The lorries had to complete several trips to move the 10 tons of bullion, reaching Gjemnes before the fishing vessels, which forced Haslund to hide the bullion in various secret locations. This amounted to some 287 boxes of bullion with cash and valuables split between five iron boxes, five wooden crates and seven smaller wooden boxes. Despite this considerable load the transport was achieved without too much fuss and the soldiers attached to the transport guarded the gold, supported by soldiers from the Gjemnes area.

By April 30th the situation on the west coast had rapidly deteriorated with yet more bombing and this continued unabated into May. Margaret Reid, secretary to Captain Frank Foley, the British Secret Intelligence officer who had assisted General Ruge and regularly transmitted messages to the British government, describes the frantic events in her diary whilst at Molde on Tuesday April 30th.[154]

> We were left in a little wood above the town of Molde. It was many times larger than Åndalsnes and showed the ravages of heavy bombing. There were, however, still many houses standing and Captain Denny [*Senior British Naval Officer Åndalsnes & Molde*] had his headquarters in a comfortable villa on the fringe of the wood. The officers all showed signs of strain. They had had their headquarters burnt down over their heads four times already – their wireless sender had given away their location to the raiders. They were also without food. Captain Denny offered us a tablet of chocolate – I refused saying we had had supper before we left – but these men in an abandoned town had had nothing to eat all day. They were in hiding. The Germans thought the town had been deserted since the King and Government had left the day before.
>
> Traitors had been busy giving the enemy information about the Royal Party's movements. At the moment when a British destroyer [*sic*] slipped up to the jetty and the Royal Party went on board, waves of bombers came over the town and dive-bombed the harbour...
>
> When dusk began to fall we moved down the road to the quay. It

was only about ten minutes through the town…passed through empty streets, picked our way over shattered glass – hardly a house had a window to it – and skirted smouldering embers where fire had broken out. I thought of Keats's lines:

"And little town thy streets for evermore will silent be
And not a soul to tell why thou art desolate shall e'er return!"

We waited in the lee of a big building which had been a hospital, but which like the rest was partially burnt out…Near the quay a coke dump blazed furiously; it must have been visible for miles and was an excellent guide for bombers as the ships had to moor alongside.

Margaret Reid and Captain Foley were evacuated on the *'Ulster Prince'* whilst General Ruge was later evacuated to Tromsø on HMS *Diana* courtesy of Captain Denny. Sadness and resignation descended over the Commander-in-Chief as he left behind a shattered Molde taking passage north in the destroyer in an attempt to carry on the fight.

Haslund's task though, was far from over. Molde which for a short but distinguished time had been the nation's capital, now lay in bombed, burnt-out ruins and was finished as a military post. General Ruge moved his Supreme Command to Furset, and it was here that he addressed his Norwegian forces from the Mission House at Batnfjordsøra.[155]

Soldiers! The British and French Governments have decided to withdraw their forces from South Norway for reasons of which we are not yet fully aware. As we cannot count on further support in this part of the country, the Norwegian Government has decided to give up the struggle in South Norway for the time being, but to continue in North Norway. It is painful to have to give up such an important part of our country, but without aircraft, tanks and heavy support weapons we cannot carry on the fight.

I thank you all for your services and for the great effort each of you has made. I begged the Government to be allowed to stay here with my troops, but the Government has decided that I must take over as Supreme Commander of the Norwegian Forces in North Norway and I am therefore leaving for the north today. Consequently, I bid you farewell and discharge you herewith. Thank you for your devotion to duty.

We all hope that continuation of the struggle will finally defeat the enemy and that we may meet again in a free and peaceful Norway. We have probably many a hard days' struggle ahead before

that point is reached. But whatever happens, let us remember:
God is on our side!

Unlike Keats's words, General Ruge's final address was very prophetic,
and although he did not know it at the time it was to be five very long
years before they would all meet again in a *free and peaceful Norway*.
His words gave succour to those who assembled there on that fateful day.
Perhaps unknown to General Ruge at that moment in time, the fight
back had already begun.

Haslund, meanwhile, took his leave of Molde travelling towards
Gjemnes. Having only journeyed a short distance he was accosted by
a Norwegian Army officer, Captain Malterud of the Military Treasury
office, desperately seeking representatives of Norges Bank. Malterud,
having learnt that Haslund was connected to the treasury in some way
explained his circumstances. The captain revealed that he needed cash
to pay the troops – about 1 million Norwegian Krone. Haslund was
now in a difficult position; he knew that payment to the troops was
right and just, but without being able to confirm the officer's intentions
as honourable and bereft of any accompanying cash he could do little.
Haslund considered the matter carefully and replied that he would meet
again with the Captain at Gjemnes that evening and that the officer
would need to bring the required requisitions and receipts so that a legal
process could ensue. This delay gave him time to carry out the necessary
checks on the man's identity and authority to request such a sum of cash.
Haslund later spoke of the experience.[156]

> After I had confirmed Malterud's identity I asked him to come to
> Gjemnes in the evening…He was accompanied by a Sergeant. In
> the company of both men the locks were opened on two iron boxes
> and the money counted and paid out. The money, in 5Kr & 10 Kr
> notes, was placed roughly equal in two potato bags.

The officer thanked Haslund, turned and the two walked off. The troops
would get their deserved pay.

Haslund's attentions now turned to the small fishing vessels that he
had earlier requested. Although *Driva* could have taken the bullion to
Tromsø it would have been too great a risk. Five fishing vessels had been
procured. Three boats came from Bud, whilst the other two came from

Hustad.[157] The fishing boats, known more commonly as *'puffers'* due to the sound of their single stroke engine, arrived at Gjemnes ready to play their part in the transport. Rumours abounded that the Germans were close by and so people went about their business confused and uncertain as to what was going to happen next. An atmosphere of nervousness and fear enveloped the community, but Haslund kept his focus on moving the gold away from Gjemnes to Tromsø.

Unloading of the trucks and stowing the bullion onto the fishing vessels by the guard soldiers took place in the dark – not a single light was shone to give the game away, but this in itself brought problems of seeing where to tread safely and Haslund later commented that it was pure good fortune that people or boxes did not fall overboard. To compound matters further refugees thronged around the pier seeking any means possible to get away. Later, during the night the *Driva* arrived with her exhausted crew and she was emptied of her 260 boxes of bullion. Loading of the puffers continued with four of the vessels being laden with bullion boxes, 547 in total. The fifth puffer was designated to carry passengers and soldiers only, although all the puffers would have a small guard onboard. To assist with the passage, planning and what to do in an emergency each puffer was to have their own 'commander'. For the purposes of the journey these were to be Fredrik Haslund, Einar Gerhardsen, Kristian Gleditsch, Major Bjørn Sunde and Sgt Pettersen, who was ordered to command the 5th puffer. Guns were taken onboard, but kept hidden and only to be used if necessary.[158]

The soldiers were also asked to keep off the deck to avoid arousing undue interest. With everyone embarked the passage north began. After only an hour they stopped as dawn was approaching. Haslund did not want the boats caught out in the open and so close together – it would be too suspicious if not for preying local eyes then certainly for the Germans. The skippers and Haslund had concluded that it would be wise to anchor at Kvalvåg for the day and proceed north the next night.

The arrival of the puffers at the anchorage had not gone unnoticed though. Haslund knew the risks of being seen, but had calculated that it would be better to avoid the Germans as best they could. The risk of being seen by a collaborator by stopping at a port or anchorage was a gamble he had to run with. But their presence caused a stir with the local inhabitants who noted the unusual appearance of five puffers entering the anchorage at the same time. They also noted that there were a large number of people onboard the boats who were disembarking their puffers looking utterly exhausted and dishevelled.

Whilst the passengers sought shelter in the farms and local alehouse the guard soldiers kept watch on the boats from the edge of a wood. This was a sensible move as it allowed the soldiers to stretch their legs a little, but more importantly the boats would look as if they were unmanned to any snooping aircraft.

Although the weather had been poor, the morning turned into a beautiful spring day. This did not match the mood of the locals who were suspicious. Despite requests for comfort in the way of coffee and maybe a place to sleep some of the group were turned away even though they showed their passports to confirm who they were, with some locals thinking that they were spies. It was not a pleasant situation. Others were a little more fortunate and managed to find rest at a prayer house, but even here the comforts were few with a only a cold stone floor to lay down upon. Tragedy was also to strike the group when Sverre Belle, one of the Norges Bank men, suddenly collapsed and died that day. Haslund wrote about the tragic death stating that he thought Sverre Belle had most probably died of a heart attack brought about by the shock of the air attack on the *Driva* and the stresses suffered afterwards. This obviously led to concerns amongst the bank staff and perhaps it was this event plus the injury to another member of the banking staff that prompted some of them to request permission to return home. Their request was accepted and the puffers continued northwards minus the men from Norges Bank.

Looking back in retrospect it is easy for one to view this action as defeatist, but that was apparently not the case. It was clear to Haslund and the others that not all banking personnel were required for the trip and in many ways it would be easier to transport the bullion with fewer people, thereby reducing the risk of injury and worse. To get over this problem a *declaration of release* was issued stating that the bank employees had been relieved of their duties and that their participation was no longer required. To support their actions the Minister of Finance, Oscar Torp was contacted to inform him of the decision. Torp endorsed the undertaking thereby removing any doubts as to the integrity of the bank employees.

It would seem, though, that misgivings might have been expressed after the war as Einar Gerhardsen later wrote seeking to give an explanation:[159]

> Unfortunately somebody died, and this made a great impression and I believe it was the catalyst for most of the employees of Norges Bank in wanting to go home. This was not easy, however, and the worst was the uncertainty. We held a counsel of war and agreed that each employee of the Norges Bank be paid 3 months salary for their duty. We had quite a lot of money as together with the gold there were two big crates of cash. I later learned that they contained a total of 12 million Krone. Who opened one of those boxes I do not know. I just know that never in my life had I seen so much money. Everyone, of course, had to sign for the amount that they were given. The money to be paid was counted and issued by two men. Receipts were then placed back in the boxes with the rest of the money.

Sverre Belle was buried at Flemma churchyard. His colleagues from the bank, who attended the funeral to bid a sad farewell to a respected colleague, conducted the funeral arrangements. His resting place can still be seen today with a tall erect stone and accompanying inscription marking the spot.

The ordeal for the returning bankers was far from over. An unnamed Norwegian Army colonel advised the bankers to travel to Molde to collect travel permits signed by the Germans so that they could journey relatively unmolested to their homes. This appears a strange decision as it must have been apparent to all that the returning bankers would be interviewed about why they were all travelling together, but Haslund factored this in to his planning.

Sverre Belle's grave – Flemma Churchyard.
Picture Credit: author

The bank officials reached Molde on May 5th staying at the Retiro. Their arrival did not go unnoticed and the next day a party of Gestapo officers arrived, along with a Norwegian aide. The men were promptly arrested and questioned about their reasons for being in Molde; who were they, where had they been and where were they were going? The Gestapo permitted them to stay at the Retiro, although under house arrest. They were not permitted to leave the building and a German guard was posted to ensure that this was adhered to. Later, the Gestapo returned to carry out more interviews and interrogations. The Germans knew that the bullion and much of the country's money had disappeared, but they had absolutely no idea where it was. The sudden appearance of a group of bank employees was clearly going to draw their attention, but fortunately the interrogation techniques of the Germans had not yet been honed and it would appear from the answers given by the bank employees that the Germans were afterwards none the wiser on the whereabouts of the bullion. The Norges Bank men had given nothing away.

As the bank staff travelled back to Molde the bullion was already being moved northwards. German bombers had flown overhead searching for opportunistic targets, but fortunately no bombs fell on Kvalvåg. Haslund knew it was time to move on and during the evening of May 1st made ready his plans to depart once more. Unable to attend the funeral of Sverre Belle he was well aware of the risks of staying too long in one place and attracting too much attention. He also calculated the risks of the bank men being detained as they returned to Molde and the possibility of the Germans extracting the information from them. The odds were not favourable.

With everyone that needed to be embarked onboard their allotted puffers the convoy duly set off. Their destination was Tunsta, just off the coast of Kristiansund. The passage required very careful and skillful navigation due to the danger of small islets and hidden rocks, but the journey was fortuitously trouble free and the convoy eventually reached the relative safety of the narrow fjord that led to Tustna. Haslund later wrote about the trip:[160]

> As soon as dusk fell and we felt that the puffers could not be seen from any height we left Kvalvåg and headed outwards (westwards) to sea. The meeting next day had already been decided upon and it

would be Tustna where the puffers could split up to their various landing places. No incidents occurred that night, a huge bonfire was burning behind us…it was Kristiansund well alight. In the morning of Thursday 2nd May (Ascension Day) we arrived at Gullstein at Tustna where among others the local shop owner, Mr Guldssten, helped us to find a place to stay and to get some food. For most of us it was the first decent sleep we had had in days. The situation at Tustna, though, was much like the same chaos at Gjemnes. Large numbers of refugees had arrived from Kristiansund and several groups of military types tried to find some transport to move northwards. Others had been dismissed and had taken off their uniforms. The sizeable unknown entourage from Eastern Norway together with soldiers in military uniform and a couple with German backgrounds were met with hefty amounts of scepticism from the locals.

The two Germans were a couple; one a dentist, the other a lawyer and understandably their very presence was causing alarm, despite the fact that they were political refugees and were seeking to distance themselves from Nazism. Rumours of collaborators and spies ran rife and the two German civilians only added to the maelstrom mix of fear and confusion. The five puffers, heavily armed with soldiers also aroused suspicion. Locals attempted to question the new arrivals, but were met with a wall of silence; no one from the puffers was allowed to say who they were, where they had been, where they were going or what they were carrying. This only served to fuel the distrust of the locals, which in turn caused difficulties when the entourage attempted to find places to rest.

The situation in which Haslund and his followers found themselves in can only best be described as a frenzied, chaotic muddle of a like never experienced before and Tustna, like many other Norwegian towns and ports, had become a destination for refugees desperate to get away from the bombing. Kristiansund, only a short distance away, was in flames. Was Tustna next? No one knew, but it must have filled the thoughts of many soldiers attempting to organise themselves as best they could to carry on the fight in the north of Norway. Radio reports from London warned of *Fifth columnists*, spies and Germans dressed as Norwegian soldiers. British newspapers, with their reports from journalists in Norway, merely added to this hysteria that was sweeping the country, along with German radio reports stating that Norway had been taken with little resistance. Earlier, Vidkun Quisling had broadcasted to Norwegians via the state radio that:[161]

> England had violated the neutrality of Norway without calling more than a feeble protest from the Nygaardsvold government…the German government had offered their assistance to the government of Norway, together with solemn assurances that our national independence would be respected.

Quisling's very sudden rise to power had taken everyone by surprise, including the Germans, but his position, later sanctioned by Hitler, merely augmented ill feeling, suspicion and bewilderment.

Meanwhile at Tustna, the scenes that unfolded are cited and described in detail by Nordahl Grieg as he attempted to reason with a certain Mr Guldssten, a local shop owner, that the assemblages of people from the puffers were not German spies, but refugees en passage with Norwegians. Grieg later wrote:[162]

> I met an old shop owner with an unquenchable belief that we were Germans in disguise and Norwegian traitors at the same time. With a voice that was quite low and full of hate he gave me his arguments…we had Germans among us. Quite rightly there were two immigrants onboard and we always tried to keep them away from people, but they did not like to sleep on the floor of the building, which had been given to the others, the man [*German*] therefore had the inspiration of walking amongst the community asking in broken Norwegian if there were any beds available. He [*Guldssten*] continued – 'your officer calls himself Major Sunde, but I just heard on the radio from London a Major Sunde speaking'. I tried to tell the shop owner that there were two brothers who were both majors. The shop owner replied that the major had taken the identity papers and the uniform. [*Guldssten*]'You are so stupid, one of the women onboard the puffers always stays with that German you call Major Sunde and says it is a Major Sunde in London to whom she is married'. I wanted to tell him that actually was the case, but he looked at me with dead eyes that were full of hatred. He turned away from me.
>
> Several people on the pier agreed with him and if they had weapons available to them then they wouldn't have accepted this German rubbish among them anymore.

The circumstances that Haslund, Grieg and Gleditsch had found themselves in are clear. But bravely Haslund did not forsake his German passengers when it would have been quite easy to have handed them over to Norwegian officials or the military.

Radio reports from the BBC informed Haslund that the war was over in Southern Norway. What Haslund did not know was that these BBC reports were late in broadcasting and that due to some oversight no one from the government had informed the BBC what the latest situation in Norway was.[163] News was a little more accurate from the newspapers, but it was the radio broadcasts from London that Haslund was relying upon. The situation really could not have been more desperate; the Germans were over-running Norway with very little resistance at great speed.

A worried Haslund still believed that the best chance of success was to move northwards. As he sought to transport the bullion it had become obvious to many that the British campaign in Norway was in complete tatters and that southern and central Norway was lost to the invaders. Denny's report is clear and concise and details the moment when evacuation was advised:[164]

> During Friday 26th April, the situation deteriorated and the newly arrived Military Base Staff, under Brigadier Hogg, were able to see for themselves how precarious the situation had become. Late that night I was asked to proceed from Molde to Åndalsnes for a Base Staff Conference, and on arrival in the early hours of the 27th was informed by Captain Maxwell-Hyslop of the frame of mind of the Military Base Staff and of the signal that he himself had made to the Admiralty stating that evacuation might be necessary, timed at 0050/27. A Staff Conference was held from 0800 to 1030, at which the Staff Officers, Naval and Military, unanimously advised Brigadier Hogg to inform the War Office, and other authorities that evacuation was necessary and the sooner the better.

Subsequently, the command was issued to re-embark 'Mauriceforce' and 'Sickleforce'. Soldiers were retreating headlong towards Åndalsnes by any means that they had at their disposal; foot, train or lorry. For many Norwegian soldiers skiing was the only option. According to Kersaudy (Norway 1940) the situation became close to a catastrophe on several occasions, with two armies in full flight. The Gudbrandsdal valley and all of southern Norway was now in the hands of the Germans, despite the many brave and heroic battles by Norwegian and British troops at places such as Lillehammer, Tretten and Kvam. It would be wrong to give the impression that it was complete rout, which was far from the case. However, the Allies were without air-cover, heavy armour and a wealth of essential war material usually needed to put up a fight and as a result the Allied troops began the process of evacuation from Åndalsnes on May 2nd. The fight was still being carried on in the north of Norway, but even from here the British and French troops were later to be evacuated. The sombre flight from Norway was taking place. Unfortunately the Norwegians were not initially made aware of the intentions of the Allies. This policy did not rest easy with the British commanders in the field: it was a dark time for Norway…and Britain.

Haslund was unaware of what was happening with the British, but fully realised that there was no time to lose. He later wrote:[165]

> On the night of the 2/3rd May we left Tustna heading to Titran on Sør-Frøya. I had a memo from the Tustna coastguard station to the Titran coastguard asking them to help us to find new puffers for onward transport. It had now become quite obvious that it would be difficult to convince our current puffer captains to move northwards from Frøya. They were of the opinion that they had been requisitioned for short trips in known waters and had no willingness to enter the waters northwards. At Titran there was quite a mess when we arrived in the early morning of the 3rd May. There was a great fear of spies and the people were quite scared of all these strangers arriving at such a little place. We succeeded, however, in finding quarters in some local Bed & Breakfasts – school houses and so on. We also found new food and supplies.

Upon landing, Haslund immediately sought out the senior officer of the Titran coastguard station. Reports were needed of the military movements along the coast and Haslund knew it would be foolish to sail again until he had some insight in to what was happening at sea. He goes on to describe events:[166]

> The coastguard station said that British warships had been observed at sea the day before and we believed that it was worthwhile to make contact in order to have some escort going northwards. Kristian Gleditsch and Nordahl Grieg volunteered to give it a try. Skipper Alf Larsen of the fishing vessel *Roald* volunteered to take them

out.[167] [*Kristian*] Gleditsch and [*Nordahl*] Grieg were equipped with warm clothes and dressed like fishermen and we put some fishing equipment on-board on the deck so as to fool the Germans of their intent. The plan was to put to sea outside Frøya, where the British warships had been observed the day before, to try and meet them to ask for assistance. From Titran coastguard station the people had been issued with signal flags to be hoisted in case of visual contact. The four signal flags were to read 'I am in need of immediate assistance and seek communication with you'.

In addition to the fishing equipment they also took with them a powerful torch so that they could flash an SOS signal in case they met a ship. The hope was that if the party managed to make contact with the Royal Navy then Haslund was to hand over a formal note, written in English, requesting their immediate assistance in transporting valuable equipment and secret documents to the Norwegian authorities in Northern Norway. It was agreed beforehand that Kristian Gleditsch would be the representative of the Royal Norwegian Government, which was also stated in the note. The mission with the fishing vessel was supposed to be secret, but somehow word got out and by the time the *Roald* slipped out of port a crowd had gathered to witness the event. Frustration and immense apprehension must have filled Haslund's mind as the boat made its way out of port, but he wanted to believe that all would be well and that luck would favour the brave. Gleditsch later wrote:[168]

> Actually we were supposed to leave quietly, but whoever had written the letter in English had whispered to his friend, who had whispered to their friend and so on, and by the time we left in the afternoon half the entourage was standing, waving watching us leave. Probably most of them never expected to see us again. It was difficult to understand why the Germans with their meticulous patrolling of the skies, were not interested in attacking fishing vessels, which were heading north.
>
> We headed out to sea and rounded the southern tip of Frøya and then headed northwest. When we were so far out it was advisable for us to turn northeast and then run parallel with the coast. In the morning we turned southeastwards again and around 5–6pm we came back to Sauøy in Froan, which was our assigned meeting place. It was a brilliant trip with a flat sea and the sun setting into the ocean, but we didn't even see a hint of smoke from British warships.

Meanwhile, whilst Gleditsch and Grieg were at sea searching for the Royal Navy a memo had been dispatched to the Bank of England from the Admiralty discussing the whereabouts of the remaining bullion. Officials in the UK had absolutely no idea where it was. One consignment was safe in the vaults of the Bank of England and the other was inbound to the UK aboard HMS *Glasgow*, but a further consignment was still unaccounted for. The following memo gives an insight on the confusion:

```
Military Branch,
Admiralty, S.W.1.
2nd May, 1940
M.07972/40

                    SECRET.

Dear Bolton,

  We have heard that one of H.M. Ships has onboard
about 23 tons of Norwegian gold and will probably bring
it to the Clyde within the next few days. I will phone
exact details when known, and no doubt you will tell us
how to dispose of it.
  We do not yet know where the remaining gold is.
Apparently there are some 11 tons more to trace.
```

Meanwhile, whilst concerns were being raised in the UK, Haslund took the opportunity to contact various officials to discuss the best possible route to get the bullion northwards and away from the Germans. If Gleditsch and Grieg failed in their attempt to find an allied ship then he reasoned that it would be wise to have a back-up plan of some sort. As a result the Mayor of Sør-Frøya and the local police chief were located and invited to discussions with Haslund and his boat skippers to thrash out some sort of plan. Haslund's report goes on:[169]

> After several discussions with the skippers of the puffers and the local authorities I decided to split the expedition in two, one for the gold and one for the passengers. If it was the case that the Germans had been informed about the transport then there was the possibility of loss of life especially since the expedition consisted of 70–80 people. Besides, experience had told us that it was difficult to find places to stay and food to eat for all these people at the places we arrived at.

The decision to split the transport in two was a judicious one. In an effort to reduce the numbers of travellers further, Haslund, via Major

Sunde, dismissed the military guard and saw to it that the men were paid off properly ensuring that they were rewarded for their service and had enough cash to enable them travel back to their homes. Before they took their leave the final duty of the soldiers was to load the two fishing boats with the bullion.

Constant loading and unloading of the bullion had been a backbreaking affair yet the soldiers shouldered their fiscal freight without complaint. They had completed their duty for Norway, but a number of years would pass before their part in the transport would be fully recognised.

Some soldiers wanted to continue the journey north hoping to meet up with the remains of the Norwegian army and carry on the fight against the Germans. Sergeant Alf Pahlow Andresen was one such soldier and he recounts his feelings and observations at that time:[170]

> It was an untenable situation for the gold. We kept looking for the British, but they were not looking for us. The journey continued from Titran and Frøya. Every hour was valuable. Haslund and Gerhardsen agreed that the gold and the people should be split up. At Titran we said goodbye to Nordahl Grieg – the strangest, happiest, eager soldier you have ever known and the most useful. The last image I have of him was with his arms full of signal flags and heading down for a boat to look for the Royal Navy. Throughout the whole journey, independent of miserable conditions, there had been a wealth of humour and uncompromising optimism. The soldiers from Gudbrandsdal adored him and they all lit up when he came and they missed him when he left. The transport of personnel now separate from the gold, Gerhardsen gave a masterly speech considering the dangers of travelling northwards. After the speech most people preferred to go back to Oslo or wherever they came from in the east. There were 16 of us left to travel to Tromsø and we just about filled up the boat. At the same time the guard troop that was dismissed were each given 100 Krone from one of the large boxes as a thank you for the job. That must be quite below the going rate for the job. I myself received 200 Krone since I was an officer. Most of the money I spent on buying some decent boots and therefore could look forward to continuing the journey with dry feet. I had almost forgotten what it was like to be dry and warm around my feet.

With the dismissal of the majority of the military guard the passenger numbers had now been reduced somewhat. Also, others had decided to either return to Oslo or make for elsewhere other than north, which enabled Haslund to work out how much sea-transport was required to carry the bullion and remaining passengers northwards.

It was envisaged that three large boats were needed. At this point Haslund called upon the local Lensmann, Hans Ruø, who assisted by using his influence to secure vessels. A plan was discussed and it was decided that two of the fishing boats, *Alfhild II* and the *Stølvåg* would take the bullion, around 9–10 tons each. *Alfhild II* was approximately 20 metres in length (65ft) with the *Stølvåg* being slightly shorter. The third vessel, a passenger boat named as the *Snorre* had been detailed to carry the travellers and this particular vessel was commanded by Einar Gerhardsen, who had requisitioned some cash from Haslund so that he could secure equipment as well as purchase food for the journey.

Having being driven to the meeting point by car the entourage boarded the boat and they sailed forth to Tromsø in favourable weather arriving on May 10th. Gerhardsen and his motley bunch of passengers had made it safely and without incident.

Haslund's thinking was once again proved right. He removed various risks such as the passengers and the dismissal of the guard soldiers, but he also ordered the telephone lines to be cut, temporarily at least, until the bullion had been embarked and the boats sailed for Sauøy. Rumours of Germans close by, traitors and *Fifth columnists* abounded with despairing regularity and Haslund had to ensure that the bullion sailed without it becoming known immediately to the enemy.[171] Radio broadcasts were unreliable, as was word of mouth and it was plain to Haslund, and others, that the situation in Norway was virtually unsustainable. He had to play it his way. As an engineer he knew there could be no half measures: it was either success or failure.

With the return of Gleditsch and Grieg, Haslund went about securing food, clothes and equipment. It was agreed that the skipper of the *Roald*, Alf Larsen, could depart with his boat and scout for any enemy activity and to report back at once if he spotted anything unusual or hostile. The remaining puffers, once provisioned, could leave at two-hour intervals, but then meet up later at Langsundet near Vikna. The initial passage would be between the islands and skerries, which would afford a little protection from German eyes and then on to the Langsundet.

Stølvågs commander was to be Haslund with Grieg as his second officer, whilst on *Alfhild II* Gleditsch was in charge with the lawyer, Aake Ording as his No 2 and Nini Gleditsch, who was responsible for the food. It's worth pointing out that Nordahl Grieg was now the only soldier to accompany the gold.

With Alf Larsen of the *Roald* reporting back that the way was clear for the boats Haslund gave the orders to leave port and on the evening of May 4th the boats set out from Sauøy maintaining their discreet distances between each other. No incidents of note occurred and once again, fortune smiled graciously upon Haslund and his band of gold smugglers as they reached Viknasundet on Sunday May 5th. Alf Larsen, skipper of the *Roald* was now paid off and he duly returned to Frøya with his boat.

Despite their successes Haslund now had a problem that was beyond even his control – daylight. The month of May was well into her stride and the long winter nights had been replaced by fine spring weather and pleasant days. In Norway as summer approaches the hours of darkness become much shorter with each passing day and mid-summer was but a few short weeks away making it more and more difficult for the boats to hide away from the prowling Luftwaffe. Haslund decided to chance his luck and ordered the boats to push on and make for Bjørn On Dønna arriving there on May 6th.

With no radio to contact the authorities to determine the current situation Haslund was left with no alternative but to risk his security, and that of the transport, by stepping ashore to investigate whether any households possessed a telephone that he could borrow. Again, fortune smiled and Haslund, persuading a house owner to lend him their telephone, managed to make a call to the Police in Sandessjøen. As a consequence of that call Haslund travelled to the village whereupon he was informed of the desperate situation Norway was in, but that the north was still free. Reports indicated that the government was at Tromsø – as was the Royal Navy and that meant that to protect the north from the Kriegsmarine there would be mines and understandably, no one had considered the needs of a small flotilla of fishing vessels carrying gold bullion puffing its way up the west coast.

Haslund returned to his fishing vessel and immediately ordered the boats to split up, but to meet at Vågsøyan, a small port just north of Bodø.

On Tuesday May 7th the two fishing vessels rendezvoused as arranged at the port; Haslund stepped ashore alone. Managing to secure the services of a car he took a short ride to Bodø to seek out the military commander for the area, Captain Gløersen. Haslund needed to know exactly what minefields the British had lain at Vestfjord and whether he could get through with his two fishing vessels. Once again security and safety was uppermost for Haslund. It would have been easier for the flotilla to have sailed for Bodø in the first place, acquire provisions and then make ready for passage north again, but Haslund didn't want to court unnecessary attention and have to answer awkward questions. He just could not take that chance. It would have only taken one call to the Germans from a sympathiser to have totally ruined the operation.

Having acquired the information he was seeking, as well as enough provisions for the journey, Haslund returned to the boats. The flotilla moved off on the night of May 8th crossing Vestfjord and arriving at Svolvær whereupon they established contact with a Norwegian guard ship and its commanding officer, Captain Myrseth. At this point Haslund was completely exhausted. He was desperate for a pilot to guide them through the final phase of the journey. To his huge relief, Myrseth stepped into the breach and a short while later Haslund had his pilot onboard steering the small flotilla safely through the waterways and sounds towards Tromsø. The journey passed without incident…well, almost. The fishing vessel *Stølvåg*, whilst crossing Andfjorden, found itself following in the wake of a submarine periscope. Understandably, this caused some alarm on the boat, but the sub appeared not to have seen the fishing vessel and it took no action against it. Haslund later wrote:[172]

> As we crossed the fjord we spotted a submarine in front of us, about 20–30 metres away. It paid no attention to us and we assumed that we had not been spotted. We crossed to land and reported what we had seen to the authorities via telephone. An hour or so later we saw an aircraft approaching. We also signaled a British destroyer that picked up speed and headed straight for the position we had given them. After a while we believed we could hear some distant explosions from depth charges.

Stølvåg and *Alfhild II*, with their precious cargo intact, arrived safely together at Tromsø. It was May 9th. Haslund's task was almost over.

14

Welcome Arrivals

Just seven weeks earlier, Oscar Torp, the Finance Minister had been searching for a leader to take on the task of denying the Germans 50 tons of Norwegian gold. His 'job description' demanded someone with qualities of honesty, leadership, vision, and a resolve to successfully complete the job whatever the conditions. Given the need for urgency, Torp's choice of Haslund had been a remarkable one.

The mission was almost over, but there was still the issue of transporting the gold back to the UK before Norway was completely over-run. The emotions of those involved with the final phase of the transport have not been recorded so one can only speculate upon the utter relief that must have been felt by all. Haslund, having completed his task with getting the gold away to safety, considered his duty was now almost over. Little did he know at that time that his services would soon once again be in demand.

Torp was already at Tromsø when the bullion flotilla arrived. His faith in Fredrik Haslund and his ability to come through had been unshakeable, but even Torp's sighs of relief must have been audible to those near him. The following day, May 10th, Haslund met with Torp to verbally deliver his report concerning the transport. Discussions naturally ensued on what to do with the gold. The decision was made to keep the bullion on the fishing vessels for now, but it was agreed that the cash would be handed over to the Tromsø branch of Norges Bank, and this was done the next day. Norges Bank had now been re-organised and Tromsø was regarded as the Main Office with Arnold Ræstad head of Norges Bank. With the cash handed over, Torp took the opportunity to visit the two fishing boats, at that point anchored in Telegraph Bay. The skippers and crews were gathered together and were thanked profusely for their endeavours on behalf of the Norwegian Government, but Torp had something else to say and he chose the occasion to inform Haslund and Grieg that they would be staying with the gold and would escort it to the UK on a British warship.

For the next few days the gold bullion resided in the hold of the *Alfhild II* anchored in Telegraph Bay. To move the bullion shore side was seen as unnecessary as events in Norway were deteriorating by the day and there could be a need to move out at short notice. Furthermore, it was deemed that the bullion was just as safe on the boats as it was on shore – perhaps more so. There was simply no need to take risks at this stage. Meanwhile, some of those who had assisted in the transport now sought jobs elsewhere, desperate to help out where possible. Norges Bank in Tromsø took on Ording, whilst Kristian Gleditsch became a translator for the French at Harstad. Nini Gleditsch took employment with the Ministry of Trade. Nordahl Grieg, despite being placed on readiness to sail with the bullion back to England, occupied himself with what he was best at – inspired and imaginative prose; born from that dark, sombre and chaotic period was a poem so beautifully written that when Grieg later read it out in person over the radio it reduced many Norwegians to tears. The poem, titled *'Today the Flagpole is Naked'* is regarded by many as a classic of its time.

NB Nini Gleditsch was not the only woman onboard the puffers as they made their way to Tromsø. Kari Berggrav, an assistant with the Norwegian Information Office, took part in the operation. She was working as a photographer and had taken many pictures of the war in Southern Norway. Unfortunately, these images were later lost in a fire.

With the remaining gold safe at Tromsø, word had been received in the UK that the bullion had been located and was safe, but that transport to a safe haven in the UK was required quickly. The Admiralty, in accordance with its promise to keep the Bank of England informed dispatched the following signal to Mr Bolton.

```
Military Branch
Admiralty, S.W.1.
12th May, 1940
M.07972/40
```

<u>SECRET AND PERSONAL</u>

Dear Bolton,

We are informed that the remaining Norwegian gold – about 20 tons – has been located in Northern Norway, and the Norwegian Government would like it removed to the United Kingdom as soon as possible.

We have given instructions accordingly to the Naval Authorities.

I will let you know of its arrival in due course.

Yours sincerely,

```
G. F Bolton, Esq.,
Bank of England
Threadneedle Street,
E.C.3.
```

During the night of May 19th and the early hours of the 20th the authorities decided, for operational reasons, that the bullion from the fishing vessel *Stølvåg* should be transferred with immediate effect to *Alfhild 11,* which with the extra weight left her understandably low in the water. Astonishingly, not all the gold was transferred and it wasn't until the crew of the *Stølvåg* checked the manifesto that they found around 20kg of gold had been left behind in the hold. The matter was reported to Gleditsch and the situation quickly remedied.

Transferring the bullion freed the *Stølvåg* for use by the Norwegian authorities for other missions and a little later she slipped out of port. Interestingly, *Alfhild 11* did not remain at anchor in Telegraph Bay, but went to sea with the other local fishing boats as if she was also fishing. This ruse prevented any suspicion as to why the same fishing boat was not acting normally.

On May 21st, Captain Kjær and Consular Cumming ordered Haslund to take *Alfhild 11* out into Tromsø Sound and to lie up beside HMS *Enterprise* so that the bullion could be transferred. That night *Alfhild 11* left her moorings and took up position beside the cruiser on the stern

```
SECRET              M E S S A G E.   1914/21st May

From F.O. i/c Narvik                Date 21.5.40.
                                    Time 2121



                  NAVAL CYPHER (D) by W/T.
_____

Addressed  C.S.I. repeated R.A. Narvik.

IMPORTANT.
     H.M.S. ENTERPRISE will be leaving for England
shortly.  Request you will arrange for her to
embark Norwegin Government Gold for passage forthwith.
                                    1914/21


     Advance Copy sent Ops. U.W.R. & O.I.C.
```

port quarter at 00:45 on May 22nd. Already onboard was the British Consul to oversee matters. Strangely, the loading of the gold, according to the ship's log did not commence until 04:00, but was rapidly completed within half an hour with the cruiser making full use of her crane to load the bullion safely and quickly. At 04:40 the British Consul left, having seen the gold safely embarked without mishap.

Prior to *Enterprise* embarking the remaining bullion initial uncertainty had lingered about which warship would bring the remaining gold back to the UK. On May 13th a signal was despatched to HMS *Devonshire* ordering her to Scapa in company with two destroyers, but to also to enquire at Tromsø whether she '*should transport 20 tons of gold to UK.*' A day later (May 14th) and the order was rescinded stating that '*HMS Devonshire is to remain in the north for the present*'. But it wasn't until May 21st that the order went to HMS *Enterprise* to carry out the transportation to the UK.[173]

15

HMS *Enterprise*

HMS *Enterprise* was laid at down John Brown's shipbuilding yard in June 1918. She was launched in December 1919 and completed in April 1926 at Devonport. She displaced 7,580 tons with a top speed of 33 knots. Initially she was fitted with seven 6in single mounted guns, although a twin 6 in was later fitted to the No I position, three 4 in AA, and two 2 pounder singles. She also carried twelve 21 in torpedo tubes set out on the main deck as four triple banks. During the 1930s *Enterprise* was also fitted with a catapult and added a Kingfisher aircraft to her inventory.

Until 1934 *Enterprise* was part of the 4th Cruiser Squadron serving in the East Indies. She was placed in 'care and maintenance', but then was given a major refit and restored to the East Indies, departing for the UK in late 1937. During 1938 *Enterprise* took on the role of ferrying crews to the China Station, but once more returned home to be paid off

HMS *Enterprise*

in September 1938. However, fortunes changed for the cruiser and she was re-employed on Atlantic escort duties during 1939/40. She was then transferred to the Home Fleet for the Norwegian Campaign.

Enterprise had been part of the Narvik force (April operations in the Harstad area) – Lord Cork & Orrery's naval command of HM Ships: the battleship *Warspite*; cruisers *Southampton*, *Effingham* and *Aurora*, the aircraft carrier *Furious*, repair ship *Vindictive* and various destroyers. *Enterprise's* operation with the naval force was a close shave as she was attacked by U65 on April 19th, but was fortuitously saved by a premature fuse. It would not be her last scrape with German forces, particularly the Luftwaffe.

By May 10th, HM anti-aircraft cruisers *Cairo, Coventry* and *Curlew* as well as the carrier *Ark Royal,* which replaced the battered and bomb damaged *Furious,* had joined the force. The plan was to avoid an opposed landing at Narvik and to bombard the Germans into surrendering and then invade. Time was running out for the Allies, though. The bombardment lasted three hours, but to the dismay of the Allies no surrender flag came and the follow up Allied invasion never materialised. The weather was atrocious at that time, which no doubt contributed significantly to the decision to withhold the landing. *Enterprise*, for her part, shelled both sides of the harbour entrance.

On May 12th *Enterprise*, with the sloop *Fleetwood* and freighter *Margot*, landed 820 reinforcements near Mo, despite constant air attacks, and then with five destroyers gave fire support for French landings in Herjangsfjord near Narvik.

Enterprise's short time in Norway had been a dramatic and fraught affair. She was riddled with splinters after surviving the onslaught of around 150 bombs from German air attack and by the time she embarked the gold at Tromsø it is fair to describe her as in poor state, yet she was still seaworthy.

Very little has been recorded about *Enterprise's* role in the bullion affair. Her logbook gives few details and despite extensive searches time appears to have taken its toll on those who served with her. However, making use of the War Diary of Vice Admiral JHD Cunningham Commanding First Cruiser Squadron, it has been possible to piece together her time just prior to embarking the gold.[174]

The diary records the following on May 18th:

> At 2400 "ENTERPRISE" returned with Sir Cecil Dormer, British Minister to Norway, General Marion, [and] visiting Norway on behalf of General Gamelin.'

A further entry on May 21st states:

> Colonel Otto Rugg, [*sic*] the Norwegian Commander-in-Chief, arrived in Tromso [*sic*]. Received Flag Officer, Narvik's instructions for "ENTERPRISE" to proceed to England shortly and to embark some 19 tons of Norwegian Government Gold then at Tromso [*sic*].

During the early hours of the following day, May 22nd, the gold was embarked on *Enterprise*, although she did not sail immediately. Instead she remained fastened to her station in harbour taking on food and water and generally being prepared in readiness for departure. Then, just prior to midnight on May 23rd *Enterprise's* anchors were raised. Crews and control parties were placed at the ready and a little after midnight she slipped away from Tromsø harbour immediately commencing a zig-zag course for Harstad arriving there at 03:15. A short time later she secured herself alongside an oiler. At 06:45 five aircraft were spotted, but strangely it wasn't until an hour later that *Enterprise* was attacked by German bombers. Seven bombs fell, but fortunately all missed and the '*all clear*' was sounded at 07:55.

Another air raid commenced at 10:23 but this lasted only 20 minutes before the aircraft were seen off by *Enterprise's* defences and with little taste for a fight the Luftwaffe hastily departed. The bombers had fortunately missed their opportunity as shortly afterwards an ammunition ship secured alongside *Enterprise* to re-supply her. Aircraft were once again spotted; no attacks commenced, but to err on the side of caution the ammunition ship quickly cast off.

What was left of the morning hours passed uneventfully and just after midday *Enterprise* recommenced her zig-zag journey back to the UK varying her speed between 15 and 25 knots. She passed various trawlers during her passage as well as HM destroyers *Bedouin* and *Foxhound*. Her initial orders were to make for the safe anchorage of Scapa Flow, which she duly reached at 18:15 on May 26th. Provision boats were soon fastened alongside and she commenced taking on water and food. *Enterprise* then remained at her berth (A1) until 16:00 on the 27th when she left Scapa and made for Devonport. This was a risky trip to make as the other two cruisers *Galatea* and *Glasgow* had made for Rosyth and Greenock in Scotland respectively. *Enterprise's* course took her down the west coast of the UK and unlike *Glasgow* she was without destroyer escort and in a poor ship state due to bomb and splinter damage. There was no 'stand down' and crews remained on constant alert, but the weather was fair and only one unidentified aircraft was spotted after leaving Scapa. The remainder of her journey south proved uneventful. *Enterprise*, despite her condition, made reasonable time, docking at Devonport (Plymouth) at 06:20 on May 29th and according to the ship's log: 09:35 *'finished disembarking special cargo'*. *Enterprise* had valiantly played her part.[175]

The bullion was immediately transferred to box rail vans belonging to the Great Western Railway (GWR) and with armed policeman escorting the bullion the train headed for London arriving, again without incident, at London's Paddington Station whereby the bullion was at once taken by covered lorries to the strong vaults of the Bank of England.[176]

There is a very small postscript to this affair, which again highlights the confusion that existed during that traumatic time, particularly as the evacuation of Norway was about to commence. HMS *Devonshire* was still at Tromsø awaiting the embarkation of King Haakon when news reached the cruiser that there was a further shipment of material to be made before sailing. In the War diary of the Vice Admiral Commanding, First Cruiser Squadron he notes on the June 6th that:[177]

> At 2355 I received a message from my Liaison Officer to the effect that evacuation was now practically certain, that arrangements had been made to embark 14 tons of bullion and that present weather at Tromso [*sic*] was favourable due enemy air activity.

The diary later notes: *'The bullion subsequently proved non-existent'*.

Interestingly, the confusion spawned a rumour that persisted into the present and years later the rumour reached the author that hidden somewhere in Tromsø was a substantial amount of gold that should have been evacuated on *Devonshire*. Whilst not wishing to dampen the hopes of treasure seekers it would appear on this occasion that the rumour is just that.

16

The 'Sealed Cargo' Arrives in the UK

Prior to the gold arriving at the Bank of England, plans were being put into place ready for the acceptance of the consignments, or so the Norwegians thought. Messrs Raeder and Sunde, the Norwegian representatives, had visited the Bank of England to request that the bank make arrangements for the transportation and acceptance of the bullion, but curiously unknown to them the first consignment was already in the UK having been transported by HMS *Galatea*. Arriving at Rosyth in Scotland on April 26th, the bullion was immediately transferred to railway trucks and plans set in motion to rail the bullion to London. The boxes had been delivered by *Galatea* sealed and in good condition, except for box numbered 551, which had had its seal broken. All the boxes were marked NB. The instructions from the Bill of Lading were clear:

> To be forwarded to the Bank of England for the Norwegian Government in the care of Mr Øyvind Lorentzen together with the Norwegian Minister in London.

On the 3rd of May 1940 a letter was sent to The Chief Cashier at the Bank of England from the Foreign Exchange Office declaring that:

> £2¼ million gold coin has arrived at the Bank and has been set aside for the Norwegian Government. A further '23 tons will be brought to the Clyde in the next few days' and 'there are some 11 tons more to trace'.

The letter went on to debate the merits of insurance, but that they were unsure if the gold on the other ships would arrive at all inferring it could be lost en route. It also stated the Royal Navy was keen to hand over the metal as soon as possible and… *'this may mean dumping them* [the bullion] *on the quay pending collection.'* The Royal Bank of Scotland was to undertake the collection, but the letter warned that it might be some time before a bank representative would be on the spot! It was decided in the end not to insure the bullion as the authorities had no idea of the bullion's port of departure, the type of naval vessel involved or if it was boxed (although *Galatea's* arrival and off-loading of the bullion must have given them a clue). A final, and probably the most pressing reason, was they wanted to avoid publicity. Insuring the bullion could have led to breaches of security and it was decided that Police escorts would be sufficient insurance from port to the Bank of England. On May 6th HMS *Glasgow* brought her consignment in.

Foreign Secretary Koht noted in his book:[178]

> We entered the Firth of Clyde in the afternoon of Saturday 4th May, and the cruiser docked at Greenock. There, men from Bank of Scotland came onboard and took away the Norwegian gold that had been carried over by *Glasgow*. It was sent to Bank of England in London – and the jokers there asked how on earth we had managed to convince the Scots to give the gold away again, after they had got hold of it.

Meanwhile, to assist in the banking of the bullion, the Norwegian Prime Minister, Johan Nygaardsvold put into place a statement of attorney. It reads:

```
                    POWER OF ATTORNEY
                    -------------------


I, Johan Nygaardsvold, Prime Minister of Norway, in the
name of the Norwegian Government, hereby authorise and
empower Mr Øyvind Lorentzen, together with the Norwegian
Minister and Legation in London to deposit in the United
Kingdom the gold belonging to the Bank of Norway which
is to be carried in British Warships, and to exercise
the rights of the bank relative to the said gold.

                    Norway, 22 April 1940.
                    (S) Johan Nygaardsvold
```

Letters containing information about the Norwegian bullion were shuttling backwards and forwards between various government departments and the Bank of England. Mr Laverack of the Bank of England penned one such letter:

> The consignments were landed in Scotland [from HM ships Galatea & Glasgow]. We received short notice from the Admiralty of these arrivals so the Royal Bank of Scotland, London, (Mr Whyte - General Manager) were asked to contact the naval vessels and arrange to escort the metal to London.
>
> The first consignment arrived at Rosyth on the 26th April. The Edinburgh Branch detailed Messrs' Small and Sutherland (Inspectors) to bring the boxes to London, travelling overnight. A second large consignment (795 boxes) arrived at Greenock about 4pm on Saturday, 4th May and Messrs' David F. Low and James Fraser (of the Glasgow Branch) took over the metal: they arrived at the Bullion Office nearly 30 hours later. The joint managers at Glasgow, Messrs' Robert L. Mudie and J.A. Bogie, met the naval authorities at Greenock and gave every assistance.
>
> The London, Midland & Scottish Railway were particularly helpful with their transport arrangements. Messrs' T.W. Royle (Chief Operating Manager), R.O. Bannister (Assistant Passenger Trains Department) and - Knott (Cartage Inspector) took an active part in the work. I would add that Mr Bannister maintained continuous contact with Edinburgh from his home address during Saturday and Sunday 4th and 5th May, and passed to me all information as to the progress of the second consignment.
>
> Signed: F.W.R Laverack
> 7th May 1940

NB *Glasgow's* gold left for the South at 03:40 Sunday morning. It should have arrived at Euston at 15:30 next day, but delays meant arrival was at 18:35. The bullion was stowed away in Bank of England without incident by 22:00 – receipts given.

No sooner had the gold from *Galatea* and *Glasgow* been deposited within the vaults of the Bank of England than the serious business of counting began. The following is a memo issued by the Bank of England accounting for the two deposits:

```
MEMORANDUM

TO THE CHIEF CASHIER

NORWEGIAN GOLD

1. Both consignments of Norwegian gold have now been
   opened. The approximate value is as follows:-

   Consignment    No. 1    £2   m.
        "         No. 2    £6½  m.
                           £8½  m.

   and represents 1,141 bars and 2,579 bags of gold
   coin.

2. It has not been possible yet to weigh any of the
   gold but the work will be commenced as soon as
   possible. In this connection I would mention that
   each bag is sealed and bears a label, and I would
   like to have a ruling as to whether the bags are
   to be opened and the contents net weighed. If this
   is done the fine gold contents can be set aside as
   sundry gold coin.

7th May 1940
```

Nonetheless, despite the memo recording the consignments and their values not all the gold was safe in the hands of the Bank of England. Aside from *Enterprise's* consignment, which had not yet arrived, a bagful of coins had been stolen whilst the bullion was being embarked at Molde. A Royal Marine, taking advantage of a damaged keg, managed to smuggle a bag of 1000 coins away. The coins were carefully hidden in one of the rear gun turrets of the cruiser ready to be collected when the ship docked. The offending marine, keen to keep an eye on his loot, also manned that particular turret. It must have been with some relief for the marine when *Glasgow* berthed at Greenock and her load of the bullion disembarked.

Unfortunately for the Royal Marine word was spreading around the ship that some of the gold had disappeared, but no one knew who the culprit was or how much had been stolen. In the haste to get the bullion away from Molde there had been no time to make an accurate count. It was known that one keg was broken, but it was not known how many bags should have been in the keg. However, enough suspicion had been raised for the Police to be informed.

Despite lengthy investigations by the author it would appear little in the way of official records exist to describe events, but what is known is that the Liverpool Police eventually recovered 704 gold coins of the *'Type 20 Koranas'*. The action by the Liverpool Police strongly indicates that the Royal Marine had somehow managed to smuggle the gold off *Glasgow* whereby he made for Liverpool. The bag originally contained 1000 coins meaning that 296 coins were, and still are, missing; in fact the missing coins were never recovered. The Police investigation subsequently revealed that the culprit was a long serving three badge Royal Marine named as Saunders.[179]

The following message was sent:

Copy

Secret
Addressed: Admiralty.
From: Glasgow

Your 1344/7. 704 Gold Hungarian coins inscribed 20
Koranas (sic) were stolen from a keg by Marine A.E.
Saunders during the shipping of the Norwegian Bullion
in H.M.S. GLASGOW on 29th April, and have since been
recovered. In accordance with instructions from Flag
Officer-in-Charge, Liverpool, the Norwegian Consul in
Liverpool was informed and all coins have been handed
over to him and a receipt obtained. Marine Saunders was
awarded 90 days detention summarily. Written reports
have been forwarded to Flag Officer-in-Charge, Liverpool.
. . . .

It is worth noting the dates from the letters and memos that the gold had been missing for well over a month. It is not recorded what Saunders had done with the coins, but rumours abounded amongst the crew on *Glasgow* that Saunders had tried to sell the coins to a pawnbroker and that the shopkeeper, suspicious of such a large amount of coins, had promptly called the Police. Their quick attendance had supposedly caught Marine Saunders red-handed. Subsequent research has been unable to confirm or deny this rumour. It is also not recorded what happened to the coins after they had been handed over to the Norwegian authorities although the following memo gives an insight on how the matter was dealt with.

```
From: The Agent,
Bank of England Branch,
Liverpool 2.
6th June 1940
                              To: The Principal
                              Branch Banks Office,
                              Bank of England, EC2
```

GOLD

Mr. Hill, the Deputy Chief Clerk, reports as follows:

"Concerning the bag of gold which was the cause of the Norwegian Consul's visit to the Bank yesterday, I was informed this afternoon by Mr. Glover, the Deputy Chief Constable that the Police were not prepared to give any information concerning the circumstances under which the gold came into their possession.[180]

The only definite information I was able to obtain was:

1. That another department was involved.
2. That the bag of Gold was handed over to a Naval Paymaster by the Police this morning.
3. That if the gold came into the possession of the Norwegian Consul he was entitled to hold it.

I inferred that the "other department" was the Admiralty. And that the gold would, in fact, reach the Norwegian Consul, and I gathered in the course of conversation that a prosecution had been contemplated but would not materialise.

The Police immediately handed over their investigation to the Royal Navy and Marine Saunders was summarily punished and given 3 months detention by a military court. For some this would seem a light punishment for the offence, but at that time Britain had its back to the wall and every soldier, sailor, airman, and Royal Marine for that matter was desperately needed. Indeed, it would have served little purpose to dismiss the long serving Saunders from the Royal Marines. Ironically, after serving his sentence Marine Saunders was seen to be working in the Naval Paymaster's Office at an unnamed Royal Navy establishment. It would appear that someone in the Navy had a sense of humour and that for Marine Saunders old habits die hard.

Marine Saunders's treasure. Not all of it was recovered by the Police

By the time the second consignment of gold was safely in the UK Norwegian administration had become more organised and a system was implemented whereby only certain designated signatories could sign for the bullion. One of those nominated signatories was Ole Colbjørnsen and once *Glasgow's* consignment of bullion had been safely delivered to London he formally recorded the event:

```
I confirm having delivered to the Royal Bank of Scotland
for transmission to the Bank of England, London the
following packages:
39 - thirty nine - small casks
439 four hundred and thirty nine - small cases
317 - three hundred and seventeen - large cases all said
to contain gold bars or coins. A number of the seals are
not intact.
These packages were delivered ex H.M.S. "Glasgow".

                    5th May 1940
                    Ole Colbjørnsen

Special Representative of the Norwegian Ministry of
Finance
```

As events in London were playing themselves out a third consignment was still to arrive. On May 24th a signal was sent to Home Fleet informing them of HMS *Enterprise's* departure from Harstad for the safe anchorage of Scapa Flow. Her speed was advised as 25 knots.

Interestingly, a *'Most Secret'* naval signal from the Admiralty was sent to HMS *Enterprise* on May 26th asking her if she had bullion onboard, and if so, how much. The signal had been signed *'for Head of M'*.

Subsequently, a Lieutenant Commander Hutchinson informed *'M'* that there were 19 tons onboard and that his information had been received from the duty captain. He went on to say that the ship would be heading south for a home port and that the Bank of England, and in particular, Mr Laverack, would be kept informed on the movement of the vessel.

Eventually HMS *Enterprise* docked in Plymouth. On May 27th *'M'* wrote to Commander J. E. Jacobsen, the Norwegian Naval Attaché in London.

> The Secretary of the Admiralty presents his compliments
> to Captain Jacobsen, and informs him that HMS Enterprise
> arrived in this country on the 26th May, with 19 tons of
> Norwegian gold. Mr. Haslund, Secretary of the Norwegian
> Ministry of Supply was in charge of the gold and was
> accompanied by three Norwegian assistants.
> HMS Enterprise sailed for Plymouth a little later where
> she is expected to arrive in the course of tomorrow
> Tuesday.
>
> Mr. Haslund has requested that the following message
> might be passed to the Norwegian Legation.
>
> Begins. Please arrange for Ole Colbjoernsen [sic] to
> receive luggage, Haslund Grieg. Ends.

HMS *Enterprise* eventually departed Scapa on the 27th at 16:05 and made Plymouth on the 29th. On May 28th there was message from the Admiralty C in C Western Approaches expressing:

> 19 tons of gold in ENTERPRISE should be handed over to Mr.
> K.H. Hopkins agent of Bank of England.

It was signed 'for Head of M'.

On the May 31st the Commander-in-Chief Western Approaches sent another telegram this time informing the recipient of the following:

```
812P.302 large boxes (approximately 100lbs.) and 245
small boxes (about 50lbs.) said to contain gold, brought
from Narvik [sic] in ENTERPRISE were disembarked on
Wednesday forenoon, 29th May, 1940, and loaded into two
G.W.R. trucks for conveyance to London, accompanied by
Bank of England official.
```

However, it didn't take long for a small amount of the gold to be released from the vaults of the Bank of England. The Norwegian authorities in London requested that five cases of gold be delivered in to their care.

```
The undersigned, Norwegian Minister in London, hereby
authorises Mr. Johan Georg RÆDER, Commercial Counsellor
to this Legation, to receive on my behalf from the Bank
of England five cases containing gold belonging to the
Royal Norwegian Government.
London, 12th June 1940
Erik Colban
```

The reference to the luggage was code for gold bullion and was a term composed by the Norwegians at the beginning of the transport with the bullion originally being known as the 'heavy luggage'. The 'light luggage' was code for Norwegian cash.

When HMS *Enterprise* reached Plymouth on May 29th her bullion was immediately unloaded and transferred to two railway box vans of the Great Western Railway whereupon the vans were sealed and the train commenced its journey to London with Bank of England Agent Mr K. H. Hopkins on board. The consignment arrived at Paddington station without undue incident.

17

Pimpernel Gold

Having invaded Norway on April 9th, albeit delayed in taking Oslo due to the sinking of the Blücher, the Germans had an opportunity to take Norway's King, parliament and gold bullion in one move. In reality they lost all three and a battle cruiser to boot. Like the UK, and many other countries, Norway had moved the majority of her gold out of the country before hostilities had begun. Approximately 50 tons of it remained behind, but one of the advantages the Norwegians had was that Nicolai Rygg had ensured that the bullion was boxed and ready in advance for it to be moved. That requirement came sooner than expected.

Although the Germans arrived at Norges Bank Oslo on April 10th it took them quite some time to work out what had actually happened to the bullion. The bank was immediately placed under armed guard and a preparatory meeting held with the remaining bank officials including NB Director, Sverre Olaf Thorkildsen, second only to Nicolai Rygg, where the question of gold and deposits in foreign countries was raised. On April 11th around noon another meeting was held and this time it was attended by a Major Fr. W. Neef, an officer with the Wirtschaftstab – a German economic exploitation group – as well as a liaison officer with the OKW for the political leadership and Herr Walter Weber of the German Legation.[181] Thorkildsen was also in attendance.[182] It is not known what the Germans initial reaction was when they realised that the gold holding in the bank was less than expected, but it could hardly have been a joyous moment when it dawned on them that a considerable amount of gold was probably elsewhere. Discussions took place and an agreement was reached that the Norwegians would not act against joint German and Norwegian interests. This agreement was formalised in writing by the next day. It is pertinent to assume that the Germans would have made a thorough search of the banks in Oslo and interrogated various officials and bank employees in an attempt to gain clues as to the location of the bullion, but the priority of the invaders in the first instance was to secure the capital and the immediate surrounding area. With that particular mission carried out their attentions would have turned northwards.

On April 15th Nicolai Rygg was back in Oslo but more importantly he had returned to the bank where he met up with a four man German delegation including Ministerial leader Sarnow, who wanted to know where the gold was and demanded assurances that it would not be taken out of the country. Sarnow 'reassured' the assembled Norwegians that the gold would only be used in the interests of Norway. Meanwhile, reports had filtered through to the German authorities that the gold was now at Lillehammer. Upon questioning, Rygg agreed that the gold had been moved there, but added that there were no new plans to move the gold again. The Germans, understandably, were not totally convinced that the gold was safe at Lillehammer and returned to the question several times. There were also concerns that the 'old government' as the Germans termed them, would somehow spirit the gold to Sweden. The bank denied this would happen and the meeting concluded with the armed German guard being dismissed from duty.

On April 24th, Neef returned to the bank again to confirm that the gold remained at Lillehammer, but it wasn't until the next day that the Germans realised that something was amiss and that perhaps the gold had disappeared. It would appear that the Germans involved were not quite as sharp as perhaps they could have been: the interrogations began.

What is known is that the Germans had absolutely no firm idea where the bullion had been moved. Their primary concern in the days following the invasion was to arrest King Haakon and his entourage and if they couldn't accomplish that then bombing the area of the King's last reported whereabouts was to become the norm. It has been long debated whether collaborators were passing on information to the Germans or whether the Germans were listening in to telephone messages and radio broadcasts or perhaps just relying on rumours. However they were receiving the information on the King, wherever he appeared, an uncannily short time later the bombers would arrive overhead.

It wasn't until the German capture of Lillehammer on May 1st that evidence was gathered by the Germans on what had happened to the gold. Employees from the town's banks were arrested, questioned and bullied about their knowledge of the bullion, but no one gave the game away and no one had any knowledge of how to open the vault. Eventually, the Germans hired a locksmith and the lock was drilled open, but to the dismay of the invaders the vault was bare, with the exception of a bunch of keys.

The Germans, having found nothing, reviewed their methods of investigation. It was clear to them that the operation to move tons of bullion from Oslo must have been well organised and have involved many people. It could not have been the sole operation of bank staff; there must have been external assistance. With the southern and central half of Norway secured from the Allies, intelligence began to filter through to those investigating the disappearance of the bullion. Focus now turned logically towards the railways. Unfortunately for the Germans what they didn't know was that the majority of the bullion was now in the UK having been transported there via HM cruisers *Galatea* and *Glasgow*. Unbeknown to them their cause was already lost.

As the German's attentions focused on the railways, a number of employees were arrested and interrogated, but like the bank workers no one breathed a word.

With the taking of Åndalsnes by the Germans on May 2nd more Norwegians were questioned. Gradually, the Germans were coming to realise that Molde had been the destination for at least some of the bullion, but again they had no idea where it actually was, if it had been taken north or hidden elsewhere. Even the crews of the local ferries were questioned – had they seen any boxes of valuables or unusual cargo? Yet again, no one knew anything.

Although Åndalsnes had been taken on May 2nd it was another three days before the Germans appeared in Molde – four days after *Glasgow* had left the port with her bullion consignment along with the Norwegian King, government and various VIPs. The Germans really had missed the boat. Nonetheless, once the Germans had secured Molde they began to interrogate various high-ranking people from the town in the hope that they could glean more information.

The interrogation was led by a German called Erich Opitz, an Abwehr radio operator who had worked closely with Major Berthold Benecke (Senior Abwehr agent in Norway) of the German Legation in Oslo.[183] Opitz's cover was that of a commercial attaché with the German Legation. Initially, he operated from the Grand Hotel and then from other less obvious abodes sending messages direct to Berlin. Clearly, prior to the invasion Opitz had been taking measures to be careful with his transmissions, but he wasn't careful enough as he failed to consider the radio skills of the Norwegian radio amateurs who duly reported their findings to the Norwegian General Staff. On April 4th, and as a direct consequence of these reports, Opitz and Benecke were considered to be 'persona non grata' by the Norwegian Ministry of Foreign Affairs and the men were requested to leave Norway at the earliest opportunity. However, the invasion on April 9th radically changed the situation and the two remained in Norway to 'extend their interests'.[184]

The interrogation experiences of the Norwegians must have been frightening, but again little was given away and credit must be given for having forestalled the Germans as long as they did. What was more worrying for the Norwegians though, was the use of a Norwegian collaborator who appeared to work closely with Opitz. This man was later named as 'Sandersen'. Apparently, this man was well acquainted with the gold transport; he appeared to know about telephone conversations that had taken place with regards to the identity of the puffers and, even more worryingly, he also had names of accomplices to the transport. The telephone system clearly had been infiltrated, but it would appear only after the transport had left Molde.

NB Subsequent research has failed to reveal the real identity of this Norwegian.

Abwehr Officer Opitz's interrogations widened. It was clear to him that the transport had been carried out using a variety of transport methods and he could see a pattern emerging. Further Norges Bank employees were arrested and questioned. Some were questioned only for a short time, but others received more rigorous questioning often being interrogated throughout the night.

There ended the German's frustrated attempts to locate the gold. Thwarted at every turn, Abwehr agent Erich Opitz had failed to break down his captives enough to obtain the information he was after. It was now clear that the bullion, or at least the majority of it, had left Norway for the UK and it became pointless to interrogate the Norwegians further. The Germans, for their part, had developed some of their techniques of interrogation. Those methods would come to haunt many Norwegians in the years to come and in some cases would kill them.

18

Atlantic Sailings

With the gold safely ensconced in the UK and the threat of German invasion uppermost in British and Norwegian minds, it was decided to ship the bullion to Canada and America as soon as possible. After all, Churchill had spirited away the UK gold reserves prior to the start of the war and it was clear to most people, especially after the miraculous Dunkirk evacuation of the British Expeditionary Force (BEF), that the German invasion was only days maybe just hours away. A palpable sense of anxiety lay across the country like an all-encompassing fog. Fortunately, the fear of invasion did not paralyse those charged with the safe keeping of the bullion. Mr Laverack, of the Bank of England, along with Ole Colbjørnsen and Fredrik Haslund at once set about planning to ship the bullion once more on several freighters. Matters concerning the gold were now in full swing as can be seen from the following letter sent to the Bank of England by the Norwegian authorities:

£2½ million to New York and similar to Montreal
We agree to your spreading the New York consignments over more than two vessels. We agree that the insurance should be effected in pound sterling and the journey from London to the British port should be included. The gold to New York should be consigned to the Federal Reserve Bank, New York, to be kept in safe custody for and on behalf of the Norwegian Government. The Norwegian Minister in Washington, Mr. Wilhem Morgenstierne is authorised to dispose of the gold for the account of the Royal Norwegian Government…the 2.5 million pounds to Montreal should similarly be consigned to the Bank of Canada, Montreal, to be kept in safe custody, for and on behalf of the Royal Norwegian Government…

The letter, three pages in length, confirmed that not all of the bullion would be shipped out.

> ...as explained to Mr Laverack these 547 cases (302 big and
> 245 small) which were recently landed at Plymouth, are
> for transhipment to Canada in our own steamers and should
> not be opened. Mr. Colbjørnsen and Mr. Haslund will take
> with them a first consignment of 250 cases (130 and 120
> small) on the M/S "Bomma" which is now being sent from
> the EC [East Coast] to Glasgow (she was actually headed
> for Leith) and is expected to be ready to leave in a few
> days time. There will be no other cargo onboard...at the
> same time we ask you to forward to the Royal Norwegian
> Legation, 10 Palace Green, London, W8, 5 - five - of the
> big cases. Kindly phone the Legation (the Minister or
> Mr. Raeder) so that a convenient time for arrival can
> be agreed upon. The remaining unopened cases 292 in all,
> whereof 167 big and 125 small, about equal quantities on
> two further Norwegian steamers...

Erik Colban and Øyvind Lorentzen signed the letter.

As a direct consequence of the letter and its instructions, the gold was taken by rail, part of which was originally from HMS *Enterprise,* to the port of Falmouth, in Cornwall on June 12th whereupon the boxes were loaded onto a tug to be taken out to the M/S *Bomma*, which had arrived safely and was now anchored in Falmouth Harbour. For security reasons it was decided to use more than one port for embarkation and to ensure that all went smoothly Colbjørnsen and Haslund were to sail with the *Bomma*. The bullion was embarked, but three days were to elapse before she sailed along with a convoy of other ships to Baltimore, which she duly reached on June 28th – again without incident. Once there the Americans provided an armed watch over her as she lay anchored in the outer harbour. On July 1st *Bomma's* precious cargo was unloaded and then conveyed via rail to the Federal Reserve Bank in New York and to the Bank of Canada in Ottawa.

With their part of the operation completed Colbjørnsen and Haslund travelled to Washington to begin making arrangements for the storage of the gold. Meanwhile, other shipments followed: M/S *Ida Bakke*, M/S *Bra Kar*, M/S *San Andres*; British liners *Duchess of York* and the *Duchess of Bedford* and sister ships *Western, Eastern* and *Northern Prince* among others.

London 10th June 1940

Dear Sirs,

Gold consignments for the Royal Norwegian Government

We have instructed the Bank of England to forward to you in two or more consignments with British liners bullion to the amount of 2.5 million pound sterling, to be kept by you in safe custody for and on behalf of the Royal Norwegian Government.

Confirming hereby our request to you, we beg to inform you that any two of the following four gentlemen shall be entitled to give orders for the disposal of the gold on behalf of the Royal Norwegian Government: M. Daniel Steen, Norwegian Consul General in Montreal, M Erik Colban, Norwegian Minister in London, M. Øivind Lorentzen, Norwegian Shipping Director in London and M. Ole Colbjørnsen, member of the Norwegian Storting and Special Representative of the Norwegian Ministry of Finance.

Trusting you will carry out this commission and thanking you in advance, we remain,

Yours faithfully,

Erik Colban   Øivind Lorentzen
Norwegian Minister in London   Norwegian Shipping Director

Bank of Canada,
Montreal.

Due to facilities not being available in Montreal the gold was held in Ottawa. As the ships arrived in Canada and the boxes counted, Mr Marble of the Bank of Canada sent cables and telegrams confirming safe arrival to Bolton of the Bank of England.

The final consignment took place on the July 18th when 30 boxes (box Nos. CO.159/188) were loaded onto the *Cameronia*. The operation was over: Norway's gold was safe and more importantly for the exiled Norwegian Government in London it could now be seen as an equal partner in the fight against tyranny, a task that it competently met and often exceeded.

For Haslund became the Social Welfare Officer for Norwegian sailors in America. But it was to be his leadership, resolve and utter persistence in transporting the gold that he would be most remembered for. Oscar Torp had chosen the best man possible.

19

The Issue of Gold

The significance of gold reserves had not been lost on the British, who at that time were desperate for the purchasing of war material. America possessed many of the answers to Britain's pressing needs, but in return the Americans wanted gold or dollars, despite President Roosevelt's sympathies. As far as Britain was concerned it didn't need to look too far for a willing partner and as early as July 1940 Norway was formally requested to present Britain with her complete gold reserves, estimated then at being some £13 million pounds sterling, although this figure was revised several times. Britain's stance was understandable, but the Norwegians had their own reasons to decline to assist. The exiled government had to remain strong; it couldn't be seen to be caving in to British demands to hand over state gold to purchase war material even if it would be in their joint interests to do so. For the Norwegians they had their people to consider – not just in Britain but also in occupied Norway and their status and position could have been placed in jeopardy if a nation's gold was handed over to a foreign power, albeit a friendly one. During one meeting dated November 4th 1940, the Norwegian Foreign Minister replied to Britain's Chancellor of the Exchequer and stated that:

> ...the Norwegian Government were prepared to do for the common cause all that was within their power, but it was their political duty to keep their gold reserves intact as much as possible. Although feelings in Norway were strongly in favour of the King's Government and hostile to Quisling, it would be a great mistake to under-estimate the possible effects of German propaganda. If the Government were now known to have handed over the gold, which was regarded as a national possession for which the Government were only trustees, great capital would be made of this in Norway and there was reason

to fear that, even if the Allies were victorious, the effect on public opinion in Norway would be fatal to the prospect of a restoration of the present Government after the war.

Norway though, did want to be seen as an equal partner in the fight against the Germans. It was a difficult dilemma which required tact and diplomacy if the Norwegians, and Britain for that matter, were not to lose face. In late September further meetings were held and it was put to Norway that they *pool their resources of gold and foreign currency* with Britain's.[185] The idea was for Norway to put the whole of their resources of gold and currency, whether owned by the Government or privately, at the disposal of Britain. In return Britain would undertake to supply the exiled Government with military and other supplies as well as currency if required. The British knew there was little chance of the Norwegians agreeing to this, but the seemingly endless meetings wore on. It was even suggested at one point that *'the Norges Bank be treated as "resident" and thus be subject to surrendering its foreign exchange'* ... to Britain's Exchange Control.[186]

The Norwegian Government sensibly decided to withhold their gold holdings and the Norwegian Minister of Finance, Oscar Torp firmly resisted the persistent heavy overtures of His Majesty's Treasury; the rebuff was taken by the British as rather unfriendly and for a time the relationship between the two countries was difficult. Britain was currently running down its own gold reserves in America and Canada as it sought to purchase war material and urgently needed to obtain more gold. Finally in March 1941 the British entered into an agreement with the Americans that became more commonly known as 'Lend-Lease' whereby material was obtained with the premise that it would be paid for after the war. The pressure was now off Norway. Such was the cost that Lend-Lease has only recently just reached its conclusion when the last payment to the Americans was made on 29th December 2006.

Norway also had its merchant fleet and this brought in welcome revenue under the NOTRASHIP agreement. Britain looked enviously at the dollar receipts the Norwegians were earning and despite some educated guesswork the Norwegian Government were cautious in advising Britain about how much they were receiving. But it should be pointed out that Britain received a favourable rate for the use of the Norwegian ships, in fact below the accepted merchant hire rate. With the income from NOTRASHIP, Norway was more than able to pay its way throughout the remainder of the war, but there was a heavy price to pay and like the UK the loss of ships and merchant marine-men was high. Nearly 600 ships and approximately 4500 sailors were lost to the ravages of war. In Britain there were murmurs of discontent at the amount of money the Norwegians were receiving from their merchant fleet, but this was hard won currency, earned in often tragic circumstances. What was not so well known was that in return the Norwegians paid significant figures for their armed forces in the UK; for the bases they flew from and the ports they sailed from, all without complaint. Norway was more than just an ally she was also an equal partner and one that sought no favours and certainly no credit.

On May 8th 1945 Norwegian and British troops landed in Norway bringing to an end hostilities in that country. On May 13th Crown Prince Olav and representatives of the Norwegian government returned to Norway followed by King Haakon on June 7th 1945 – exactly five years to the day after he left the country – returning to great scenes of jubilation throughout the country. But as the festivities gradually diminished so began the investigations into the role and participation of the various civilian administrations and armed forces that were involved throughout the war and as a result committees were formed to carry out those investigations. It wasn't just the Norwegian authorities that were asking questions – so were the British when they realised that Norges Bank was moving back to Norway.[187]

With the bank duly returned to Norway, a semblance of normality resumed once more as the country slowly began to rebuild itself. During the autumn of 1947 a committee was established and tasked by parliament to investigate the role of the bank whilst in exile in the UK as well as under occupation in Norway. Some, including various officials in the UK saw Norges Bank's role as trading with the enemy. But by 1948 the investigations were concluded that prior to the invasion the bank had prepared adequately, in fact probably better than most. Nicolai Rygg was a visionary and he had been absolutely correct in his actions. After the war, Rygg and his colleagues received recognition for their actions with the gold and for the manner in which they conducted the bank's business

```
        F. 1878/09

                                        8th June, 1945

Dear Mantle,

     The Bank of England tell us that the Norges Bank which
established its Head Office in this country on the occupation
of Norway by the Germans, has closed its office in London as
from the 26th May and has returned to Oslo.  When the Norges
Bank established its Head Office in London in 1940 the Bank
of England were issued with an authority by the Treasury under
T.W.E. legislation to place the assets of the Norges Bank
which are in the form of balances securities or gold at the
disposal of the Norges Bank established in London.

     The Bank of England now ask for a formal authority under
T.W.E. legislation which will enable the Bank to continue to
accept monies for the credit of Norges Bank's accounts with the
Bank of England and to act on instructions emanating from the
Norges Bank in Oslo signed by the existing signatories or any
new authorised signatories. At the same time the Bank will
require a Treasury authority to continue for the time being
to regard Norges Bank accounts with the Bank as those of a
resident of sterling area for D.F.R. purposes.

     I should like to establish with you the proper procedure
to be followed in cases of this kind, because we are likely
to get a number of them.  We have already had the cases of
Belgium and Greece, and in the latter case you issued the

                                              /authorities

P.J. Mantle, Esq.,
     Trading with the Enemy Dept.,
        24, Kingsway,
           W.C.2.
```

Author archive

whilst under occupation. For its part the bank had acted properly at all times and had actively sought to protect the monetary system that had been forced upon them. With complete sincerity and integrity the bank came through, paving the way for a peacetime economy.

It was not until December 1st 1987 that the Norwegian Government finally brought home the remaining gold that had been residing in the Federal Reserve Bank since 1940. SAS, Norway's principal airline was tasked with the job of transporting the remaining bullion back to Norway. The occasion was made even auspicious with the King of Norway, King Olav accompanying the bullion on the non-stop flight to Oslo landing at Fornebu airport (now closed). The following day a second flight arrived

The obverse and reverse of King Oscar II – King of Norway and Sweden.

carrying bullion, but this time from Ottawa in Canada. After 47 years of being cared for abroad the gold of Norway was finally home.

On January 28th 2004 Norges Bank issued a press release confirming that the bank had sold its shares of gold reserves amounting to some 16 tons. Further sales of gold bars were planned, but added that seven gold bars would be withheld from sale along with a substantial amount of coins that were part of the gold transport. The bars and coins would become part of an exhibition.

The sale of the gold brought about an income of 1½ billion Krone that was in turn given over to Norges Bank's foreign exchange reserves. At the end of 2003 Norges Bank's gold reserves totaled some 37 tons and were made up of 3½ tons of coins and 33½ tons of gold bars. The gold was eventually sold on the international gold market in London.

APPENDIX

Per Prag's Diary

During the research for this book an article in *'Aftenposten'* concerning the gold transport was written by the journalist Hilde Harbo asking people to come forward with their stories on the gold transport. As a direct result, Mr Muus Falk whose father was a friend of Per Prag's, via the Norwegian Resistance Museum, Oslo, has kindly donated the following story.

When the Germans invaded in 1940, I was stationed in Molde on the west coast as regional secretary of the Conservative Party, and I was 29 years old. I took my car to drive southwards so I could report for duty, and arrived in Lillehammer, famous tourist resort, 120 miles north of Oslo. I got a room at the Victoria Hotel, and soon realised that it was full of diplomats, government officials and military big shots.

In the evening I was approached by a senior civil servant, who asked whether I could drive a Frenchman to Ålesund on the west coast. I said I had already covered most of the way, and would do the job provided it would help the war effort. Shortly afterwards I was introduced to the French Ambassador, who gave me a pass signed by the Prime Minister, Johan Nygaardsvold. I told him I would have to go through the military roadblocks, and I did not think that the military would take kindly to a pass signed by a socialist prime minister.

After midnight I woke up by a knock on my door, and it was the French Ambassador who handed me a new pass. I believe I must be the only person who has received an ambassador in long johns! The pass was signed by General Otto Ruge, Commander-in-Chief of the Norwegian Armed Forces. Then I realised my task was highly important.

I met my French passenger, Monsieur Charles Gobinot, early in the morning. He was a pleasant man in his sixties. He had been wounded twice during the First World War. He brought a suitcase and two small bags, like those used by the doctors. I put his suitcase in the boot, but he sat himself in the rear seat with a black bag on either side.

At Otta I was flagged down by 25 year old Asbjørn Flatøy, who had been stranded on his way to Trondheim. I gave him a lift, but realised at the next stop that Gobinot was uneasy about accepting a passenger who had not gone through security. As events turned out, it proved to be a stroke of luck to have Asbjørn with us.

Having reached Rosten Bridge on top of the Gudbrandsdal Valley, we were stopped by three men, who told us that German parachutists had just landed north of us at Dovre. To my surprise, Charles Gobinot knew two of the men – Arne Sunde,[188] later to become Norway's first ambassador to the UN, and Benjamin Vogt, son of the Norwegian Minister in London.

Arne Sunde asked me to return to Otta with a message for the telegraph manager, who would relay it to the War Council in Lillehammer. At Otta, I had just read the message on the phone, when I met Birger Ljunberg, the Minister of Defence. I told him about the German parachutists, and he asked me to return to Rosten Bridge and to tell Arne Sunde that Norwegian troops would be on their way shortly. When he heard that I was travelling with Charles Gobinot – and he obviously knew about our mission – he said it would be too dangerous for Gobinot to remain where he was. He promised to ask the telegraph manager to arrange for a safe place for us until the Germans were captured. So I took Gobinot and Asbjørn with me back to Otta, where we were directed to an old but comfortable farm in the Ottadal Valley.

After a couple of days at the farm, the telegraph manager informed us that Norwegian forces would rush the Germans that evening, and we should be able to proceed the next morning. We motored up to Kirkestuen Hotel at Dovre, where we got rooms for the night. The small hotel was chocker-block full of 50 men from the local Red Cross ambulance, mostly sleeping on the floors.

I woke up about 5 in the morning, when somebody called my name. I rushed to the window, and saw Trygve Lie outside. He shouted to me to open the door, and I registered that this was the second time I presented myself to a big shot dressed only in long johns.

It transpired that the only guests left at the hotel were Gobinot, Asbjørn and myself. The 50-strong ambulance team had fled – along with the hotel's staff. There had been some considerable shooting, but we had not heard it.

Trygve Lie[189] asked if I could make some coffee in the kitchen, and by that time we were joined by the Foreign Minister, Halvdan Koht,[190] who proved to be a great friend of Gobinot. I invaded the empty kitchen, and made coffee – which was the best coffee I have tasted at five in the morning, as the Foreign Minister complimented me.

The position between the Germans and the Norse was not quite clear that morning, and Trygve Lie asked me to take him northwards to a safe point. I did, and we returned to Dovre church, where Trygve Lie took up a stand at the porch. I remained in my car, when I heard shots, and I thought that Trygve Lie had been hit, but he shouted to me "start up the car". I tried, but the car would not start, and Trygve Lie shouted, "switch on the ignition"! Which I did, and then he flung himself into my car and I accelerated beyond the reach of the Germans.

On the way back to Kirkestuen Hotel, we were stopped by two men – and to my surprise they were Crown Prince Olav and Arne Sunde. I gave them a lift in my car and wondered whether anybody had ever given a lift to the Crown Prince of Norway. Further down the road we were halted by a number of cars, whose passengers were changing into snow-white deceptive clothing. I could see King Haakon among them.

Charles Gobinot then had some serious meetings with members of the government and afterwards he told Asbjørn and I that he had decided to drive through the German lines – because "Germans don't shoot civilians"! And this was in 1940!

We set out in the morning, and passed the point where Norwegian troops had fired at the Germans, and the ground was littered with spent cartridges. I believe some Norwegians had been killed there.

Further on, we saw the farmhouse where the Germans had sought refuge. Some of them came out, carrying machine guns at the ready. I was driving very slowly, and when I looked back at the rear seat, I saw that Gobinot had opened both black bags and held a hand firmly inside both of them. Then we were stopped by a truck, which had blocked the road.

'Get out of the car and move the truck' said Gobinot. 'But I have never driven a truck', I said. 'Do it now', replied Gobinot. I clambered over the snowdrifts and approached the truck from its left-hand side. What I saw made me vomit. Blood was splattered everywhere and it was obvious that no amateur could move the truck. The Germans – about half a dozen of them – were now standing on the other side of the fence. I returned to my car, and without a word being said, I started to back out of there, until I found a spot where I could turn and start on the way back. Going downhill I stopped at a point where I knew the Germans could no longer see us, and I lit a cigarette. 'Donnez moi un cigarette aussi', said Gobinot and I handed him the pack with a match box, and I had the personal pleasure of seeing that his hands shivered just as much as mine.

Back at the telegraph office in Otta, the manager told us that the government now wanted us to proceed across the mountain plateau on skis to Geiranger, and every effort would be made by his friends to speed up the journey. He certainly did fulfill his promise. Our feet were measured for ski boots, and we started the drive up the Ottadal Valley. At one spot we were flagged down by a young boy whose name was Per (I met him 12 years later), and he gave us boots and skis, which fitted admirably. We followed instructions and drove on to Pollfross where we were met by a young boy with a reindeer and sledge. This was where we put on our skis. Gobinot had never been skiing, but it only took a few strides on the snow before he got the idea. That Frenchmen had guts! Our luggage was loaded on to the sledge, but before Gobinot released his two black bags I had to get the boy to promise that he would never get out of eyesight of Gobinot.

We reached Grotli Hotel on the mountain plateau, only 24 miles from Geiranger, and decided to sleep a few hours before tackling the steep descent towards Geiranger. As we left in the morning, we met two Norwegian ship-owners, who were on their way to New York. They were heading for Stryn on the west coast and asked why I had chosen Geiranger. "Because the boy and his reindeer have opted for Geiranger", I said. As it turned out, we arrived in Geiranger 24 hours before the ship-owners did. But then, their journey had not been planned by the telegraph manager at Otta!

At the end of the long frozen lake we were ambushed by 5 armed men, who turned out to be telegraph workers, alerted by the telegraph manager at Otta. They took the lead and escorted us down the steep slopes above Geiranger. We sat on our skis and scrubbed with our feet, finally reaching the bottom of the descent. Here, we were met by a horse and sledge and further downhill we were transferred to a truck, which took us right down to the quay. The post boat to Ålesund had been kept waiting for us for more than an hour, but the overnight trip took us to Ålesund in comfort. Asbjørn and I had a real treat, when Gobinot opened a bottle of strong spirits, and treated us to a really welcome drink.

On arrival in Ålesund, Gobinot was unable to walk, and we got him a lift in the van of Grand Hotel, which took us to the military office, where I got an official receipt for the safe delivery of Monsieur Charles Gobinot.

So what was this secret mission all about? I had my own guess at the time, but I did not know the truth until I met Charles Gobinot again – strolling the deck of the British cruiser HMS *Devonshire*, which transported

King Haakon and his Government from Tromsø beyond the Arctic Circle to Scotland. Gobinot told me that the Allies had decided that Vigra radio station near Ålesund should be the focal point for communications between Allied fleets and the ground forces in Norway. And the French Ambassador had been entrusted to bring the Allied codebooks to the radio station.

But how could you take the risk of driving right into the hands of the German parachutists, I asked Gobinot. No, said Gobinot. They would shoot the driver first – and that was you – and that would give me a split second to flick my thumbs, which would activate the explosives in both bags, and we would all be blown to kingdom come – including the code books! It was not until the bombing of London that I felt so close to death! Asbjørn and I had to return the same way via Geiranger to pick up the car at Pollfoss, and we drove down to Otta, where we reported for duty at the Telegraph manager's office. He said there is another secret job waiting for you, check in at the Grand Hotel and ask for a CA Stang, a barrister from Oslo. We met him, and he said he had been asked by the Minister of Finance to locate the Head of the Bank of Norway. Stang had reason to believe that the bank chief was in Tønset, where the Government had appointed a new governor (Fylkesmann). So we started up the Fampus road past Rosten Bridge and Kirkestuen Hotel, until we reached Dombås rail junction of tracks to Oslo, Trondheim and Åndalsnes. We stopped at Dombås Tourist Hotel for lunch, we thought, but the Germans then started to bomb the railway station – where they killed the American military attaché, as he was standing just outside the railway tunnel. We escaped by driving on the Dovre mountain plateau.

We arrived at Tynset and were given a splendid supper, during which I went to sleep through sheer exhaustion. I woke up by the Governor shouting that the Germans were coming, and he dropped me in my long-johns and other clothing unceremoniously in to my car, whilst his staff got Stang and Asbjørn pushed into my car. I did not even have time to put on my trousers, because I started the car as the Germans entered the village from the south.

We travelled northwards from Tynset, and had a slight accident, when I went to sleep at the wheel, but the car luckily stopped in the snow in the roadside. When we reached Ullsberg, my passenger CA Stang was arrested by a young army lieutenant. I did not know at the time, but after waiting an hour or so, I walked up to the local HQ and asked the young lieutenant why he kept my passenger as a prisoner. He said it was a peculiar mission to try to locate the whereabouts of the Chief of the Bank of Norway, but when I showed him my "passport" signed by the Commander-in-Chief of the Norwegian Army, General Otto Ruge, he reluctantly let us go.

We then motored via Oppdal and the entire length of the Sunndal valley to Sunndalsøra, where we were met by an unbelieving array of army officers, who told us that the entire road had been bombed by a German aircraft for about an hour before our arrival. We knew. We had seen and heard them!

So we arrived in Molde. My flat was in fine shape, but somehow we knew that the Germans were around, because the King and Government were staying in Molde. Asbjørn and I reported to Einar Gerhardsen (later to become Prime Minister), and he asked Asbjørn to return to Oslo to get the families of the Government members to travel northwards. I never met Asbjørn again until we were both bombed in London in December 1940. Gerhardsen asked me to report for duty at the office of Fylkesmann (Governor) Trygve Utheim.

My first job at the Fylkesmann's office was to take care of the foreign diplomats stranded in Molde by the Government. Luckily, the father of two of my girlfriends in Molde owned timber huts on a small island north of Molde, and I accommodated the Hungarian Ambassador and his wife in one hut, the other being occupied by the Finnish Minister and Count Douglas of Sweden plus CA Stang and myself.

I returned to the island every evening – by rowing across the sound until one evening, when all hell broke loose. The Swedish count had decided to return to Oslo, but the Finnish minister objected and used his fists to knock out the Swedish Count. I told the contestants that there was precious little to fight about, because the Germans were expected to land in Molde the next day.

Next morning I was asked by Governor Utheim to drive to the innermost part of the Romsdal Fjord to pick up the wife and children of Sigbjørn Mustad, MP, who was staying with us on the island. I got there in the nick of time, because the Germans were on the other side of the fjord, thanks to the fact that good Norwegians had kept the ferry on the other side of the fjord.

Finally, I stood in the Governor's office, when a German naval plane landed on the Molde fjord. The Governor had a stand-by fishing boat at Vevang, and I implored him to come with me to the boat, but he said he had to stay behind to safeguard Norwegian interests. So I left alone in my car and drove to the island, where I picked up Mustad and Stang, and then on to Vevang to join the fishing boat. I met Governor Utheim in London several months later, when he was appointed a member of the exile government.

There were five of us on the boat, escaping from Molde to north Norway. One of them was Lars Evensen, prominent trade union leader, later to become a member of the post-war Norwegian government. As days went past, we were talking about what would happen in Norway before the war was over, and it was almost uncanny how Lars Evensen proved to be correct. He said – and named – dissidents in the Labour Party who would step forward and offer their services to the Nazis. I cannot remember names, but his forecast was accurate.

It took a week to journey from Vevang to Tromsø, and we had several incidents en route. During a short stay at Harstad we were bombed, but survived. In Tromsø we rented a house that belonged to the former Nazi mayor – and the tenants consisted of Professor Karl Keilhau, barrister C A Stang, Miss Unni Diesen (daughter of the admiral and secretary to the Foreign Minister), Finn Hansen (private secretary to the Prime Minister) and myself. Keilhau arranged for me to get a dual job – as assistant to the board of Bank of Norway, and as secretary – to the board of Norwegian Broadcasting. My boss in both jobs was Dr Arnold Raestad, twice foreign minister in the late liberal government.

The war in Norway took a turn for the worse in early June 1940, and I remember that Dr Raestad took me aside and asked whether I wanted to continue the fight in England. I answered YES – unhesitatingly – and I went to the chief of police to get a new passport. On Thursday June 7 – Norway's Flag Day we left Tromsø on board the British cruiser, the HMS Devonshire, 105 of us, including King Haakon.

I forgot to tell you about an incident, which happened a couple of weeks before withdrawal from Norway. During a board meeting at the Bank of Norway we had a frenzied phone call from the manager of the Bank of Norway branch in Bodø, saying he had run out of cash. The chairman, Dr Arnold Raestad, authorised J Nørve, a member of the board, to proceed to Bodø with five million Krone in bank notes, and asked me to accompany him. We set off in a small fishing boat with two local boys. As we entered Bodø harbour, the Germans started bombing. Nørve and I climbed to the very top of Landego Island, where we had a bird's eye view of the wanton destruction of Bodø. Afterwards, we tied up in the port and contacted the local Bank of Norway representatives, who received the cash. Then we returned to Tromsø. Professor Keilhau received a phone call late at night from the manager of Bank of Norway in Harstad, saying he had thirty thousand pounds sterling in his vault, and, knowing about the impending withdrawal, he asked what we could do about it. I told Keilhau that the Navy had an aircraft which called at Tromsø twice a day, and I would be willing to accompany it to Harstad to pick up the cash. Professor Keilhau phoned the naval office, but was told that the admiral was asleep, and nothing could be done. So much for wartime red tape: and in due course the Germans got the cash.

HMS *Devonshire* steamed northwards from Tromsø and skirted Spitsbergen, because it was evident that the Germans were out in full to hit King Haakon and his Government.

We were treated well onboard ship, and it felt like being cruise passengers, until 5am one morning we woke up to the sound of heavy guns firing. Nothing happened to us, but at midday I was told by Charles Gobinot that the German battleships Gneisenau and Scharnhorst had sunk the British aircraft carrier Glorious and two destroyers, sailing about 30 miles behind us. Obviously, the Germans had thought that the King and Crown Prince and Government were on board the aircraft carrier. This mistake had probably saved our lives.

We were transferred from HMS *Devonshire* on board a lighter, and then we stood on firm ground again – in Scotland. It was only when we stood there, we realised for the first time that now we were exiles. The problem was made clear when a well-meaning immigration officer started to stutter the names of the exiles. Then, almost as out of another world, the President of the Storting, J. C. Hambro, stepped forward, and gently took the list out of the hands of the immigration officer, and said "Perhaps I can make the job easier for you" Hambro then started in his most stentorian manner from the Storting to read out the names of the refugees. Mine was the second last name to be called. Hambro started by ringing out the name of "Prime Minister Johan Nygaardsvold", and the Premier shouted "HERE". And so it went on, the list involving 105 names. From Gourock, we travelled in a most luxurious train, which proved to be the personal train of King George VI. We had wonderful food and plenty of drinks – until we arrived at Euston station about 10 pm. King George turned up in person to greet King Haakon, and took him to Buckingham Palace… On arrival in London, we were met by officials from the Norwegian Embassy, and all non-government officials were taken to South Kensington Hotel.'

Per Prag

Map Routes
of the Gold Transport

Notes

1   Haarr, G, *The German Invasion of Norway:* Seaforth Publishing, Barnsley, 2009, p. 3. NB this publication is now widely regarded as the most definitive account of the German invasion. If the reader wishes to understand more about the complexities and events of April 1940 then this book is heartily recommended.

2   Taylor, A.J.P. *The Second World War – An Illustrated History:* Penguin, London, 1976, p. 17.

3   Ibid.

4   Knight, N, *Churchill – The Greatest Briton Unmasked:* David & Charles, Newton Abbot, 2008, pp. 96–97.

5   The League of Nations had been set up when peace negotiations began in October 1918; President *Woodrow Wilson* of the USA stated that the *Fourteen Points* plan should serve as a basis for the signing of the *Armistice.* The League of Nations had no armed forces and relied on boycotts if nations contravened the rules. There were sixty nations signed up to the agreement including Britain, Germany, France and Norway. Germany resigned from the League in October 1933. France resigned in April 1941. The League of Nations was replaced by the United Nations in 1945.

6   Taylor, A.J.P. *The Second World War – An Illustrated History:* Penguin, London, 1976, p. 30.

7   Ibid., p. 32.

8   Radio broadcast from the Prime Minister of Great Britain & Northern Ireland Neville Chamberlain on 3rd September 1939. Directly after his speech the air-raid sirens sounded in London. It was a false alarm.

9   Belgium had declared herself as neutral.

10 Gilbert, M. *The Churchill War Papers – At the Admiralty Vol 1:* Heinemann, 1993, p. 6. Churchill had previously been forced to resign his original Admiralty post in 1915 as a result of the failures of the Dardanelles campaign.

11 Gilbert, M. *The Churchill War Papers – At the Admiralty Vol 1:* Heinemann, 1993, p. 6.

12 Gilbert, M. The Churchill War Papers – *At the Admiralty Vol 1*: Heinemann, 1993, pp. 120–121. This comment by Churchill was not factual. No mines were actually laid.

13   Robert, A. *The Holy Fox – Biography of Lord Halifax:* Weidenfield & Nicholson, 1991.

14   Churchill, W.S. *The Second World War, vol 1:* Cassell, London, 1948, p. 424. Please note that Churchill's account was written after the war and is not 100% consistent with the minutes taken at the meeting.

15   The *Deutschland* class *Graf Spee* was one of three heavily armoured cruisers. The term 'pocket-battleships' was coined by the British due to the ship's main armament of six 11inch (280mm) guns. The Kriegsmarine later classed them as heavy cruisers.

16   Kersaudy, F. *Norway 1940:* Collins, Glasgow 1990, p. 24.

17   Ibid., p. 62.

18   Rankin, N, *Churchill's Wizards – The British Genius for Deception 1914–1945:* Faber & Faber, London, 2008, p. 233.

19   Beesly, P. *Very Special Intelligence – The Story of the Admiralty's Operational Intelligence Centre 1939–1945:* Chatham Publishing, 1977, p. 37.

20   Denham, H. *Inside the Nazi Ring (A Naval Attaché in Sweden):* John Murray, London, 1984, pp. 2, 4.

21   Haarr, G, *The German Invasion of Norway:* Seaforth Publishing, Barnsley, 2009, p. 56.

22   Lieutenant Commander Gerard B. Roope was later posthumously awarded the Victoria Cross for his deeds.

23   *Plan R4* was an initiative to pre-empt a possible German reaction to the mining of the Norwegian Leads. British troops were embarked in HM cruisers and troop ships ready to sail to the ports of Trondheim, Narvik, Stavanger, and Bergen. The plan was not implemented due to the German invasion of April 9th 1940.

24   Weser is the name of a river in Germany.

25   *Brassey's Naval Annual.* 1948. H.G. Thursfield, ed. New York: Macmillan, 1948.

26   This order originated from Commanding Admiral Diesen. During the evacuation of Norway, Admiral Diesen was transported to Britain on the *Ulster Prince.*

27   Also known as Räumboote. Used mainly for minesweepers and escort duties. Designed to operate in shallow waters. Similar in size and shape to the 'C' Class British motor launches.

28   Part of transcript of Mr Fevang's interview carried out by Stian Trovik, Lillehammer.

29   Report from First Lieutenant Fregattenkapitän Erich Heymann, with thanks to Geirr Haarr.

30   It was the Polish submarine *Orzel* (meaning Eagle in Polish).

31   Kersaudy, F. *Norway 1940:* Collins, Glasgow 1990, p. 65.

32   Michael, M. *Haakon King of Norway:* Allen & Unwin, London, 1958.

33 National Archives reference: FO371/24829.
34 The time Koht and Bräuer met was approximately the same time that *Blücher* received hits from the batteries at Oscarsborg Fort.
35 Koht, H. *Norway Neutral and Invaded:* Hutchinson, London, 1941, pp. 66–67.
36 Ibid., p. 76.
37 Haarr, G, *The German Invasion of Norway:* Seaforth Publishing, Barnsley, 2009, p. 177.
38 Gilbert, M. *The Churchill War Papers – At the Admiralty Vol 1:* Heinemann, London, 1993, p. 991.
39 Sir John Colville, CB, CVO was a British civil servant who kept wartime diaries of his time with the then Prime Minister, Winston Churchill. He died November 1987.
40 Dik Lehmkuhl, *Journey to London:* Hutchinson, London, 1942, p. 49. Lehmkuhl writes that the simple code completely hoodwinked the Germans.
41 *The War Illustrated* – April 1940, Vol 2 No 34.
42 *The War – Incorporating War Pictorial* – April 19th 1940, No. 26, p. 777.
43 National Archive reference: T1/12177. NB the paragraph, originating from one of Hambro's agents in Norway was copied and included in the letter.
44 Nicolai Rygg was born the son of a shoemaker on the 29th February 1872. His background clearly did not restrict him though, and eventually he rose to become an economist and Professor in state economy and statistics from 1910–13. Promotion as Director of Central Bureau of Statistics (Statistisk sentralbyrå) from 1913 to 1920 prepared him well for his next post – that of Governor of the Bank of Norway (Norges Bank). He held this post in Norway from 1920–1946. Rygg's hobbies included mountaineering and writing books. He was also the author of the History of Norges Bank. Married to Agnes they had one child, Else who tragically only survived for two weeks (25.9.1911–7.10.1911). Rygg passed away in 1957 and is buried at Vestre Gravlund Cemetery, Oslo.
45 A gold bar weighs about 400 ounces or 11.3 kg, but the bullion markets will accept bars ranging from 350 ounces to 430 ounces. Most bars, however, are close to 400 ounces so an imperial ton (2000 pounds or 32,000 ounces) contains about 80 bars of gold. A bar of gold is assayed and the actual purity of the gold is stamped on the bar together with a registration number. A bar of gold considered to be 'good delivery' will not be less than 995 parts gold in 1000 parts. The amount of gold that was rescued from Norway was approximately 50 tons and was made up of 818 large crates at 40 kg per crate, 685 smaller crates at 25 kg each and 39 kegs weighing in at 80 kg each. The kegs were filled with 5 bags of bullion and each bag contained 1000 coins.
46 National Archives reference: T 236/215.
47 Armed bank guards were employed by Norges Bank. They trained with their firearms at Akershus Fort, Oslo prior to WW2.

48 *Orienteering,* 1990 – Norges Bank in-house magazine.

49 Ibid.

50 Quisling made his first broadcast at 19:32. The meeting at Hamar broke up around 19:40. Nobody from the government at Hamar heard that broadcast.

51 Radio broadcast by Vidkun Quisling on April 9th 1940.

52 Koht, H. *Norway Neutral and Invaded:* Hutchinson, London, 1941, pp. 79–80.

53 Rognes, according to some, later became closely associated with the gold transport; although to date the author has been unable to prove this. However, Rognes did become instrumental in setting up early resistance in Norway, being one of the pioneers of MILORG, the Norwegian military resistance group. His exploits rapidly came to the attention of the British and eventually he was brought to the UK in Feb 1941. Initially, Rognes was posted to the Shetlands to work with other Norwegians with the famed *'Shetland Bus'* and became known as *'Kapteinen på Shetlands'* – 'Captain on the Shetlands'. His involvement with the resistance, including such famed fighters as Max Manus and later with Norwegian SOE has never really been fully appreciated.

54 Kersaudy, F. *Norway 1940:* Collins, Glasgow 1990, p. 80.

55 Pettersen was accepted on the Norges Bank Board in 1939 and Skurdal in 1935. Source: Ole-Johan Olsen of Norges Bank.

56 A diversionary force of 350 Royal Marines – *'Operation Henry'* – was landed at Namsos on the 14th April.

57 Lieutenant Diesen was Admiral Diesen's son.

58 Some reports have suggested as few as 8–9 Ju-52 aircraft arrived over the Dombås area. However, Geirr Haarr's account is finely detailed and it is his figures I have made use of.

59 National Archive reference: ADM199/482.

60 Colonel Thue, officer commanding Infantry Regiment 11 (IR11), around April 23rd, handed over to Trygve Lie the sum of one million, one hundred thousand kroner in cash. This cash was presented to Lie in suitcases with a full inventory of the contents. Receipts were also signed and handed over. Apparently, the cash had been stored in a farm cellar.

61 The question raised in the House also requested information about the Danish gold reserves. Sir John Simon, later The Right Honourable Viscount Simon, was a liberal politician and Chancellor of the Exchequer from 1937–1940. He resigned in May 1940 to become Lord High Chancellor of Great Britain. He never served in Churchill's War Cabinet. Reference: *HC Deb 16 April 1940 vol 359 c792.*

62 Jøstadmoen camp was situated close to the town of Lillehammer. The camp is still in use.

63 Albert Viljam Hagelin (1881–1946) was a Minister of Domestic Affairs in Quisling's National Samling Government. He was shot at Akerhus Fort, Oslo

in May 1946 after being found guilty of treason during the Norwegian Post-War Trials.

64 An English translation of Grieg's original text by unknown transcriber. Document resides in the Imperial War Museum, London. Ref: 8934 Misc 16 (356).

65 Many people left the party after purges by the NS. The organisation had become concerned about those not fully supporting Quisling.

66 This is an English translation of Grieg's original text. The transcriber is unknown, but this document resides in the Imperial War Museum, London. Ref: 8934 Misc 16 (356).

67 Haslund gave four radio broadcasts from Boston, USA in 1940 describing the events that surrounded the gold transport.

68 There were 10 type G3 rail trucks and two passenger coaches. Source: Norwegian Railway Museum.

69 Harnes, P.A. *Gulltransporten – dramaet dag for dag:* Romsdal Sogelag, 2006, p. 30.

70 This is an English translation of Grieg's original text. The transcriber is unknown, but this document resides in the Imperial War Museum, London. Ref: 8934 Misc 16 (356).

71 Harnes, P.A. *Gulltransporten – dramaet dag for dag:* Romsdal Sogelag, 2006, pp. 31–32.

72 Churchill had made an arrangement with the Admiralty to issue to him first all telegrams on Norway, thus he was in a position of knowledge long before his contemporaries. Source Kersuady, 1990.

73 This transmitter was apparently offered to Foley by the Colonel commanding Åndalsnes district HQ. Source: Margaret Reid's War Diary, Gyldendal Norsk Forlag, 1980 (English Translation), p. 35.

74 Kersaudy, F. *Norway 1940:* Collins, Glasgow 1990, p. 109. Authors' note: Francis Edward Foley was a British Secret Service agent (joined in 1918). His designated code was A1. During the evacuation of Norway, Foley, along with his secretary Margaret Reid, was transported to Britain on the *Ulster Prince*. After the Norwegian Campaign he was given the task of questioning Rudolph Hess. In 1949 Foley retired to Stourbridge (there are memorials to him in Stourbridge, his birthplace Highbridge, the Foreign & Commonwealth Office, London, Israel and Berlin). He is reputed to have saved over 10,000 Jews in his role as a Passport Control Officer in Berlin. He passed away in 1958.

75 Ibid., p. 81.

76 Derry, T. K. *The Campaign in Norway:* 1952. Author's note: the complete book is available to download on-line.

77 The railway is a branch line of the Oslo to Trondheim main line.

78 Andresen, AP, *I Natt Og Tåke Mot England*, Cappelen, 1992 p. 18.

79   Donald, W. *Standby for Action – A Sailor's Story:* William Kimber, London, 1956, p. 22.

80   Ibid., p. 23.

81   The Admiral was in fact Rear Admiral John Guy Protheroe Vivian KBE, CB.

82   Authors note: HMS *Black Swan* later received a direct hit that passed through the quarter-deck, right through the wardroom, passed through a fresh water tank, exited the aft magazine and between two ratings who were carrying shells and out through the hull between the two propeller shafts. The bomb fortunately failed to explode, although some members of the crew were badly hurt. HMS *Black Swan* was patched up to make her seaworthy and she duly made for Scapa Flow. She survived the war.

83   *The War Illustrated' May 17th 1940.* Author's note: it is possible that this quote is purely propaganda and therefore must be treated with caution.

84   Andreas Lund's report to Norges Bank dated 21st June 1946. Source: Norges Bank, Oslo.

85   Author's personal interview with Ove Voldsrud in 2007 at his home in the presence of his family.

86   Some aircraft were lost to anti-aircraft fire over Åndalsnes whilst others crashed due to possible mechanical faults.

87   The Royal Norwegian naval vessel *Trygg* was eventually lost to a bomb that passed through the ship, but fortunately did not explode. However, *Trygg* was severely holed and as a result she sunk.

88   National Archives reference: ADM116/4680.

89   Admiral Sir Philip Louis Vian GCB, KCB, KBE, CMG & DSO with two bars, St Olav's Medal with Oakleaves. Vian was perhaps most famous for his rescue of 299 prisoners from the German ship 'Altmark' in Feb 1940.

90   Captain Michael Maynard Denny, RN (later Sir): the Senior Naval Officer (SNO) in charge of Åndalsnes and Molde. He was made Captain in 1936. Awarded the following recognitions: Companion of the Order of the Bath for services at Åndalsnes & Dunkirk in 1940; the St Olav Medal in February 1943 for his part in the Norwegian campaign; Commander of the British Empire in the New Years Honours List of 1944; Mentioned in Dispatches for his part in the attack on the Tirpitz in April 1944; Distinguished Service Order (DSO) for his part in Operation Iceberg of October 1945; Knight Commander of the Order of the Bath (KCB) in Her Majesty's Birthday Honours List of 1950 and finally Knight Grand Cross of the Order of the Bath (CGB) in Her Majesty's Birthday Honours List of 1954. Born October 1896 he passed away in April 1972. He was Senior Naval Officer, Åndalsnes landing, Norway; Chief Staff Officer, evacuation of Dunkirk – both 1940 and from June 1940 he was Flag Captain, HMS *Kenya* (cruiser) & Chief Staff Officer to Rear-Admiral Commanding 10th Cruiser Squadron (Malta and Russia convoys, Vaagso Raid, Norway 1941). Denny was evacuated from

Molde on 30th April at 22:45 on the *Ulster Prince*. Source: National Archives ADM/196/56.

91 National Archives: CAB 44/72.

92 Ibid.

93 Ibid.

94 Ibid.

95 National Archives reference: ADM199/482.

96 Author's note: Kristian Gleditsch was born in 1901 and died in 1973. He was a graduate engineer and later became director of the Norwegian Graphical Survey. During the invasion Gleditsch and his wife, Nini, followed the government to Lillehammer. When appointed to become Haslund's deputy he duly followed the gold transport from Åndalsnes to Tromsø. His wife returned to the UK on HMS Devonshire, along with the King and government, but Kristian Gleditsch took a more circuitous route via Russia and Canada and eventually entered the UK four months later. Gleditsch remained in London until the end of the war whereupon he returned to Norway.

97 Martin Linge was an actor prior to the war, but was perhaps better known as Captain Linge, the commander of 'Linge Company' also known as 'Kompani Linge' and NORIC1 (Norwegian Independent Company No. 1) – a Norwegian Special Forces group used exclusively by the Special Operations Executive (SOE) for operations in Norway. Captain Linge tragically lost his life on 27th December 1941 during 'Operation Archery' – the raid on Måloy on South Vågsøy, Norway.

98 Foreign & Commonwealth Office publication 1996. When Britain declared war on Germany in September 1939 Germany was sorely in need of funds to fuel her war economy and her economic base was still too weak to enable a protracted conflict. Germany had already acquired gold from Austria, Czechoslovakia and Danzig. To add Norwegian bullion to fund the German war machine would have been very welcome.

99 Kristian and Nini Haslund Gleditsch worked for the Norwegian Aid Committee to Spain during the Spanish Civil War. Kristian Gleditsch was secretary from 1936–1937. Nini remained in Spain from 1937–1939 organising medicine and food for children. She later worked with the victims and refugees of the conflict.

100 HMS Galatea – Captain Brian Betham Schofield, RN (27th February 1940 – 1st March 1941).
    Source: National Archives: ADM/196/118.

101 The brother of Major Bjorn Sunde, Major Arne Sunde was onboard HMS *Galatea* (and this was to cause some dramatic confusion later amongst some Norwegians), along with Ben Vogt and Vice-President Øyvind Lorentzen, who were later to be instrumental in the NOTRASHIP agreement.

102 National Archive reference: T236/215.

103 Ronald Palmer later became Chief Writer of the Pay Office – the most senior rating of the Lower Deck serving on HMS Galatea when war broke out. He had joined the 'Senior Service' prior to WW2.

104 HMS *Galatea* was lost to a torpedo strike by U557 on 15th December 1941 with a resultant heavy loss of life. 22 officers and 440 ratings went down with the ship, but 144 men were saved. U557 was lost the next day to an accidental ramming by the Italian motor torpedo boat *Orione*. There were no survivors from the German submarine.

105 John Henry Godfrey was born in Handsworth, Birmingham, in July 1888. He was educated at King Edward Grammar School, Birmingham, and Bradfield College. In 1903 he served on HMS *Britannia* as a naval cadet, being promoted Midshipman (1904), Acting Sub-Lieutenant (1907), Sub-Lieutenant (1908) and Lieutenant (1909). He served on the destroyers *Welland* (1909), *Bramble* (1910–12), *Blanche* (1913), *Charybdis*, (1914) and *Euryalus* (1914–16). He was promoted to Lieutenant-Commander (1916) and served in the Mediterranean and Black Sea (1917–19). He was also mentioned in dispatches and awarded the Légion d'honneur (Chevalier) and the Order of the Nile. After his appointment as War Staff Officer in the Home Fleet in 1919, and promotion to Commander in 1920, he served in Plans Division (1921–23), and at the Staff College, Greenwich (1923–25). He was appointed second in command of *Diomede* in New Zealand (1925–28), promoted to Captain in 1928, was Deputy Director, Staff College (1929–31), and commanded *Suffolk* in the China Station (1931–33), before returning as Deputy Director, Plans Division (1933–36). He commanded HMS *Repulse* in the Mediterranean (1936–38) and then served as Director of Naval Intelligence and Rear-Admiral (February 1939–December 1942). In 1942 he was appointed Vice-Admiral. Godfrey was subsequently appointed Flag Officer commanding the Royal Indian Navy in February 1943. He had been placed on the retired list and promoted to Admiral (September 1945) but continued to serve in his old rank until March 1946. He returned to England and after leave finally retired in September 1946. Godfrey was awarded CB in 1939. He died in August 1971 at Eastbourne. Source: www.janus.lib.cam.ac.uk

106 Gleditsch, Nini and Kristian, *Glimt Fra Kampånene*, Dreyers Forlag, Oslo, 1954, p. 47.

107 Ibid., pp. 47–48.

108 Fannestranda is a roadway that emerges from the centre of Molde out towards the end of the fjord. Large summer houses line the route.

109 Letter to author.

110 The Norwegian Government and Royal party arrived in Molde on the 23rd April.

111 Grieg, Nordahl. *Flagget,* Gyldendal, Oslo, 1945 p. 23.

112 Per Bratland (1907–1988), photographer. Bratland is well known for his picture

of King Haakon and Crown Prince Olav standing by a Silver Birch tree during a lull in the bombing of Molde. The article appeared in rbnett and was written by Per Kåre Tveeikrem and published 28.04 2010 – the anniversary of King Haakon and the famous picture. See website for further details: http://translate. google.co.uk/translate?hl=en&sl=no&u=http://www.rbnett.no/krigsvaaren/ article212139.ece&prev=/Dimvns&sa=X&ei=JZGWUOffCejE0QW3mICQ Ag&sqi=2&ved=0CC4Q7gEwAg

113 Bratland, Per. *Er Vi Slik?* Aschehoug & Co., Oslo, 1971, pp. 54–72.

114 The Vecko Journal, a Swedish a weekly publication in 1940 but now published on a monthly basis.

115 In Harnes' book, *'Gulltransporten – dramaet dag for dag'* he mentions that during the autumn of 1941 Per Bratland was visited in London by Nordahl Grieg and asked about the history behind the photos at Molde. Grieg, as we know, had been there in the area on the same day and his thoughts after that had been on the expression of King Haakon as they appeared on the photos. In 1942, inspired by what he saw, Grieg penned the famous poem, *'The King'* in which he describes the mood at Glomstua from his own experiences and Bratland's photos. Grieg, along with other members of the transport had been quartered at a secondary school at Rauma, not far from Glomstua. Later the King personally signed the back of the poem "With warm thanks for the beautiful poem, Haakon R". Later, in 1942, King Haakon celebrated his 70th birthday by issuing 20 copies of a special edition of his book *"All for Norway"*. They were presented to government officials, royalty and…to Per Bratland, signed by the King giving his personal thanks.

116 Molde suffered a devastating fire in 1916 when approximately 1/3rd of the city was lost to fire. In 1940 the fires started by incendiaries destroyed approximately 2/3rds of the city. Subsequently, much of Molde was re-built after the war.

117 Ræstad's background was very interesting and it would appear his appointment was a sound and natural choice. Having been a lawyer and author on law and economics he had answered the call of politics during the 1920s being appointed Foreign Minister in Otto Blehrs government. From 1933 until the invasion Ræstad had been leader of the Norwegian Broadcasting Board, but his counsel was also sought on other important state matters such as Notraship – the merchant shipping agreement between Norway and Great Britain. His knowledge of legal matters would certainly have been put to good use.

118 National Archives reference: T236/215.

119 National Archives: T236/21.

120 National Archives reference: AIR 20/1085.

121 Lotte, a Finnish name was given to women volunteers in honour of Lotta Sværd, a Finnish national heroine. Later, during the *'Winterwar'* between Finland and USSR the Finnish female volunteers became well known for their

humanitarian work. Norway's 'Lottes' were based on the Finnish model and was originally established in 1928.

122 National Archives reference: ADM199/482.

123 Michael, M. *Haakon King of Norway:* Allen & Unwin, London, 1958, p. 163.

124 National Archives reference: CAB 44/72.

125 Ibid.

126 Author's note: I have been unable to find any documented evidence or eye witness account to any espionage activity in Molde, although unsubstantiated rumours of espionage still surface from time to time.

127 Author's note: the political and public outcry, had it become known that Britain's gold reserves were being moved out would have been substantial and probably very damaging. Churchill had taken a gamble, albeit a calculated one, risked his political career and had got away with it. Yet it had been a close run thing as an article appeared in the French newspaper *'Le Soleil'* detailing the movement of Britain's gold. Fortunately, either it passed without notice or there were some very deft and nimble secret service initiatives that meant the story failed to run in the UK.

128 National Archives reference: ADM 199/474.

129 Harnes, P.A. *Gulltransporten – dramaet dag for dag:* Romsdal Sogelag, 2006, p. 67.

130 Author's note: this was probably the moment when a Heinkel 111 flew over very low and HMS *Glasgow*'s gunners opened fire. According to the 'Ship's Log' only one aircraft was recorded as flying over the cruiser. One small Norwegian vessel and four naval trawlers are recorded as being alongside the ship. Some unconfirmed reports state there was more than one bomber.

131 Harnes, P.A. *Gulltransporten – dramaet dag for dag:* Romsdal Sogelag, 2006, 70–71.

132 Author's note: Captain Legernes had been promised that he would be paid for the trips to Glasgow, but no recompense was ever received.

133 http://www.regjeringen.no/en/archive/Bondeviks-2nd-Government/the-office-of-the-prime-minister/Taler-og-artikler-arkivert-individuelt/2004/speech_at_commemoration_of_hms.html?id=268518

134 National Archives reference: ADM 199/474.

135 The report is reproduced with the kind permission of Lady Cuthbert, wife of Commander Cuthbert RN, and historian Graham Salt.

136 Harnes, P.A. *Gulltransporten – dramaet dag for dag:* Romsdal Sogelag, 2006, pp. 68–69.

137 Koht, H. *Fra Skanse til Skanse:* Tiden Norsk Forlag, 1947, p. 100.

138 Written interview with Tom Morton RN.

139 Written interview with Don Edwards RN.

140 Written interview with John Kelleher RN.

141 Written and personal interview with Bill Watts RN.

142 Written interview with Cyril Milner RN.

143 Imperial War Museum ref: 1018401/23/1.

144 Personal interview with Horace Grant RN. Horace was the final *Glasgow* veteran to be awarded the Norwegian Participation Medal. This was issued to Horace in 2007 by Commander Paal Hope of the Royal Norwegian Navy for services in Norway and to its people. HMS *Glasgow*'s crew is the only Royal Navy ship's crew to be honoured with such an award indicating the high esteem in which King Haakon held the ship and her crew.

145 Royal Naval Museum reference: 1983.1251/2.

146 National Archives reference: FO371/24834.

147 Written interview with Jack Hall RN.

148 Paymaster Commander Laurence Arthur Boutwood RN was in charge of supplies, secretariat, signals and censorship.

149 National Archives reference: ADM116/4680.

150 *Driva* was built in Trondheim in 1909. Registered to take 343 passengers she served also as a postal steamer operating in the Trondheim area. In 1920 she plied her trade from Molde and was eventually taken out of service in 1950 whereupon she was laid up. Sold in March 1956 she was eventually broken up. Source: www.warsailors.com.

151 Haslund's report to the Minister of Finance, Oscar Torp.

152 Gleditsch, Krsitian and Nini. *Glimt fra Kampårene*: Dreyers Forlag, Oslo, 1954, p. 53.

153 Professor Wilhelm Keilhau was born in Oslo in 1888. He held a variety of academic posts specialising in politics and science. Later during the 1920s he became involved with the discussion on the Norwegian Monetary policy. During the war years Keilhau worked in London as a director with Norges Bank. After the war he maintained his interest in monetary matters and had numerous works published. He passed away in 1954. Thore Boye was Secretary of the Foreign Ministry. He escorted the gold on a fishing boat. He escaped to the UK and served with the Norwegian Government in London. In 1942 he worked for the Norwegian Ministry of Defence. After the war he continued his work with the Foreign Ministry eventually retiring in 1981. Source: Aftenposten 26th June 2006.

154 Margaret Reid's War Diary, Gyldendal Norsk Forlag, 1980 (English Translation), pp. 116–117.

155 Ibid., p. 122.

156 Haslund's Report to Finance Minister Torp dated 9th August 1940, see page 22.

157 Three fishing vessels were registered in Bud: M-27–BU – 'Heimdal 2', M-76–BU – 'Bard 2', M-33–BU – 'Svanen'. The following boats were all registered from the town of Hustad: M-40–HU – 'Leif', M-58–HU – 'Gudrum'.

158 Einar Gerhardsen, born 10th May 1892, was a member of the Labour Party.

At the end of the war he became Prime Minister of Norway leading the post-war economic recovery. Gerhardsen held the post on two further occasions and is considered by many to be the 'Father of the Nation'. He passed away on September 19th 1987.

159 Harnes, P.A. *Gulltransporten – dramaet dag for dag:* Romsdal Sogelag, 2006, pp. 85–86.

160 Haslund's report to the Minister of Finance, Oscar Torp, p. 29. In the report, Haslund refers to the man as Mr Guldssten, but Harnes, P.A. *Gulltransporten – dramaet dag for dag:* Romsdal Sogelag, 2006 refers to him as Mr Gullstein.

161 Radio broadcast by Vidkun Quisling on April 9th 1940.

162 Grieg, N. *Flagget:* Gyldendal Norsk Forlag, 1945, p. 26–27.

163 Havers, R. *Here is the News – The BBC and the Second World War:* Sutton Publishing, 2007.

164 Captain Denny's Proceedings sent to the Admiralty and dated 5th May 1940.

165 Haslund's report to the Minister of Finance, Oscar Torp, p. 30.

166 Ibid, p. 32–33.

167 ST-97–SF: –'Roald'. Skipper: – Alf Larsen

168 Gleditsch, Nini & Kristian, *Glimt Fra Kampårene*, Dreyers Forlag, Oslo, 1954, p. 59.

169 Haslund's report to the Minister of Finance, Oscar Torp, p. 31.

170 Andresen, AP, *I Natt og Tåke Mot England,* Cappelens Forlag, Oslo 1992, p. 23

171 The phrase 'fifth column' was originally termed during the Spanish Civil War in 1936 by Emilio Mola Vidal, a reactionary who announced on radio that he had four columns of forces waiting outside Madrid with a fifth column inside the city ready to rise up for their cause.

172 Haslund's report to the Minister of Finance, Oscar Torp, p. 38.

173 National Archives reference: ADM116/4680.

174 National Archive reference: ADM199/388.

175 National Archive reference: ADM53/112157.

176 Sir Charles Hambro was at that time Chairman of the Great Western Railway, but was unfortunately still in Sweden having escaped there after being chased out of Oslo by the Germans on April 9th. Apparently, he had been negotiating trade agreements with his Norwegian counterpart. Having escaped to Sweden he met up with his cousin, Carl J. Hambro – President of the Norwegian Storting in Stockholm. During this meeting discussions took place about the Norwegian merchant fleet, regarded as the most modern in the world. Those discussions centred on an organisation called NOTRASHIP. Sir Charles was also Chairman of Hambros Bank in London and it was his bank that supported NOTRASHIP financially. Sir Charles was a Director of the Bank of England and worked for the Ministry of Economic Warfare. Later, he was to become Head of the Norwegian section of the Special Operations Executive

and eventually head of the whole organisation. It was Sir Charles who later coined the names *'Gunnerside'* and *'Grouse'* as the operational names for the famous SOE 'Heavy Water' raid at Rjukan. Unfortunately, very few records exist of his participation in various aforementioned enterprises even in the Bank of England or the National Archives. His final wish just prior to his passing in 1965 was that all of his personal records were to be destroyed *'in the interests of democracy'.*

177 National Archive reference: ADM199/388.

178 Koht, H, *Frå skanse til skanse:* Tiden, 1947 p. 109.

179 The term 'three badge marine' indicates a long service award.

180 William Egerton Glover gained the rank of Assistant Chief Constable. After 40 years service he retired on 18th June 1946, passing away on 21st November 1967.

181 Norges Bank under okkupasjonen, Oslo 1945, J.Chr. Gundersen, Boktrykkeri.

182 The war economy specialists were coordinated under Major Neef and assimilated into the staff of group XXI on March 20, under the title "Group War Economy". Major Neef had arrived by plane on April 9th, but did not reach Oslo until April 11th. Initially, for the first few days after the occupation, the German Ambassador Dr Braeuer remained the political plenipotentiary of the Fuehrer – effectively a foreign diplomat with full powers to act independently. Ministerial Director Sarnow, as Foreign Office commissioner who dealt with economic problems, was attached to him. However, their success was limited and both Braeuer and Sarnow were recalled to Germany on April 22. Reference: Avalon Project – Yale Law School – Lillian Goldman Law Library: Nazi Conspiracy and Aggression Volume IV Document No. 2353.

183 Berthold Benecke was born in Hanover in 1889. In July 1937 he was undertaking an extensive tour of Scandinavia using the cover of Nordic representative for the German company, Ruhrstahl AG. Benecke was particularly interested in Norwegian iron ore. In 1938 he returned to Norway under the alias of Dr Altvater, but in truth he was working for the Kreigsorganisation. Benecke was very critical of Vidkun Quisling and filed several reports warning of the Norwegian opposition to Quisling. However, Benecke was subsequently removed from his post in June 1940 for his criticisms.

184 Professor Tore Pryser.

185 National Archives reference: T236/215.

186 Ibid.

187 National Archives reference: T236/216.

188 Arne Toralf Sunde, born 6th December 1883, was known as a politician, Olympian and reservist army officer. During the invasion of April 1940 he took part in the Battle of Dombås fighting against German parachutists. Later, having been evacuated to the UK he served in the exiled Nygaardsvold

Government from 1940–1945. He also served as the Norwegian Ambassador to the United Nations and later became President of the UN Security Council in 1950. Arne Sunde passed away on 30th July 1972.

189 Trygve Halvdan Lie was born 16th July 1896. He joined the Labour Party in 1911 and was appointed to the Norwegian Parliament in 1937, holding the positions of Minster of Trade (from July to October 1939), Minister of Supply until 1941 and then Foreign Minister with the Norwegian Government-in-exile. In 1946 he became the first Secretary-General of the United Nations, a position he held until 1952. Trygve Lie passed away on the 30th December 1968.

190 Halvdan Koht was born on 7th July 1873. Koht can be described as a politician, historian and biographer. Initially a liberalist he joined the Labour Party in 1911. He rose to become Foreign Secretary from 1935 until 1941. Koht was also a member of the Norwegian Nobel Committee from 1918–1936. After he had resigned from the Nygaardsvold Government-in-exile, he spent the remaining years of the war in America. He passed away on 12th December 1965.

Bibliography

Abelsen, F. *Norwegian Naval Ships 1939–1945:* Sam & Stenersen, 1986.

Adams & Whitehouse. *Royal Air Force Stradishall 1938–1970:* The RAF Stradishall Memorial Trust, 1986.

All For Norway (Alt For Norge). Published on the occasion of HM King Haakon's 70th Birthday. Royal Norwegian Government's Information Office 1942.

Andenaes, Risre & Skodvin. *Norway and the Second World War* – 5th ed., 1996.

Arthur, M. *Forgotten Voices of the Second World War:* Imperial War Museum, 2004.

Ash, B. *Norway 1940:* Casell, 1964.

Baden-Powell, D. *Pimpernel Gold – How Norway Foiled the Nazis:* Robert Hale, 1978.

Baden-Powell, D. *Operation Jupiter – SOE's Secret War in Norway:* Robert Hale, 1982.

Bailey, R. *Forgotten Voices of the Secret War:* Imperial War Museum, 2008.

Barker, R. *Blockade Busters:* Pen & Sword, 1976.

Bassett, R. *HMS Sheffield – The life and Times of 'Old Shiny:'* Arms and Armour Press, 1988.

Beesly, P. *Very Special Intelligence – The Story of the Admiralty's Operational Intelligence Centre 1939–1945:* Chatham Publishing, 1977.

Beesly, P. *Very Special Admiral – The Life of Admiral J H Godfrey C.B:* Hamish Hamilton, London, 1980.

Bennett. R, *Behind the Battle – Intelligence in the War with Germany 1939–45:* Pimlico Books, 1999.

Beretnin Fra Direksjonen For Norges Bank (22 April 1940 til 13 Juli 1945) – Oslo *Norges Bank 1946* (Report from the Directors of Norges Bank).

Binney, M. *Secret War Heroes – Men of the Special Operations Executive:* Hodder & Stoughton, 2005.

Borgen, J. *Nordahl Grieg:* Gyldendal Norsk Forlag, 1945.

Bowman, M. W. *The Bedford Triangle: US Undercover Operations from England in World War Two:* Sutton Publishing, 1989.

Boyce & Everett, *SOE the scientific secrets:* Sutton Publishing, 2003.

Brady, M. Ed, *Nordic Gold – The Facts of a Record:* Norsk Numismatic Forlag, Oslo, 1989.

Bramsen & Wain, *The Hambros 1779–1979:* Michael Joseph, 1979.

Brassey's Naval Annual. 1948. H.G. Thursfield, Ed. New York: Macmillan, 1948.

Broch, T. *The Mountains Wait:* Michael Joseph, 1943.

Brown, D. ed. *Naval Operations of the Campaign in Norway:* Frank Cass Publishers, 1951.

Bryant, A. *The Turn of the Tide:* Collins, 1957.

Buckley, C, *Norway and the Commandos Dieppe:* HMSO, 1952.

Cantwell, J. D. *The Second World War – A Guide to Documents in the Public Records Office:* 1998.

Churchill, W.S. *The Second World War, vol 1:* Cassell, London, 1948

Clark, F. *Agents by Moonlight (The Secret History of RAF Tempsford During World War II):* Tempus Publishing Ltd., 1999.

Clarke, D. *Seven Assignments:* Cape, London, 1948

Cookridge, E. H. *Inside SOE – The Story of Special Operations in Western Europe 1940–45:* Arthur Barker Ltd., 1966.

Cookridge, E. H. *Set Europe Ablaze:* Pan Books, 1969.

Corrigan, G. *Blood, Sweat and Arrogance:* Orion Publishing Group, London, 2006.

Cruickshank, C. *SOE in Scandinavia:* Oxford University Press, 1986.

Dalzel-Job, P. *From Arctic Snow to Dust Of Normandy:* Alan Sutton Publishing, 1991.

Dear, I. *Sabotage & Subversion:* Arms & Armour Press 1996

Delaforce, P. *The Polar Bears – Monty's Left Flank:* Sutton, 1995.

Denham, H. *Inside the Nazi Ring (A Naval Attaché in Sweden):* John Murray, London, 1984.

Derry, T. K. *The Campaign in Norway:* 1952.

Donald, W. *Standby for Action – A Sailor's Story:* William Kimber, London, 1956.

Draper, A. *Operation Fish:* Cassell Ltd., 1979.

Edwards, G. *Norwegian Patrol:* Airlife Publishing, 1985

Evensen, K. *Oscarsborg* Knut, 1992

Foley, T. *I was an Altmark Prisoner:* Aldor, London, 1940

Foot, M. R. D. *S.O.E. The Special Operations Executive 1940–46:* BBC Publication, 1984.

Frischauer, W, Jackson, R. *The Navy's Here – The Altmark Affair:* Gollancz, London, 1955.

Gallagher, T. *Assault in Norway – The True Story of the Telemark Raid:* Purnell Books, 1975.

Gilbert, M. *The Churchill War Papers – At the Admiralty Vol 1:* Heinemann, 1993.

Gotaas, B. *Fra 9 April Til 7 Juni:* Jacob Dybwads Forlag, 1945.

Grieg, N. *Flagget:* Gyldendal Norsk Forlag, 1945.

Gundersen, J.Chr. *Norges Bank under okkupasjonen*, Boktrykkeri, Oslo 1945,

Hambro, C. J. *I Saw it Happen in Norway:* Appleton-Century, 1941.

Harnes, P. A. *Gulltransporten – dramaet dag for dag:* Redigering og trykk: ekh.no, Molde 2006.

Hart-Davis, D. *Peter Fleming – A Biography:* Jonathan Cape Ltd., London, 1974.

Hauge, E. O. *Salt Water Thief:* Duckworth, 1958.

Haukelid, K. *Skis Against The Atom:* North American Heritage Press, 1989.

Havers, R. *Here is the News – The BBC and the Second World War:* Sutton Publishing, 2007.

Holman, G. *Commando Attack:* Hodder & Stoughton, 1942.

Howarth, P. *Undercover – The Men and Women of the SOE:* Routledge & Kegan Paul, 1980.

Howarth, D. *We die Alone:* Collins, 1955.

Howarth, D. *The Shetland Bus:* Thomas Nelson & Sons 1957.

Irvine, J. *The Final Curtain:* A. Irvine, Lerwick, 2004.

Irvine, J. *The Waves Are Free:* Shetland Publishing Company, 1988.

Jackson, R. *The Royal Navy in World War II:* Airlife Publishing, 1997.

Jensen, Ratvik & Ulstein, *Kompani Linge* Vols 1&2: Gyldendal, 1948.

Jorgensen, C. *Hitler's Espionage Machine:* Spellmount Ltd., 2004.

Kersaudy, F. *Norway 1940:* Collins, Glasgow 1990.

Kjedstaldli, S. *Hjemme Strykene:* Aschehoug & Co., 1959.

Koht, H. *Norway Neutral and Invaded:* Hutchinson, London, 1941.

Koht, H. *Frå skanse til skanse:* Tiden, 1947

Knight, N, *Churchill – The Greatest Briton Unmasked:* David & Charles, Newton Abbot, 2008.

Kynoch, J. *The Naked Soldiers:* Charnwood Publications, 1995.

Kynoch, J. *Norway 1940 – The Forgotten Fiasco:* Airlife, 2002.

Lambert, J. *The Fairmile 'D' Motor Torpedo Boat:* Conway Maritime Press 2005.

Lebor, A. *Hitler's Secret Bankers:* Simon & Schuster UK, 1999.

Lie, T. *Leve eller Do – Norge I Krig (Live or Die – Norway in War):* Tiden Norsk Forlag, 1955.

Lucas, L. *Voices in the Air 1939–1945:* Arrow Books, 2003.

Macintyre, D. *Narvik: 1959.*

Mackenzie, W. *The Secret History of SOE: Special Operations Executive 1940–1945:* St Ermin's Press, 2000.

Mann & Jorgensen, *Hitler's Arctic War:* Ian Allan Publishing, 2002.

Manus, M. *Underwater Saboteur:* William Kimber, 1954.

Marks, L. *Between Silk And Cyanide – The Story of SOE's Code War:* Harper Collins, 1998.

Mears, R. *The Real Heroes of Telemark:* Hodder & Stoughton, 2003.

Michael, M. *Haakon King of Norway:* Allen & Unwin, London, 1958.

Moland, A. *I Hemmelig Tjeneste – Kompani Linge sett med britiske oyne:* Orion Forlag, 2001.

Moulton, J. L. *The Norwegian Campaign of 1940:* Camelot Press, 1966.

Munthe, M. *Sweet is War:* Duckworth, 1955.

Munthe-Kaas, O, *Operasjonene gjennom Romerike-Hedemarken-Gudbrandsdalen-Romsdalen:* Bind I og II, Oslo, 1955

Nielsen, T. *Inside Fortress Norway – Bjorn West – Norwegian Guerrilla Base 1944 –*

1945: Gyldendfal Norsk Forlag, 1992.

Nilsson & Sandberg, *Blockade Runners – Sweden's lifeline in the Second World War:* Gullers Forlag (Sweden), 1996.

Norge I Fest: Mittet, 1946.

Nyquist, R. B. *Fighting Norsemen* – Royal Norwegian Government Information Office.

Nyquist, R. B. *Sons of the Vikings* – Royal Norwegian Government Information Office.

Oliver, G. D. *In Peace and War: The Story of HMS Glasgow 1937–1958.*

Peter Moen's Diary: Faber & Faber, 1951.

Petrow, R. *The Bitter Years (The Invasion and Occupation of Denmark and Norway April 1940 – May 1945):* Hodder & Stoughton, 1974.

Pope, D. *The Battle of the River Plate:* Chatham, London, 1956.

Poulsson, J. A. *Aksjon Vermork – Vinterkrig pa Hardangervidda:* Gyldendal Norsk Forlag, 1993.

Rankin, N., *Churchill's Wizards – The British Genius For Deception 1914–1945:* Faber & Faber, London, 2008.

Reynolds, L. *Dog Boats at War – Royal Navy D Class MTBs & MGBs 1939–45:* Sutton Publishing (IWM) 1998

Rhys-Jones, G. *Churchill and The Norway Campaign:* Pen & Sword, Barnsley, 2008.

Richards, B. *Secret Flotillas (Clandestine Sea Lines to France & French North Africa 1940–1944:* HMSO Publication, 1996.

Richards, D. *Royal Air Force 1939–1945 - The Fight at Odds:* (Vol 1) HMSO, 1953.

Riste & Nokleby, *Norway 1940–45 The Resistance Movement:* Tanum Norli 1970

Robert, A. *The Holy Fox – Biography of Lord Halifax:* Weidenfield & Nicholson, 1991.

Ruge, O, *Felttoget, erindringer fra kampene April – Juni 1940:* Aschehoug, Oslo, 1989

Salvesen, S. *Forgive – But Do Not Forget:* London, Hutchinson, 1958.

Scott, P. *The Battle of the Narrow Seas (Light Coastal Forces 1939–45):* Country Life Ltd.

Secret Agent's Handbook of Special Devices: Introduction by Mark Seaman. Seaman, M. (ed.) – Crown Copyright 2000 – Public Record Office

Shores, C. *Fledgling Eagles:* Grub Street, 1991.

Sivertsen, S. C. *Jageren "Sleipner" i Romsdalsfjord Sjoforsvarsavsnitt april 1940:* 1999.

Smith, M. *Foley – The Spy Who Saved 10,000 Jews:* Hodder & Stoughton, 1999.

SOE Operations in Scandinavia, National Archives, 1998

SOE Syllabus – Lessons in ungentlemanly warfare, World War 11: Secret History Files (National Archives), 2001

Somme, S. *A Biologist On The Run:* rewritten by Ellie Targett, 1991.

Sønsteby, G. *Report From # 24:* Barricade Books, 1999.

Sorvaag, T. *Shetland Bus Faces and Places 60 Years on:* The Shetland Times Ltd., 2003.

Stafford, D. *Secret Agent – Britain's Wartime Secret Service:* BBC Worldwide, 2002.

Stevenson, W. *A Man called Intrepid:* Macmillian, 1976.

Taffrail, *The Navy in Action:* Hodder & Stoughton, 1940.
Tevnan & Horsley, *Norway Invaded:* Withy Grove Press Ltd., 1940.
Ulstein, R. *Englands Farten – Bok 1 & Bok 2:* 1965
Warwicker, J. Ed. *With Britain in Mortal Danger – Britain's most Secret Army:* Cerberus Publishing, 2002.
Wiggan, R. *Hunt the Altmark:* Robert Hale, London, 1982.
Wilkinson & Astley, *Gubbins & SOE:* Leo Cooper Publishing, 1993.
Young, P. *Commando:* Pan Books, 1969.

Combined Operations – 1940–1942

Coastal Command
His Majesty's Submarines
There's Freedom in the Air – Official story of the allied air forces from the occupied countries.
Before We Go Back – Norway's Fight since April 1940
Fleet Air Arm – The Admiralty account of Naval Air operations
Bomber Command
The Royal Marines – The Admiralty account of their achievement 1939–1943

Magazines

After The Battle – Telemark – Operation Freshman – Issue 45
After The Battle – The Shetland Isles – Issue 67
After The Battle – Sinking of the Blücher – Issue 101
After The Battle – The Raid on Vaagso – Issue 109
After The Battle – The Norwegian Campaign – Issue 126
The War Illustrated' March 1st 1940

Films

'*Shetland Gjengen*' film of the Shetland Bus starring David Howarth, Leif Larsen and many of the original crews from the famous wartime base.
Kampen om Tungtvannet A black & white film in Norwegian language only.

Research Papers

An Analysis of the Norwegian Resistance During the Second World War
By Major Kim M. Johnson
March 1997

Unpublished Sources

Vice Admiral Hans B. Gundersen RNorN (1958?) An account of the 30th & 54th Norwegian Flotilla.

Colonel John Skinner Wilson – two unpublished accounts of the history of Norwegian SOE (1945) – believed to be kept at Hjemmefrontmuseet, Olso

Randall Tomlinson DSM – To the Shores of Scandinavia (1994)

Index

Numbers in italics denote pages with illustrations